Ruth A. Baer is professor of psychology at the University of Kentucky. She has written and published extensively on mindfulness and is the editor of two books for professionals: *Mindfulness-Based Treatment Approaches: Clinician's Guide to Evidence Base and Application*, and *Assessing Mindfulness and Acceptance Processes in Clients: Illuminating the Theory and Practice of Change*. She teaches and supervises several mindfulness-based treatments, including Acceptance and Commitment Therapy (ACT), Dialectical Behaviour Therapy (DBT), Mindfulness-Based Cognitive Therapy (MBCT), Mindfulness-Based Stress Reduction (MBSR), and Mindfulness-Based Relapse Prevention. She lives in Lexington, Kentucky, with her husband.

Praise for *Practising Happiness*

... an experienced ... nician, internationally-renowned ... mindfulness practitioner a ... brilliant teacher who combines warm humour, deep intelligence and em ... thic gentleness of heart.'

Mark Williams, Professor f Clinical Psychology and
Wellcome Trust Principal Research Fellow, Oxford University,
co-author of *Mindfulness: A Practical Guide to Finding Peace in a
Frantic World* and *The Mindful Way Through Depression*

'This book is like a mindfulness walk. It seamlessly integrates the best of mindfulness training from the major evidence-based care approaches, giving it a sense of breadth of vision, as if you can see across vast distances on your walk. It gently and calmly steps through many domains of self-exploration (rumination, emotion, self-criticism, values, and so on) and yet it never wanders. Each step is small but each step is purposive, as if you are being guided on your walk by a very wise person who knows where she is going but is willing to let you set your own pace in getting there. And when you are done you feel alive and whole, as if you have come home, and you are simply happy to be there. This is a walk worth taking – and a book worth reading. Highly recommended.'

Steven C. Hayes, Foundation Professor of Psychology,
University of Nevada, author of *Get Out of Your Mind and into Your Life*

'Anyone who struggles with difficult emotions or gets trapped in rumination will benefit enormously from this book. Written by one of the leaders in the secular approach to mindfulness, Ruth Baer guides readers through the different facets of mindfulness and explains how these can be used and practised to help us find inner calmness, reduce self-criticism and attain happier states of mind. Knowledgeable, accessible

D0415755

'and practical, this book will be of immense help to many people in how to deal with our rather chaotic, emotional minds.'

Paul Gilbert, Professor of Clinical Psychology, University of Derby, author of *The Compassionate Mind* and *Overcoming Depression*

'*Practising Happiness*, Ruth Baer's latest book, is an open invitation to finding out for yourself how mindfulness can add immeasurably to your quality of life. Written with a reassuring, supportive tone, this workbook moves seamlessly between the problems and the promises each of us encounters as it describes how awareness, willingness and kindness can open truly new vistas of well-being.'

Zindel V. Segal, University of Toronto, *The Mindful Way through Depression*

'Bringing attention to our experience with compassion, patience and equanimity can be radically transformative. You will be in the hands of a gentle, authoritative guide as Ruth Baer draws on her extensive clinical, scientific and personal experience to set out a path of mindfulness practice and inquiry. *Practising Happiness* is an accessible and practical guide to the transformative power of mindfulness in everyday life.'

Willem Kuyken, Professor of Clinical Psychology, co-founder of the Mood Disorders Centre, University of Exeter and the Exeter Mindfulness Network, co-author of *Collaborative Case Conceptualization*

'In this wise and compassionate book, Ruth Baer integrates up-to-date research, effective contemporary mindfulness-based approaches and her own deep knowledge and understanding of the psychology of human distress and of mindfulness meditation practice. Lucid and compelling, the book offers a practical step-by-step guide to awareness, insight and transformation through mindfulness, enlivened by vivid personal stories and delightful touches of humour. A pleasure to read.'

Melanie Fennell, University of Oxford, author of *Overcoming Low Self-Esteem*

'This is one of the most carefully designed and written handbooks on mindfulness to date. The author is a senior mindfulness researcher who has sifted through the burgeoning scientific literature to present the essential psychology and practice of mindfulness in a palpable, jargon-free, highly accessible manner. Strongly recommended for anyone, regardless of background or experience, who wishes to live a happier, less encumbered life.'

Christopher Germer, clinical instructor, Harvard Medical School, author of *The Mindful Path to Self-Compassion*

'For many, happiness is an elusive state. Each fleeting moment leaves us clamouring for more. Chasing after happiness can become an exhausting and discouraging enterprise, as our most familiar strategies often backfire. Fortunately, this book offers an extremely effective alternative. Drawing on her extensive experience practising and researching mindfulness, Baer provides compassionate and practical advice to those seeking to enhance their sense of satisfaction and purpose. Full of extremely practical tools and engaging case examples, this book provides us with the guidance we need to truly enjoy all that life can offer.'

Susan M. Orsillo, Suffolk University, co-author of *The Mindful Way through Anxiety*

'*Practising Happiness* weaves together the rigour of science, the beauty of art, the wisdom of reflection and decades of lived clinical experience to offer us one of the most compelling books on how to cultivate greater happiness and wellbeing in our lives. Dr Ruth Baer lucidly and brilliantly offers a book that has the power to transform our individual and collective lives.'

Professor Shauna L. Shapiro, Santa Clara University, co-author of *The Art and Science of Mindfulness: Integrating Mindfulness into Psychology and the Helping Professions*

'In *Practising Happiness*, Ruth Baer draws from decades of her own and others' research, as well as her personal experience, to provide concise, accessible tips for living a meaningful, satisfying life. She clearly illustrates the natural human habits or 'traps' that can interfere with our wellbeing, while providing simple, step-by-step guidance to promoting new habits that will enhance and expand readers' lives. Vignettes and worksheets bring concepts to life and help readers apply them immediately to their own lives. This book may be life-changing for those who have never practised mindfulness, and will also provide valuable structure and guidance for those who have practised but not yet seen the benefits they seek and useful reminders even for seasoned practitioners. I highly recommend *Practising Happiness* and plan to buy copies for many people I know.'

Lizabeth Roemer, University of Massachusetts Boston,
co-author of *Mindful Way Through Anxiety:*
Break free from chronic worry and reclaim your life

Practising Happiness

Ruth A. Baer

ROBINSON

Constable & Robinson Ltd
55-56 Russell Square
London WC1B 4HP
www.constablerobinson.com

First published in the UK by Robinson,
an imprint of Constable & Robinson Ltd., 2014

A copy of the British Library Cataloguing in Publication Data
is available from the British Library

Important Note
This book is not intended as a substitute for medical advice or treatment.
Any person with a condition requiring medical attention should consult a
qualified medical practitioner or suitable therapist

ISBN 978-1-78033-438-7 (trade paperback)
ISBN 978-1-78033-439-4 (ebook)

Printed and bound by CPI Group (UK) Ltd, Croydon, CR0 4YY

13 5 7 9 10 8 6 4 2

Contents

Part 4:
Putting It All Together

Acknowledgements

Immersing myself in the leading research-based mindfulness programmes has convinced me that each has important wisdom to contribute to people wishing to improve their lives. This book is heavily indebted to the following colleagues who pioneered the development and scientific study of mindfulness-based treatment approaches: Marsha Linehan for dialectical behaviour therapy; Jon Kabat-Zinn for mindfulness-based stress reduction; Zindel Segal, Mark Williams and John Teasdale for mindfulness-based cognitive therapy; Steve Hayes, Kirk Strosahl and Kelly Wilson for acceptance and commitment therapy; Jean Kristeller for mindfulness-based eating awareness training; Sue Orsillo and Liz Roemer for acceptance-based behaviour therapy; Alan Marlatt, Sarah Bowen and Neha Chawla for mindfulness-based relapse prevention.

I thank all of you for your innovative thinking, compelling research, insightful books, outstanding training workshops and friendly support of my professional development. It has been a privilege to learn from you. Your influence pervades my work, this book, and how I've come to see the world.

I am also deeply indebted to the many other psychologists who have influenced my work through their inspiring research on topics included in this book, including David Barlow, Kirk Brown, Linda Carlson, Sona Dimidjian, Barbara Fredrickson, Paul Gilbert, Willem Kuyken, Sonya Lyubomirsky, Christopher Martell, Kristin Neff, Susan Nolen-Hoeksema, Carol Ryff, Shauna Shapiro and Ed Watkins, among many others.

I thank my friend and colleague Martha Wetter, without whom I wouldn't have ventured into DBT, where I first encountered mindfulness. I thank Cindy Sanderson and Charlie Swenson for outstanding professional training in DBT and for inspiring my initial suspicions that mindfulness might be important in the world of scientific clinical psychology.

I am grateful to the teachers at my first professional mindfulness retreats and trainings who accepted with understanding and patience my initial difficulties with intensive meditation and helped me find my way, especially Jon Kabat-Zinn, Zindel Segal, John Teasdale, Ferris Urbanowski, and Mark Williams.

I thank the many teachers at the Insight Meditation Society in Barre, Massachusetts, who have shaped my practice and understanding of mindfulness: Guy Armstrong, Rebecca Bradshaw, Christina Feldman, Joseph Goldstein, Michael Liebenson Grady, Michele MacDonald, Susan O'Brien, Larry Rosenberg, Sharon Salzburg and Steven Smith. I especially thank Sharon and Joseph for making IMS an ideal environment for this purpose.

I am indebted to the students in my classes for doing their mindfulness homework in the spirit of interest, exploration and open-mindedness, and writing wonderful accounts of their experiences, some of which I adapted for this book. I also thank the many clients in the groups we run in our clinic, for their courage and willingness to engage with the mindfulness practices and discover their benefits, even in the midst of stress and pain. Their progress inspires me to share what I've learned.

I thank Fritha Saunders at Constable & Robinson for inviting me to write this book and guiding me through the process; Melissa Valentine at New Harbinger for insights about marketing; Jon Davies and Jasmine Star for copy-editing; Jo Stansall for editorial support; Kathy Norrish for the beautiful illustrations; and Mark Williams for the wonderful foreword. My heartfelt thanks to the non-fiction writing class at the Carnegie Center for Literacy and Learning in Lexington Kentucky, and to Neil Chethik, our teacher, for listening to many excerpts from this book, offering countless helpful suggestions, and cheering me on. I also thank Leslie Guttman, my editor at the Carnegie Center, who scrutinized every sentence and helped sustain my energy. I'm indebted to Richard Smith, my friend and colleague in the psychology department, who read most of the manuscript and offered valuable suggestions from the perspective of an accomplished academic who has written for the non-academic audience.

I'm grateful to my wonderful graduate students for their support of this project – despite the time it took away from mentoring them – especially Jess Peters, for her outstanding leadership in the lab, Paul Geiger, Tory Eisenlohr-Moul, Laura Smart, Brian Upton and Erin Walsh.

I thank my father, Donald Baer, for his many influences, especially his frequent loving reminders that the primary benefit of a tenured faculty position is the chance to pursue one's deepest interests.

I thank my mother, Ann Marshall-Levine, for her thoughtful enthusiasm for my work; and my sisters, Miriam and Deb, for their sustaining, unconditional love. I thank Trevor Stokes, my graduate school adviser and honorary member of the family, for continuing friendship and support of my professional endeavours, even when I venture into strange territory. I thank the rest of my family and my other friends and colleagues for their love, encouragement and unfailing confidence that I could write this book.

Most of all, I'm deeply grateful for the love and support of my husband Terry Schoen, who makes the journey joyful no matter what the weather on the mountain.

Foreword

Why can't we be as happy as we'd like to be? It turns out that we often trap ourselves into ways of thinking and feeling that create persistent unease. If this was not bad enough, the very ways we try to escape entangle us even more. We brood about our past mistakes and worry about our ability to cope in the future. Clinical levels of depression and anxiety, or problems in controlling emotions or impulses, can take over our lives. Happiness can seem very elusive indeed.

It is rare to find a book that would help virtually everyone who reads it and puts its advice into practice. The book you hold in your hand is just such a rarity. Ruth Baer has brought together a number of different approaches that have been proven by careful research to release those who suffer from some of the most common emotional difficulties from the traps that emotions can set. These approaches have also been found to bring about a transformation in life that allows peace and well-being to be felt deeply, sometimes for the first time in years.

How can this be? The secret is in the title. Note that it does not refer to the pursuit of happiness, the quest for happiness, or the goal of happiness, but to the *practice* of happiness. This is fundamental. As it turns out, happiness is not to be a goal to be pursued, but rather a byproduct of a certain way of living your life. As one psychologist has expressed it, it involves getting 'out of your mind and into your life' (Hayes, 2005). The essence of the mindfulness and acceptance approach to daily living involves practising fully inhabiting your life by learning, day by day and moment by moment, to first notice and then turn towards the present, with all its joys and discontents, nostalgia and regrets, plans and worries, thoughts and imaginings. It's learning that you have potentialities you never dreamed of, but that making them real involves learning, piece by piece, how to drop the myriad ways in which you try to protect yourself.

By trying to avoid or suppress discomfort whenever it arises, you get into a habit of withdrawing from your life, and you can find that you have become a stranger to your best and wisest self. This book offers you the chance to come home to your life through mindfulness.

Mindfulness is one of many translations of an ancient word that means 'lucid awareness' or 'non-forgetfulness'. Mindfulness training is the practice of remembering to wake up, moment by moment, to what is arising in the inner and outer world, as best you can. Developing such awareness takes gentle but firm persistence, as the mind quite naturally acquires most skills by making most of our behaviours automatic and habitual. Habits are normally so useful: if we still had to think deeply about how to balance when we walk or how to keep an automobile in the correct part of the highway, we'd have little energy or mental space to think of anything else. But habits are hungry: any behaviour we repeat more than once is fair game – a suitable candidate for becoming a habit. This is not itself a problem. What *is* a problem is that the part of the mind that is freed up when actions become habitual typically is not then employed to appreciate the present moment or think great or creative thoughts; rather it drifts off into daydreams, brooding about the past or worrying about the future, ruminating about our unsolvable problems or those of others, or trying to work out the meaning of life. When your mind wanders about in this way, happiness seems to elude you, and if you then turn your attention to *why* you feel less happy than you'd like to, this can make you feel even worse. So you distract yourself as best you can, and postpone happiness for another day, without realising that it was right in front of you all along. It turned out that while you were searching for the meaning of life, you missed the experience of being alive.

This is why happiness, seen narrowly as a goal to be pursued, is an illusion. Yet none of us is immune. It is an illusion that catches us in its snare again and again. We need a reliable guide to help us navigate through this path, and Ruth Baer is just such a guide: an experienced clinician, internationally renowned researcher, mindfulness practitioner and brilliant teacher who combines warm humour, deep intelligence and empathic gentleness of heart. Expect a good read, and enjoy reading this book: but also expect her to invite you to practise some new things as an experiment. This is where the action starts – and where you can begin to reclaim your life. I wish you well as you embark on this adventure in practising happiness.

Mark Williams

Professor of Clinical Psychology and Wellcome Principal Research Fellow, University of Oxford. Author of *Mindfulness: A Pracitical Guide to Finding Peace in a Frantic World*

Part 1

Introduction

1 How This Book Will Help You

'Happiness is not a station you arrive at, but a manner of travelling.'

Margaret Lee Runbeck

If you fit any of the following descriptions, this book is intended for you:

- You feel there's too much stress in your life, and you're not sure what to do about it.

- You're troubled by worries, fears and anxiety.

- You're sad, blue and discouraged, and it's wearing you down.

- You do things you regret, like overeating, losing your temper, watching too much TV.

- You regret NOT doing things: not keeping up with your friends and family, not pursuing your goals at work, not taking care of yourself.

- You wish you could find more meaning and satisfaction in life.

- You wish you could be happier.

This book is about *mindfulness* – a type of awareness that focuses on the present moment with an attitude of friendly curiosity. Research shows that mindfulness helps with all of the problems listed above. People who practise mindfulness feel less depressed, anxious and stressed. They learn to stay in touch with their true priorities, handle their problems more effectively, and find peace of mind. Their relationships are stronger. They feel more positive emotions and get more enjoyment from ordinary activities. Even their physical health improves.

You may find it hard to believe that present-moment awareness can have so many benefits. Maybe you're thinking that you're already aware of your present moments – painfully aware. Your present moments are filled with stress and difficulties. Why would you want to be *more* aware of them?

Usually, when we say we're aware of our problems, we mean that they're often on our minds, or that we constantly think about them. Thinking about problems is great when it helps us solve them. But often we get trapped in our own thinking. Thoughts go round and round in our heads, problems remain unsolved, and we feel worse.

Then we try another strategy: NOT thinking about our problems. This is harder than it sounds. Thoughts about problems come into our minds whether we want them to or not. To get rid of the unwanted thoughts, we often go to great lengths to distract ourselves. We bury ourselves in work, watch endless TV, eat, drink or shop too much. This creates more problems that demand our attention. It's hard to avoid being aware of them.

Mindfulness is a *distinctly different* kind of awareness. It's non-judgemental and compassionate, even when the present moment is stressful and difficult. Practising mindfulness teaches us to recognize harmful patterns of thinking and reacting before they get worse. It prevents downward spirals into stress, anxiety and depression. Mindfulness keeps us in touch with what really matters: our most important values and goals. It helps us manage our reactions to events and provides time to choose wisely what to do in upsetting situations. This leads to a greater sense of meaning and satisfaction.

This book explains what mindfulness is, how to be more mindful in ordinary life and how mindfulness will help you. Practising mindfulness doesn't eliminate pain and misfortune, but it will make you happier in several ways. It will put you in touch with simple pleasures and momentary joys that you may have been overlooking. It will show you how to find meaning and purpose by acting on your deepest values and most important goals, even when it's stressful, difficult, or painful to do so. It will help you find inner strength and peace of mind in the midst of serious adversity. It will wake you up to the experience of being alive.

For a detailed understanding of how this works, it's best to read the whole book and practise the exercises. As an introduction, let's consider the case of Glenn. Before he learned mindfulness skills, Glenn was extremely troubled by anxiety in social situations. He was especially fearful of speaking in groups. You may or may not share this problem – it doesn't matter. The ways of thinking and reacting that got Glenn into trouble, and the mindfulness skills that freed him, can be applied to many other types of problems.

Glenn's Story

Glenn wakes up in the morning feeling nervous. His heart is racing, his stomach tight. He knows why: this afternoon he has to lead a one-hour staff meeting. His boss is away and asked Glenn to chair the meeting. Glenn couldn't think of an acceptable reason to say no, so he agreed, despite his fear of speaking in groups.

Glenn lies in bed obsessing about the meeting. 'What if I make a mess of things? I always get so nervous. What if my voice shakes? People will hear it. They'll know how insecure I am, and they'll think I'm incompetent. I can't believe I agreed to do this. It's going to be a disaster. Maybe I should call in sick. No, that would look suspicious. Why can't I handle things better? It's only a meeting. I shouldn't get so worked up. I'll never get anywhere if I can't cope with things like this.'

After dwelling on these thoughts for several more minutes, Glenn forces himself out of bed and goes to work, alternately obsessing about the meeting and telling himself not to think about it. He spends much of the day reviewing the agenda and looking at his notes, despite having fully prepared for the meeting the day before. He walks into the conference room at precisely 3.00 p.m. and explains that he'll chair the meeting in the boss's absence.

For about forty-five minutes, Glenn works his way through the agenda. His mouth is dry, but his voice sounds OK. He keeps his eyes on his notes much of the time, looking up only when necessary. Then he sees someone yawning and checking the clock. 'People are bored,' he thinks. 'I'm making a mess of this. I should stop before it gets any worse.' A wave of anxiety comes over him. He announces that time is running short, and the rest of the agenda will be dealt with at a future meeting. People look at him oddly but are happy to rush off. 'They couldn't wait to get out of here,' Glenn thinks. 'I'm obviously no good at this.'

For a moment, Glenn feels relieved that the meeting is over, but then worries creep in. 'How will I explain to my boss that I didn't finish the agenda?' he wonders. 'I'll just have to say there wasn't time. But what if someone tells him we stopped early? I can't believe I did that! I'm such an idiot.'

Psychological Traps

What went wrong? Glenn's fear of speaking in groups, and his understandable desire to feel less anxious, caused him to fall into several *psychological traps*: patterns of thinking, feeling and reacting that seem reasonable – on the surface or in the short term – but make problems worse over time. These traps are introduced below. Each trap is discussed in more detail in later chapters.

1 – Rumination

Glenn worried excessively about the meeting, brooding and stewing about it in unhelpful ways. Psychologists call this 'rumination'. It's different from constructive thinking because it doesn't solve problems – it makes matters worse. If asked why he ruminated so much, Glenn would say it seemed necessary to be prepared. Yet he'd prepared the day before. Ruminating didn't help; in fact, the more he dwelled on the meeting, the more anxious he felt.

2 – Avoidance

Glenn thought about calling in sick – an obvious form of avoidance that he decided against. Instead, he used a more subtle form of avoidance by keeping his eyes on his notes much of the time. He was afraid of seeing boredom or impatience in his co-workers' faces. But this backfired – he didn't see when people looked sincerely interested. When he happened to catch someone yawning and checking the clock, he automatically assumed that everyone had been doing that all along.

3 – Emotion-driven behaviour

Emotion-driven behaviour is often impulsive and rash. To escape from uncomfortable feelings, we act suddenly, without considering the long-term effects. Later, we wish we'd handled the situation differently. When Glenn noticed someone looking bored, he felt so anxious and discouraged that he quickly ended the meeting. For a moment he felt relieved, but then regretted his behaviour and began to worry about the consequences.

4 – Self-criticism

Criticism is helpful when it's constructive, but Glenn judged himself in vague and unreasonable ways. He called himself an idiot, thinking that he deserved criticism, that it was the only way he'd ever improve. But he'd chastised himself about public speaking for years, and it only made the problem worse. It sapped his energy and motivation and kept him from developing his skills.

How Mindfulness Skills Helped Glenn

This was not the end of the story for Glenn. By practising the following skills, Glenn learned how to use *mindful* awareness to cope with his anxiety and handle stressful situations effectively. The mindfulness skills are introduced briefly here and described in much greater detail throughout this book.

Non-judgemental observation and labelling

Glenn learned to **observe** his present-moment experiences, including *thoughts* ('I'm making a mess of this'), *bodily sensations* (racing heart, tight stomach), *emotions* (anxiety, discouragement), and *urges* (to call in sick, end the meeting early). Instead of ruminating, he learned to **label** these experiences by calling them what they are, telling himself, 'Those are thoughts . . .' or 'I'm feeling an urge . . .' He learned to be **non-judgemental** in his observing and labelling. Rather than 'It's stupid of me to be so anxious . . . ' he simply noted the anxious thoughts and feelings when they appeared. These were important first steps.

Acting with awareness

Glenn also learned how to focus on what he's doing, while he's doing it. He learned how to be fully engaged. And so now, when running a meeting, he looks attentively around the room, listens carefully and guides the discussion. When thoughts and feelings about how he's doing come to mind, he notices them briefly, labels them as thoughts and feelings, and re-engages with running the meeting. This is a big change in the nature of his awareness.

Acceptance and willingness

Glenn learned to *accept* the presence of anxious thoughts and feelings. This doesn't mean that he likes them, approves of them or wants them to be there. Rather, he allows them to come and go in their own way and time, while still proceeding with what he's doing. He realizes that negative thoughts ('I'm no good at this') don't have to control his behaviour – he now can choose whether to act on them. Even though he feels anxious, he's *willing* to chair the meeting as best he can, without quitting early, because he values being a helpful employee and wants to advance his career.

Self-compassion

Glenn also realizes that he's not alone – fear of speaking in groups is a common problem. Rather than judging himself harshly, Glenn recognizes that his anxious thoughts and feelings are understandable, given his longstanding fear and his lack of previous experience with running meetings. He tries to help himself constructively; for example, he brings water to meetings in case his mouth gets dry, gives himself credit when he does reasonably well, and recognizes where his skills could improve.

Glenn is now much happier and more satisfied with his life. Because he learned mindfulness skills, he is *aware* of anxiety whenever it appears, but not in a brooding, self-critical and emotionally reactive way. Instead, he's *mindfully* aware. Mindful awareness doesn't get rid of Glenn's anxiety, but it helps him manage it constructively. As Glenn continues to practise mindfulness, his anxiety about public speaking will become less intense. Eventually, he may enjoy running meetings. But he'll also know that he can handle it even when he's feeling anxious. Knowing that anxiety doesn't have to control his behaviour will give him a feeling of inner strength.

If this brief description of Glenn's mindful behaviour seems odd, unnatural or unrealistic to you, that's because learning to be mindful during difficult times is like learning to swim or ride a bicycle – it takes practice and feels awkward at first. This book is full of tools to make the process easier: worksheets, exercises and personal stories of people who've benefited from practising mindfulness. If you work with this book consistently, it can teach you all the skills that Glenn used and help you apply them to your own life.

Why I Wrote This Book

I've been a professor of clinical psychology for over twenty-five years. My colleagues, students and I work with many types of people seeking help for a wide range of problems – depression, anxiety, stress, impulsive behaviour, relationship problems, and more. We're strongly committed to a scientific approach. This means that we use the latest methods that studies show are highly beneficial. We're researchers as well as clinicians and teachers; we undertake studies to learn more about what mindfulness is, how it works and how best to teach it.

During the past few decades, psychologists and other mindfulness experts have developed many programmes that teach mindfulness:

educational, skills training and therapy programmes. The programmes with the best scientific support are:

- Mindfulness-based stress reduction (MBSR).

- Mindfulness-based cognitive therapy (MBCT).

- Dialectical behaviour therapy (DBT).

- Acceptance and commitment therapy (ACT).

These programmes are summarized in the next box. Research consistently shows that they're beneficial for a wide variety of problems: depression; anxiety; stress; drug and alcohol abuse; eating problems; and health problems (insomnia, pain, the stress of having illnesses such as cancer). These programmes also increase positive emotions and general satisfaction with life.

Each programme has its own perspective and teaches mindfulness in its own way, but there's quite a bit of overlap. Having worked with these programmes for many years, I'm convinced that each has important wisdom to contribute to people who would like to learn about mindfulness to improve their quality of life. This book combines the wisdom from all of these mindfulness programmes and presents it in a self-help format.

MINDFULNESS–BASED PROGRAMMES WITH STRONG SCIENTIFIC SUPPORT

Mindfulness-Based Stress Reduction (MBSR)

MBSR is usually taught as an eight-week class. It was originally developed for people with stress, pain and medical problems, and has many benefits: reducing stress and worry; increasing positive emotions; and improving quality of life.

MBSR is also effective for professionals (doctors, nurses, therapists) who face significant stress in their work. MBSR includes short and long meditation exercises (5–45 minutes) that involve sitting or lying quietly while observing your breath, thoughts, sensations and emotions. It also includes mindfulness of daily activities, such as eating and walking.

Mindfulness-Based Cognitive Therapy (MBCT)

MBCT is based on MBSR. It was developed for people with depression and is effective in preventing and treating it. MBCT has also been adapted for anxiety, stress and health problems. It increases positive emotions and helps people gain clarity about their important goals in life. MBCT is usually taught as an eight-week class and includes meditation exercises and mindfulness during daily activities.

Dialectical Behaviour Therapy (DBT)

DBT was originally designed for people with borderline personality disorder, a condition that includes strong negative emotions, impulsive behaviour and stormy relationships.

DBT is also effective with eating problems, depression, anxiety and drug problems, and is helpful for anyone wanting to learn how to handle negative emotions. DBT can include individual therapy, group classes or both. It teaches a wide variety of mindfulness exercises, but doesn't require formal meditation.

Acceptance and Commitment Therapy (ACT)

ACT is flexible – it's provided as individual therapy, group classes or workshops. It includes a wide variety of mindfulness exercises, stories and metaphors. ACT emphasizes identifying your true priorities in life and making your behaviour consistent with them. It's helpful for many problems, including depression, anxiety, stress, chronic pain, alcohol and drug use, and health problems.

Other Promising Programmes

Mindfulness-Based Relapse Prevention (MBRP) – for substance abuse.

Acceptance-Based Behaviour Therapy (ABBT) – for anxiety.

Mindfulness-Based Eating Awareness Training (MB-EAT) – for binge eating and obesity.

How This Book Is Organized

Each chapter builds on previous ones, so it's best to read them in order the first time through. If you find that particular chapters are especially important for you, it may be helpful to return to them. For example, if you're prone to rumination, or if specific mindfulness skills resonate with you, re-reading those chapters may be beneficial. The book is divided into the following sections:

Part I – Introduction

The first two chapters introduce mindfulness and invite you to try a few simple exercises. These chapters are designed to provide a taste of mindfulness and whet your appetite for learning more. They won't give you a thorough understanding of mindfulness; that requires reading the rest of the book and practising the exercises.

Part II – Psychological traps

The next four chapters explain the psychological traps that Glenn fell into: rumination, avoidance, emotion-driven behaviour and self-criticism. These chapters describe how the traps work, why it's so easy to fall into them, and how mindfulness can get us out. The traps are very common. No matter what form of stress, worry or unhappiness is troubling you, there's an excellent chance that one or more of these traps – perhaps all four – is contributing to it. Each chapter in this section includes several tools: a short questionnaire for examining your own tendency to fall into the trap; a worksheet to guide you in observing and understanding your own patterns of thinking, feeling, and reacting; and introductory mindfulness exercises that will help you get out of the trap or avoid falling into it.

Part III – Mindfulness skills

These chapters provide a more comprehensive understanding of mindfulness skills, how to practise them and how they help. The chapters include exercises, worksheets and personal stories of people who've practised the exercises and benefited from them. Although each chapter focuses on a specific mindfulness skill, it's important to recognize that all the skills work together.

Part IV: Putting it all together

This section has two chapters. The first includes exercises that combine the mindfulness skills. This will provide a clearer understanding of how to bring everything together. The final chapter discusses happiness – what it means and how practising mindfulness will help you find it.

How to Make the Best Use of This Book

While working with this book, keep the following points in mind:

1 – It's impossible to understand mindfulness without practising it

Reading about mindfulness and talking about it with others is helpful, but practising mindfulness is a bit like skiing down a mountain, floating in the ocean, singing in a choir, riding a bicycle or walking the streets of an exotic foreign city. You don't really know what it's like until you do it yourself.

2 – Mindfulness can seem paradoxical and puzzling at first

Feeling puzzled is a normal part of the journey. See if you can adopt an open-minded, curious attitude. The nature of mindfulness, and how it can help you, will become clearer as you work with it, especially if you do the worksheets and exercises.

3 – It takes a while to see the effects of practising mindfulness

Trying the exercises just once or a few times probably won't be very helpful. Until you've had time to practise the exercises consistently, over a period of time, it's best not to draw conclusions about whether mindfulness will help you.

Frequently Asked Questions

How much practice is necessary?

No one really knows, although teachers agree that regular practice is important. In our clinic, we offer mindfulness programmes of eight weekly classes. We encourage participants to practise mindfulness nearly every day for the entire eight weeks before deciding whether it's helpful. Most people begin to see benefits within four weeks. A few people see benefits right away.

I recommend daily practice while working with this book over a period of eight to twelve weeks. That may sound like a big commitment, but it doesn't have to be. On the website for this book you'll find recordings to guide your practice of some of the exercises. Most of these take five to twenty minutes. The book also includes exercises for being mindful while doing things you were going to do anyway – eating, driving, walking, washing the dishes. Virtually any activity can be a mindfulness exercise if you pay attention to it with a non-judgemental attitude. This doesn't require any extra time.

Is mindfulness a religious practice?

Mindfulness was originally discussed in ancient Buddhist traditions, but it's about paying attention – a human ability that we all share, regardless of our religious background or beliefs. In today's modern world of psychology and mental health, mindfulness is taught as a set of skills and exercises for improving health and wellbeing. Mindfulness exercises can be practised in a completely non-religious way.

Some of the exercises in this book are based on meditation. This means that they invite you to sit quietly and focus your attention on specific things, like the sensations of your breath moving in and out of your body, or sounds you can hear in the environment. You can sit cross-legged on the floor if you like, but it isn't necessary. Many people prefer to sit in chairs.

Mindfulness meditation is a way of teaching yourself to observe your present-moment experiences with acceptance and friendly curiosity. It is NOT a way to empty your mind, stop your thoughts or numb your feelings. It develops clarity and insight about your thoughts and feelings, so that you can make wiser decisions about what to do in difficult situations.

Is a self-help book for me?

If you're interested in learning about mindfulness and willing to work with a book, then this one has excellent potential. The problems it discusses are part of being human. The mindfulness exercises are explained carefully and instructions are provided to guide you in practising them. The book is intended to be useful for people with a wide range of problems and concerns, as well as people seeking personal growth and insight.

If you have a clinically significant psychological disorder (such as severe depression or borderline personality disorder), severe drug or alcohol abuse, a traumatic background that causes you great distress, or if you're at risk of harming yourself, it would be wise to consider working with a therapist. This book is designed to be useful in conjunction with therapy, although it's important to talk with your therapist about whether it fits with the work you're doing.

What if I'm feeling sceptical about mindfulness?

It's perfectly OK to feel sceptical. I felt sceptical myself when I started learning about mindfulness in the 1990s. I had no experience with

meditation and learned about mindfulness when I did intensive professional training in dialectical behaviour therapy (see the box on pages
10–11 for a brief description of DBT). At that time, I thought mindfulness was for monks in monasteries, not for scientific psychologists. But I
needed to learn DBT for my professional work as a clinical psychologist,
teacher and supervisor, so I started practising the exercises.

To my surprise, the exercises had a big impact on me. I developed a
great interest in learning more. I read books by noted mindfulness teachers, went to mindfulness training sessions, conferences and meditation
retreats. I studied the mindfulness-based programmes described in the
box on pages 10–11. I undertook research on mindfulness.

The more I learned, the clearer it became that mindfulness was making a
huge difference in my life. I felt more appreciative of the external world,
more at ease with my inner workings. Mindfulness improved my self-
understanding and insight, clarified my priorities and made me happier.
It didn't get rid of stress and difficulties, but helped me handle them
more effectively. The same was true for the people I was working with:
clients, colleagues and students. Today, I continue to practise regularly,
using the skills described in this book. Mindfulness permeates how I see
the world and live my life.

However, this doesn't mean that I'm mindful every minute. I'm actually a somewhat absent-minded professor (as my students will tell you).
It also doesn't necessarily mean that mindfulness will change your life.
However, research shows that practising mindfulness helps a great many
people. My own research, teaching, clinical work and personal experience confirm this. I'm confident that if you work your way through this
book in the spirit of exploration and interest, there's an excellent chance
it will make a difference to you. And, like anything else, you will get
more out of it if you put more into it.

So let's get started.

2 Welcoming All Visitors to the Mind

'The content and quality of our lives depend on our level of awareness.'

Sharon Salzberg

Imagine that a winter storm has caused trees to fall on power lines all over your city. You and countless others have no electricity. Your house is cold; you can't cook, watch TV or use your computer. After dark, you rely on candles and torches. According to the newscast on your battery-powered radio, electricity won't be restored for days.

You consider your priorities and options. Do you need more candles, batteries, blankets or food that doesn't need cooking? Which shops are still open? Should you try to get a kerosene heater? Where will you find kerosene? Could you stay with friends or relatives for a few days? What would be best for your two young children, your dog, your house?

From the library, which still has power, you contact your sister, who lives 100 miles away and was unaffected by the storm. She invites you to stay with her for as long as necessary. You gratefully accept. Now you have a clear goal: to get your family to your sister's home. You start packing, preparing the car, securing your house and notifying people that you'll be away.

While handling this situation, you're in a state of mind called *problem-solving mode* – focusing on goals and thinking rationally about how to achieve them. When we're in problem-solving mode, we notice *discrepancies*: differences between the way things are (at home with no power, uncomfortable) and the way we want them to be (at sister's house, more comfortable). To reduce the discrepancies, we analyse the problems, think of potential solutions, put plans into action, keep track of progress and revise plans when necessary.

Problem-solving mode is extremely useful for managing crises. In fact, it's essential for accomplishing any complex project. Renovating a kitchen, writing a book, growing a vegetable garden – all require planning, working towards goals, checking on progress and dealing with difficulties. On a larger scale, problem-solving mode is responsible for many of humanity's great achievements, such as computers, air travel and medicine. All were developed by generations of scientists, engineers, inventors and others working to reduce discrepancies between the status quo and a desired future.

Even an ordinary day requires frequent use of problem-solving mode. Daily life is full of discrepancies between the present situation (haven't showered, dressed, fed the cats, eaten breakfast or gone to work) and the desired situation (all of that done by 9.00a.m.). Some of this behaviour is so automatic that we don't think of it as problem-solving – it's our normal routine. But the mental process is the same: noticing discrepancies, acting to reduce them and checking on progress.

Many people enjoy solving problems, large or small, one after another. Some choose a profession based on a love of skilful problem-solving. Plumbers, mechanics and doctors, among others, devote their careers to solving problems for others' benefit; many find the work rewarding and fulfilling.

Problem-solving mode is so helpful that we expect it to work for every problem that arises. Unfortunately, in some circumstances it doesn't work very well. Let's consider two examples.

Alicia's Story

Alicia is in training to become a history teacher. She's teaching her first lesson to a class of sixteen-year-olds in a few days. She feels nervous about it and wishes she felt calm. This is a discrepancy; it seems to call for problem-solving mode.

At first, problem-solving is useful; it helps Alicia think of ways to feel less nervous. She works hard on her lesson plan; she practises the lesson with fellow trainees; she chooses what to wear to feel comfortable in the classroom, which is often too warm.

But she's still terribly nervous. She reminds herself that she's well prepared, that her fellow trainees enjoyed the lesson, that it doesn't have to be perfect – it's a training exercise and her supervisor will provide feedback afterwards. She takes deep breaths and relaxes her face and shoulder muscles. In the evening, she goes for a vigorous bike ride.

These strategies help, but she's not nearly as calm as she'd like to be. Every time she thinks of the lesson, her heart races. 'What's wrong with me?' she asks herself. 'Why can't I settle down? I'll never succeed if I can't control my nerves.' She tries to stop thinking about the lesson, but it keeps coming back to her mind. Then she ruminates about it. 'This is going to be terrible,' she tells herself repeatedly. 'The students will have no respect for me.' She imagines the lesson going badly, the students rolling their eyes and refusing to participate, her supervisor having to step in. 'I have no future as a teacher,' she thinks as she gets into bed.

These thoughts make it hard for Alicia to fall asleep. She gets up and drinks two glasses of wine. This helps temporarily, but she wakes up at 4.00 a.m. and can't go back to sleep.

Alicia's attempts to feel less nervous were helpful at first, but now they're making matters worse. Why is this happening? Unfortunately, it's often difficult to get rid of negative emotions, especially in situations like Alicia's, where it's normal to be nervous. We can take reasonable steps, as Alicia did, but it's unlikely that nervousness will completely disappear. Trying too hard to get rid of nervousness led Alicia into psychological traps discussed in the previous chapter: rumination, self-criticism and emotion-driven behaviour.

Alan's Story

A week ago, Alan asked his girlfriend of two years to marry him. She declined. She's moving away to take a new job, isn't ready for marriage and doesn't want to continue the relationship. She was clear that she won't change her mind.

Alan is facing a huge discrepancy between the way things are and the way he'd like them to be. He's understandably upset. His mind automatically jumps into problem-solving mode, trying to think of ways to change the situation. He ruminates about what he could have done differently, but arrives at no clear answers. Judgemental thoughts circulate through his mind. 'I guess I just wasn't good enough for her,' he tells himself. 'I can't believe I messed this up. There must be something wrong with me.' These thoughts lower his mood and create tension. He becomes irritable, snapping at people who are trying to be supportive. Then he criticizes himself and avoids his friends. Like Alicia, Alan has fallen into psychological traps.

How Mindfulness Helps

When we need to do something important but stressful, or when facing painful situations that can't be changed, it's difficult to handle our feelings wisely. The problem-solving mode can cause trouble because it keeps us focused on trying to change things, even when change is unrealistic. In these situations, we need skills for accepting unpleasant realities. Practising mindfulness teaches us how to accept the things we can't change. Paradoxically, this leads to healthier, more meaningful change.

Let's look at what happens with Alicia and Alan after they learn the mindfulness skills taught in this book.

Alicia

Alicia recognizes that she has done everything she can to prepare for her history lesson. Ruminating about nervousness and trying to eliminate it are not helping. She adopts a mindful perspective, observing her racing heart and shaky feelings with a non-judgemental and self-compassionate attitude. When self-critical and pessimistic thoughts come to mind ('I'll never succeed if I can't stay calm'), she recognizes that they're *thoughts* –

she doesn't have to believe them or act on them. She accepts that anxious thoughts and feelings are natural under the circumstances. She reminds herself of her longstanding desire to be a history teacher and reaffirms her willingness to take the necessary steps. 'Teaching my first lesson is part of the process,' she tells herself. 'To work towards my goal, I'm willing to do things that make me nervous.'

Alicia feels much better, but not because she's rid herself of nervousness. Rather, the way she *relates* to her feelings of nervousness has changed. She has shifted from problem-solving mode to *mindful acceptance* mode, a distinctly different state of mind. She realizes that she can allow the nervous feelings to come and go on their own, while she proceeds with what she needs to do. She doesn't have to control the nervous feelings, and they don't have to control her. This understanding gives her a strong feeling of wellbeing.

Alan

Alan also shifts into mindful acceptance mode. He recognizes that the end of a long relationship is painful for most people and he needs to take care of himself. He observes his feelings of sadness, noticing the sensations of heaviness and hollowness. Other thoughts and feelings appear: anger at his girlfriend, fear of being alone. He accepts them as normal for the situation and allows them to come and go. When he has judgemental and despairing thoughts about himself, his feelings or his future ('I wasn't good enough, I'll never find anyone else') he notices them, labels them as thoughts, and doesn't dwell on them.

Instead, he asks himself what he needs: a good meal, a long walk, an amusing movie, an important task, a chat with a friend? He turns his attention to constructive behaviour, such as working on a project or making plans to see his family. He accepts that these behaviours don't change the fact that his relationship ended. They don't get rid of his sadness – the sad feelings will pass gradually, in their own time. Even so, he feels better than when he was ruminating and is less likely to lose his temper.

He recognizes that he can carry on with his life, gently and kindly, while going through a period of great sadness.

Alicia and Alan's stories illustrate important points about mindful acceptance mode. It's *mindful* because we're paying attention, not ignoring or denying the realities of the situation. Mindful acceptance is friendly and compassionate, not critical or judgemental. It differs from problem-solving mode because we're not trying to reduce discrepancies or fix anything – we're *allowing* certain realities to be as they are, even if we don't like them.

Mindful acceptance does NOT mean saying, 'I guess I just have to accept this,' and resigning yourself to hopelessness and passivity. It's not weak or spineless, and doesn't mean you don't care. It won't keep you stuck in misery. On the contrary, mindfulness increases clarity and broadens our perspective. Because we're observing closely, we're more likely to see what's actually happening – in the situation and in our hearts, minds and bodies. If we've made mistakes, a state of mindful awareness helps us see them clearly, reflect on them and learn from them. As a result, we're more likely to choose wise actions. We're better able to see opportunities for *meaningful* change, such as advancing towards an important goal or finding a new path.

Introduction to Practising Mindfulness

Practising mindfulness means focusing attention on the present moment in a non-judgemental and accepting way. In any given moment, we have many choices about what to focus on. We might choose something outside the body, such as sights, sounds or scents in the environment. If we're being mindful, we observe them with openness and acceptance, allowing them to be the way they are.

Mindfulness of sounds

What sounds can you hear right now? As best you can, observe them with interest as they come and go. See if you can bring a non-judgemental, accepting attitude to all the sounds you can hear, whether they're pleasant, unpleasant or neutral. For example, you might notice birds singing a lovely song, a lawn mower making an obnoxious noise, or footsteps passing outside the room. Do you notice a tendency to judge the sounds, or to figure out what is making each sound? Are you thinking about how to avoid the unpleasant sounds or hear more of the pleasant ones? If so, see if you can let go of these thoughts. Practise observing the sounds as they occur and accepting them as they are. Adopt a friendly, curious and open-minded attitude toward the sounds. Notice their qualities, such as pitch, volume or duration. Notice periods of silence between sounds. Close your eyes, or look away from this page, and try this for a minute or two.

Your mind is likely to wander off. This is normal. When you notice that your mind is elsewhere, gently bring your attention back to observing sounds.

Mindfulness of sensations

We can also focus our attention internally, on sensations in the body, or on thoughts, emotions or images in the mind. Try it now, with sensations in your right hand. What can you feel in your right hand at this moment? Is it warm or cool, sweaty or dry, itchy, tingly, numb or neutral? Is it touching something? Do you feel the texture or temperature of whatever your hand is touching? Spend a few moments closely observing the sensations in your right hand, with an attitude of acceptance and curiosity. Allow the sensations to be exactly as they are, even if they're unpleasant. If you don't feel very much at all in your hand, practise observing the absence of sensation and accepting that as your current experience.

Your mind will wander off. When you notice, gently bring it back. As best you can, refrain from criticizing yourself about the wandering mind. Everyone's mind wanders.

Practising mindfulness on a walk

Going for a walk provides good opportunities to observe the external world *and* notice what your mind and body are doing. Before trying it, consider the following examples of walking in a park in different mental modes:

Melinda: walking in problem-solving mode

Melinda has an important meeting a few blocks from her office. The quickest way to get there is to walk through a park. Melinda sets out with no time to spare, keeping to the stone path to avoid the damp ground and thinking of what she'll say during the meeting. Suddenly, she comes upon a work crew. They've dug up a large section of the stone path, creating a muddy mess.

'Oh no,' she thinks. 'Why didn't they put up a sign? I don't have time to turn back. I'll just have to go around.' Melinda feels frustrated and annoyed, but focuses on her goal of getting to the meeting – on time and looking professional. She detours quickly around the mud, trying to keep her feet dry. She arrives with just enough time to stop in the restroom and wipe the worst of the dirt and grass from her shoes.

Valerie: walking in mindful acceptance mode

Valerie is walking in the park during her lunch break. She's not in a hurry and has no particular destination. Her only goal is to be back in her office in half an hour. She feels the air on her skin, smells the fresh scents, watches the trees swaying in the breeze and appreciates the sounds of the birds. Thoughts and daydreams pass through her mind, but she doesn't dwell on them; instead, she returns her attention to the environment around her.

When she comes to the dug-up portion of the path, she observes the mud, looks around, decides to go back the way she came, and walks in another section of the park.

Rob: walking in shifting mental modes

Rob begins his walk in mindful acceptance mode, feeling the warm sun, seeing flowerbeds in bloom and hearing children playing. He senses the ground under his feet and feels his arms gently swinging. Someone starts up a lawn mower. For a moment, he observes the sound mindfully, noticing its pitch, volume and texture. He smells the mower's fumes and the scent of cut grass.

Then a thought comes to Rob's mind about the state of his own lawn. Another thought follows, about the neighbourhood teenager who has not mowed it lately, despite promising to do it every week. A feeling of frustration arises. Rob's body becomes tense. Soon his mind is caught up in a stream of thoughts about his lawn. He pictures it looking shaggy and unkempt and his neighbours talking about it. He imagines storming over to the teenager's house and demanding that he do his job.

Suddenly, Rob realizes that he's been carried away by his thoughts. His body is still walking in the park, but his mind has been elsewhere, working (not very constructively) on the problem of the lawn. He notices that his fists are clenched, his face is scowling and his heart is beating faster. Gently, he brings his attention back to the present environment, feeling the breeze, smelling the air, seeing the grass and trees, hearing the lawn mower. He decides that, after his walk, he will make a rational plan for dealing with his lawn. For now, when thoughts about the lawn come to his mind, he notices them in the same way he notices other things. 'Hey, there's a thought,' he says to himself. 'Oh, there's a butterfly.'

Instructions for Your Own Mindful Walk

Walk anywhere you like: in a park, your neighbourhood, even an indoor shopping mall. Choose a time when you don't have conflicting demands. Start by walking mindfully, as best you can. Choose something specific to focus on. For the first few minutes, you might observe sounds. As before, notice them with an attitude of friendly curiosity, even if you find some of them unpleasant. See if you can let go of analysing the sounds; focus on simply hearing them.

If you like, play with variations; focus on just one specific sound for a while, then switch to a different one. Then expand your awareness to include all the sounds at once. Listen for sounds ahead of you or behind you, to your left or your right. Refrain from judgements about how well you're doing. If you're hearing sounds, you're doing fine.

Then switch to seeing. Notice colours, shapes or movements in your environment. Do you notice a tendency to label or analyse what you see? As best you can, let go of thinking about what you see and focus on just observing it. For example, instead of 'That's a rose bush', notice shapes and colours, patterns of light and shadow, the textures of the leaves or petals.

As you choose, switch to observing the scents in the air, the sensations of your feet moving along, the sun on your skin, or anything else. Practise noticing without judgement, allowing whatever you observe to be just as it is, even if it's unpleasant.

Before long, your mind will wander off. This is completely normal. Minds naturally wander, so refrain from criticizing yourself, as best you can. See if you can recognize where your mind went. Were you thinking about a problem, like how to get your lawn mowed or what to say in a meeting? Were you concentrating on a goal? Did your mind travel into the future or the past? Perhaps you were daydreaming about a variety of things. It doesn't matter. When you notice that your mind has wandered, gently bring it back to observing the present moment and accepting it as it is. The more you practise this, the stronger your mindfulness skills will become.

Why It's Helpful to Practise Mindfulness

Think about what happens when you pursue the goals that are most important to you. Is it always easy and pleasant? For most people, a meaningful and satisfying life includes stressful, challenging, even painful experiences. They seem to be inescapable.

For example, parenting includes many joys and satisfactions, but good parents also have to cope with stressful events and circumstances: health problems; accidents; academic, behavioural or emotional difficulties; peer-group problems; and the ever-changing balance between closeness and independence. Likewise, a career can be rewarding and fulfilling, but with significant costs: difficult professional training; long hours; competition with highly qualified peers; and evaluation by critical supervisors.

Pessimistic thoughts, such as 'I'll never succeed at this' and 'This is too much for me' inevitably come up as we pursue our most important goals. Negative emotions arise, such as anxiety, sadness, disappointment, boredom and anger. We feel urges to give up, lash out or distract ourselves in unhealthy ways. We might prefer to avoid these unpleasant thoughts, feelings and urges, but they're a normal part of an active, engaged, satisfying life. The alternative – an inactive, disengaged life – causes its own type of unhappiness.

Practising mindfulness teaches us that we don't have to fight with painful thoughts and emotions. Instead, we can choose a mental mode. When the problem-solving mode would be useful, we can analyse the situation and work towards changing it. When the problem-solving mode is not useful, we can observe our thoughts and feelings with openness and acceptance, rather than struggling to suppress, escape or change them. Mindfulness teaches us a valuable lesson about ourselves: we are more than our thoughts and feelings. Thoughts and feelings are like visitors – they come and go. We enjoy some of them and dislike others. Either way, we may learn from them. Most importantly, we don't have to be controlled by them.

The mindful approach to thoughts and feelings may still seem unnatural or confusing to you. Or you may think it makes sense but feel uncertain of how to apply it to your own life. These reactions are common and normal. Your understanding will increase as you work through the rest of this book.

For now, it may be helpful to consider the following poem, 'The Guest House', by the Persian poet Rumi. It was written in the thirteenth century, and is popular today among mindfulness teachers. It uses a powerful metaphor to portray mindful acceptance of thoughts and emotions, especially unpleasant ones. It invites us to contemplate the idea that treating our thoughts and feelings as honoured guests can make our lives richer and more satisfying. Read it slowly and let it sink in.

The Guest House

This being human is a guesthouse.
Every morning a new arrival.

A joy, a depression, a meanness,
some momentary awareness comes
as an unexpected visitor.

Welcome and entertain them all!
Even if they're a crowd of sorrows,
who violently sweep your house
empty of its furniture,
still, treat each guest honourably.
He may be clearing you out
for some new delight.

The dark thought, the shame, the malice,
meet them at the door laughing,
and invite them in.

Be grateful for whoever comes,
because each has been sent
as a guide from beyond.

In Western culture, this is an unorthodox way of relating to negative thoughts and emotions. Meet them at the door, welcome them and invite them in. Don't try to chase them off, ruminate about them, or criticize yourself for having them. This can be very difficult without the necessary skills. We will see in the following chapters how attempting to bar the door or run away from thoughts and feelings causes us to get stuck in psychological traps, and how practising mindfulness skills can set us free.

Part 2

Psychological Traps

3 Rumination

'You'll never plough a field by turning it over in your mind.'

Irish proverb

At 8.00 a.m., Keith discovers that his car won't start. He thinks, 'Oh no, I have a meeting at 8.30! I'm going to be late. This is such a pain. What am I going to do?'

Keith thinks about who might give him a ride. First he pictures his co-workers, one by one, trying to remember where they live. Then he considers his neighbours, wondering if any are still at home and where they work. He thinks of several friends. For a moment, he imagines himself on a bicycle. He considers taking the bus.

None of these ideas seem very promising. He only knows a few of his co-workers well enough to ask for such a favour, and they don't live nearby. He hardly knows his neighbours at all. Most of his friends start work at 8.00 and have probably already arrived at their jobs. He doesn't own a bicycle. The bus service in his town is not very good; he's never used it and has no knowledge of the routes, the schedules, or even where the nearest stop is.

'I could call a taxi,' he thinks. 'But it will take time to arrive and I'll be late for the meeting.' Then he thinks about the meeting. 'How bad would it be if I missed it?' he asks himself. 'People sometimes miss this meeting and nothing terrible happens.' But then he remembers something on the agenda that he wants to discuss. 'This is so inconvenient!' he thinks. 'What else could I do? Would the boss agree to postpone the meeting?'

Postponing the meeting seems unlikely. Then Keith remembers a recent meeting in which someone who was out of town participated by speakerphone. 'Speakerphone!' he thinks. 'I'll call the office and tell them I'm having car trouble. I'll ask the assistant to set up the speakerphone. Then I can participate in the meeting, call the mechanic about the car and get to work later.'

Frank has the same problem. At 8.00 a.m., he discovers that his car won't start. But instead of considering ways to handle the situation, Frank gets caught up in a different kind of thinking.

'Why does this sort of thing always happen to me?' he wonders. 'What's wrong with me that I can't do something as simple as get to work on time? This is completely my fault. I thought the car sounded a little funny yesterday and I didn't do anything about it. Why didn't I take it to the mechanic immediately? That was really stupid. I should have known something was wrong.'

Frank remembers other occasions when he's missed work because of unexpected problems. 'I've done this too many times,' he tells himself. 'Just last winter when the pipes froze and I had water all over the house, that was a disaster! I missed two days before I got that sorted out. That was my fault, too – I forgot to leave the tap dripping.'

Then he makes pessimistic predictions. 'People are going to think this is typical of me, always so unreliable. I can imagine what they'll be saying when I walk in late. I bet my boss is wondering if I should really have this job.'

Frank's thinking becomes repetitive. He keeps telling himself he's an idiot, irresponsible and undeserving. He continues to chastise himself for not taking care of the car. He asks himself why he can't handle things better.

Helpful and Unhelpful Ways of Thinking about Problems

Keith and Frank thought about the same problem, but in different ways and with different results. Within a few minutes, Keith decided on a reasonable course of action and felt better, whereas Frank made no progress and his mood spiralled downwards. Keith was engaged in constructive problem-solving. Frank was ruminating.

Constructive Problem-solving

Keith's way of thinking included several steps shown in many studies to be useful for solving problems:

1 – Focusing on a clearly defined problem

Keith stayed focused on the specific problem: how to get to work on time, or how to handle the situation if arriving on time wasn't possible.

2 – Brainstorming

Keith thought of several ways to get to work: getting a ride from someone; riding a bicycle; taking the bus; calling a taxi. Then he thought of ways to cope with not arriving on time. Some of his ideas were not workable (he doesn't have a bicycle), but that didn't matter. At the brainstorming stage, the point is to think of many potential solutions. This increases the chances of coming up with something useful.

3 – Making a decision to try something

Keith decided to try the speakerphone option. It seemed promising: He knew there was a speakerphone in the office, the assistant could set it up, and it had been used recently and worked well.

Unconstructive Rumination

In ordinary language, the word 'rumination' sometimes means 'pondering' or 'reflection', both of which can be normal and healthy ways of considering something carefully. Psychologists, however, use the term 'rumination' to refer to the type of thinking that Frank was doing: negative, repetitive, prolonged, unhelpful thinking. Frank didn't focus on the specific problem, think of potential solutions, or make a decision to try something. Instead, he remembered previous difficulties (frozen pipes) and imagined future misfortunes (people thinking badly of him, losing his job). He criticized himself for perceived failings and asked himself vague questions ('What's wrong with me?') that didn't help with the immediate situation.

This unconstructive form of rumination – also known as brooding, stewing, obsessing, worrying, overthinking, dwelling on things, or turning something over and over in the mind – was of no help to Frank. The thoughts went round and round in his head, didn't solve anything, and made him feel worse.

Common Topics of Rumination

We can ruminate about many things: negative emotions; current problems; stressful events from the past; future disasters. Psychologists recognize several types of rumination. The topics are different, but the style of thinking is the same for each: negative, repetitive, prolonged and unhelpful. In the next box is a summary of common types of rumination.

COMMON TYPES OF RUMINATION

1 – Ruminating about sadness and depression

- Repetitive, unconstructive thinking about feeling sad, blue and dejected.

- Brooding about how exhausted or unmotivated you feel and why you feel so bad.

- Stewing about how terrible your situation will be if you continue to feel this bad.

- Obsessing over questions with no clear answers, such as, 'What have I done to deserve this?' or 'What's wrong with me?'

2 – Ruminating about anger

- Dwelling on how angry you feel and the event or situation that caused the anger.

- Replaying the incident in your mind, over and over.

- Obsessing about how unfair the situation was or how badly others behaved.

- Fantasizing about revenge.

- Having repeated mental arguments with people.

3 – Ruminating about future disasters

- Worrying about misfortunes that might afflict you or your loved ones: illnesses, accidents, losing a job, failure in school, financial or relationship problems, or anything else.

- Asking 'What if ... ?' and then imagining disastrous scenarios ('What if I get fired?')

4 – Ruminating about ongoing problems or past events

- Telling yourself repeatedly that the problem or stressful event was completely your fault (even if it wasn't).

- Dwelling on the idea that things like this always happen to you, that it's going to ruin things for you, that you can't cope.

5 – Ruminating about social interactions

- Worrying or obsessing about your behaviour with others – whether you said the wrong thing, looked foolish or offended someone.

- Replaying the conversation or interaction in your mind.

- Repeatedly imagining what you wish you'd said.

- Stewing over what others think of you now.

Bill's Story

Bill has had chronic back pain since a car accident two years ago. Every morning, he gets out of bed, feels the pain in his back and starts thinking, 'Why does this pain never get better? It's ruining everything. I can't function with this pain. I can't believe my doctors haven't found a way to control this. I'm going to be completely useless if this goes on. What if the rest of my life is wasted? What have I done to deserve this?'

Bill's thoughts continue along these well-worn tracks for long periods of time. His doctor encourages him to walk more, do gentle exercises, see his friends and resume activities he used to enjoy. Bill constantly tells himself that he should try harder, but he hasn't summoned the energy to follow his doctor's advice. He ruminates about that, too. 'Why can't I get going?' he asks himself repeatedly. 'I'm always so tired. I rest all the time, I should have more energy. What's wrong with me?' Rumination is causing Bill to feel depressed and hopeless. He spends most of his time lying in a recliner and watching TV, becoming more and more isolated.

Bill is ruminating in several of the ways described in the previous box. He obsesses about his current symptoms: pain, depression, fatigue, lack of motivation. He stews about his future. He dwells angrily on his doctor's failure to get rid of his pain.

Chronic back pain is a serious problem. If Bill stops ruminating, he'll still have back pain. But his doctor has given him good recommendations for managing it. Rumination keeps Bill focused on the most negative aspects of his situation. It lowers his mood, saps his motivation, and prevents him from focusing on constructive problem-solving. If he didn't spend so much time ruminating, he would have more energy and motivation to walk, stretch and see friends, even though he has pain. His quality of life would begin to improve.

Everyone ruminates now and then. If it doesn't happen often or persist for long periods, it probably won't do much harm. The self-test in the next box will help you examine your own tendency to ruminate. Using the rating scale provided, write the number in the blank space that indicates how true each statement is for you.

SELF-TEST: RUMINATION

1	2	3	4
Rarely true	Sometimes true	Often true	Very often true

_____ I keep thinking about how bad I feel.

_____ When something angers or upsets me, it replays in my mind for a long time.

_____ I worry about bad things that might happen in the future.

_____ I dwell on my problems for long periods of time.

_____ In my mind, I go over and over my embarrassing or awkward moments.

Add up your ratings. If you scored between 11–14, you may have a moderate tendency to engage in unhelpful rumination. If you scored between 15–20, this could be significant cause for concern.

Consequences of Rumination

Research shows that rumination has many serious consequences:

- It intensifies negative moods. Ruminating about sadness makes depression worse; ruminating about anger strengthens the angry feelings

- Rumination interferes with motivation, concentration, memory and problem-solving

- People who ruminate when they're sad or discouraged are more susceptible to serious depression, binge eating and alcohol abuse. They're more likely to develop post-traumatic stress disorder if something extremely stressful happens to them

- Anger rumination increases heart rate, blood pressure and muscle tension. It keeps the body from returning to a resting state

- Rumination harms relationships. People who ruminate when they're angry are more aggressive – criticizing others harshly, losing their temper and retaliating when they feel wronged. Constant obsessing about anything tends to annoy people, even if they want to be loving and supportive

- Ruminating about uncomfortable interactions with others lowers self-esteem and increases anxiety

Rumination is a Psychological Trap

If rumination is so harmful, why do we do it? There are several important reasons:

1 – We mistakenly believe that rumination should help

Sometimes rumination *feels* like constructive problem-solving. We think we're analysing our problems, situations or personalities, trying to understand why we're unhappy or stressed. It seems logical that this type of thinking would lead to deeper insight and better moods.

Unfortunately, this belief is mistaken. Rumination worsens negative moods and interferes with problem-solving.

2 – Rumination provides temporary protection from painful emotions

Imagine that someone has done something that hurt your feelings. Ruminating about how badly this person behaved makes you feel angry. The anger may be unpleasant, but it distracts you from the pain of your hurt feelings. Anger is often preferable to hurt feelings because it makes us feel justified or energized. We sometimes enjoy dwelling on others' misdeeds when we're upset with them. Like a prosecuting attorney, we mentally build the case against the accused, feeling stronger and more confident as we amass the evidence. This keeps us from feeling vulnerable, or thinking about painful realities, such as the role we might have played in the situation, or serious problems in the relationship that need to be resolved.

3 – Rumination distracts us from constructive but difficult behaviour

Suppose you are partly responsible for the episode in which your feelings got hurt. Perhaps the other party is not entirely to blame. To repair the relationship, it might be necessary to bring up the subject for discussion, to apologize, or to change your behaviour. This may feel awkward and painful. As long as you stay absorbed in rumination, you don't have to confront the need to do something difficult.

Rumination is a psychological trap. We get caught in the trap because of the short-term benefits and the illusion that it should help. But the price is high. In the long run, rumination worsens negative moods, saps our motivation to behave constructively, makes us more likely to do things we regret later, and keeps our bodies in an unhealthy state of tension.

Understanding Your Own Patterns of Rumination

The following worksheet will help you observe and understand your own tendency to ruminate. In order to benefit from this exercise, it's important to pay attention to your thinking processes. Try to notice when you're dwelling on repetitive thoughts about an unpleasant situation, problem or negative mood.

As you become more aware of your thinking, you may find that you're criticizing yourself for ruminating. As best you can, let go of the criticism. Instead, adopt the perspective of an explorer who takes a keen and open-minded interest in whatever is discovered. See if you can explore your own mental patterns with an attitude of *friendly curiosity*.

Here's an example of the rumination worksheet with instructions:

Worksheet: Understanding an episode of rumination

Remember to maintain an attitude of friendly curiosity

Day and time	Triggering event	Ruminative thoughts	Emotions	After-effects & consequences
When did this episode of rumination occur?	*What started your episode of rumination? Where were you? What was going on? Were other people involved?*	*What thoughts were going round and round in your head?*	*What emotions were you feeling while you were ruminating?*	*How did you feel after the episode? What happened next?*
Writing this down helps you to be specific about which episode you're working with, isolating it from other things going on in your life. If you do the worksheet several times, it will help you see patterns.	The trigger might be an event in the external world, such as being criticized at work. Or it could be an emotional state that came over you for no clear reason – maybe you woke up feeling depressed or anxious and started ruminating.	As best you can, write down your thoughts exactly as they appeared in your mind. If you had images or pictures in your mind, describe them.	You may have felt one or more negative emotions, such as sadness, anger, anxiety, guilt or shame. Note them here. If you felt any positive emotions, note them also.	Include body sensations, thoughts, emotions and urges. Also include any effects on your behaviour or interactions with others.

Let's look at a copy of the worksheet completed by Ellen (on the next page) a woman in her forties who often feels socially awkward and worries that people don't like her. She has been attending a monthly book club as a way to make new friends.

After studying Ellen's example, try completing the worksheet for one of your own episodes of rumination, using the blank version on page 44. Make extra copies of the worksheet first – the exercise is especially useful if you complete it several times. After you've done it once, be alert to future episodes of rumination and work through this exercise again. This will help you to identify negative thinking patterns over time.

Each time you complete the worksheet, choose one specific occasion to write about: an episode of rumination that occurred on a particular day at a specific time. The most recent episode might be the easiest to remember, but choose one that stands out in your mind.

Don't worry about trying to keep a perfect record. The purpose of the exercise is not to criticize yourself but to gather information, in a non-judgemental way, about your own thought processes. Using the rumination worksheet is one way of developing mindfulness skills that will help you deal more effectively with unhealthy thinking patterns.

Worksheet: Understanding an episode of rumination

Your name: <u>Ellen</u>

Remember to maintain an attitude of friendly curiosity

Day and time	Triggering event	Ruminative thoughts	Emotions	After-effects & consequences
Wednesday around 3.00p.m.	I was at my book group meeting. I was sharing my thoughts about the book when a group member checked her cell phone for messages.	I talk too much. People are noticing it takes me too long to make my point. They get bored with what I'm saying. They're not taking me seriously. No one wants me here. Why can't they listen to me? They shouldn't be so judgemental. I listen when they talk. They should pay attention when I talk.	First I felt shame and fear, then I was angry.	I was quieter than usual during the rest of the meeting. Afterwards I didn't chat with anyone or make a coffee date like I usually do. I went straight to my car. When I got home I felt lonely and had no energy. I over-ate. When my daughter called wanting to talk about her divorce, I was more impatient with her than usual. I felt hopeless about relating normally to other people.

Worksheet: Understanding an episode of rumination

Your name: _____

Remember to maintain an attitude of friendly curiosity

Day and time	Triggering event	Ruminative thoughts	Emotions	After-effects & consequences

After you've completed this worksheet several times, reflect on any patterns that may have emerged.

- Do you tend to ruminate about particular topics (how sad you feel, how badly you or others behaved, potential future disasters)?

- Do you tend to ruminate in specific situations?

- What are the usual consequences of rumination?

Mindfulness: an Alternative to Rumination

What should we do in place of rumination? We've already seen that constructive problem-solving is much more helpful: identifying a specific problem, thinking of possible solutions, and trying something that might help.

But what if there is no specific problem to be solved?

After one of her book club meetings, Ellen went shopping. She put her purchases into the car, backed out of her parking space, and hit another car in the passenger-side door, making a large dent. No one was hurt, but Ellen felt terrible. She apologized, provided all of her contact and insurance information, and made sure that the other driver's costs would be covered. She resolved to be more careful in the future.

Now there's nothing else that Ellen can do, but she's ruminating about the situation. She constantly asks herself how she could have been so careless, tells herself she's a terrible driver, and replays the incident in her mind.

Why is this happening? Ellen is feeling guilt and regret about the accident. This is normal. In fact, these feelings may help her remember to drive more carefully. But Ellen's mind doesn't want to let go of the incident. It sees a discrepancy between the way things are (*I caused an accident*) and the way she wants things to be (*I wish I hadn't*). Her mind is stuck in problem-solving mode, trying to think its way out of this discrepancy.

In this situation, problem-solving mode is not very useful. It may help Ellen to think of one or two more things she could do – for example, choosing parking spaces that she can exit by driving forward (when possible), or buying a newer car with a rear-view camera (when she can afford one). But she can't change the past. Every driver has moments of inattention that might cause an accident. Brooding about her mistake won't improve Ellen's driving. In fact, rumination will have unintended effects: she'll feel worse and be more preoccupied, *increasing* the chances of another accident.

In situations like this, mindfulness is a healthy alternative to rumination.

Using Mindfulness to Reduce Rumination

If you've been using the rumination worksheet, you've already started applying mindfulness skills to rumination. You've been observing your own thinking patterns with a friendly, curious, non-judgemental attitude. To begin building on these skills, let's revisit the poem from the previous chapter – 'The Guest House' by Rumi. (If you don't remember it very clearly, turn back to the end of chapter 2 and re-read it.)

According to the poem, unwanted thoughts and feelings are our guests. Let's think about how this mindful perspective applies to rumination. What does it mean to treat each guest 'honourably', as the poem suggests, even if we'd rather be rid of some of them?

Imagine that you operate a bed and breakfast. Some of your guests like to linger in your cosy breakfast room, getting to know each other and discussing all manner of things: the weather, the local attractions, the news of the day. A few of your guests have strong opinions about the state of the world. Some are angry about it, others are sad or anxious. These guests talk endlessly about the difficulties of the times, why things are going so badly, why we can't solve our problems, what's wrong with society, what our leaders should do about it, why these constructive steps will never be taken. These guests are ruminating. You find it unpleasant.

As the host, what can you do? Can you tell your guests to go out and enjoy the sights and leave you in peace? Perhaps you could, but it would be inhospitable, and it might not work. Some guests would rather stay indoors all day and continue the conversation. Can you persuade the guests to discuss more pleasant topics? Probably not, and they wouldn't like it if you tried. People immersed in troubling concerns often resist being steered to other topics. A guest house that discourages conversation among the guests might lose customers. This B&B is your livelihood and you love the welcoming feeling that it provides.

And so, as a gracious host, you're polite and cheerful to all of your guests. Every morning, you serve a nice breakfast. You ask your guests if they slept well. You help them with their plans for the day. Then you're free to go about your work. You don't have to participate in the unpleasant conversation. You don't have to agree with everything that is said. You can turn your attention to more pleasant guests, or to tasks that need doing in the house. You can still hear the louder guests, but their voices fade into the background as you attend to your duties in the kitchen, the guest rooms and the garden.

Now let's apply this image to your own experience. You are the guest house; your thoughts and feelings are the guests. You probably have some unpleasant guests (everyone does). Some of them are loud, critical and unreasonable. You wish they would leave or be quiet, but it's impossible to control them. Instead, you recognize that you have many guests. Arguing with the unpleasant ones doesn't seem to help, and so you turn your attention to the other guests. You continue with your activities. You look around. You can still enjoy the world and do good work even with unpleasant guests ruminating in the background.

It's important to recognize that this is difficult. Rather than in your house, ruminative thoughts are in your *head*. They feel very close. Moreover, ruminative thoughts are often about you. They're saying that you're an idiot, that you've messed things up again, that you can't cope, that things will never go your way, that other people don't treat you well. Thoughts about ourselves often feel compelling and important.

With practice, however, it's possible to see these thoughts as unpleasant guests in your internal B&B, to be treated with respect (briefly), and allowed to be themselves, while you turn your attention elsewhere. This can be a huge relief. Trying to make ruminating guests go away or talk about something else is exhausting. Practising mindfulness teaches us that the internal guest house is more spacious than we realized – there is room for many guests. We learn to welcome them all, regardless of whether we like what they have to say. We learn that we don't have to fight with them or try to control them. We can allow them to come and go in their own time, while directing our attention as we choose, pursuing activities that we value, and appreciating the breadth and depth of present moment.

What does this mean for Ellen? When she sees ruminative thoughts (*How could I have been so careless? I'm a terrible driver*) she recognizes them. 'Ah,' she says. 'There are the ruminating guests again.' She realizes that it's natural to feel regret after a car accident, that making mistakes is part of being human. She accepts the feeling of regret as an unpleasant guest, but one with a useful purpose: it reminds her to be attentive when driving. For a moment, she might ask herself if there's anything else she can do about the accident. 'No,' she says. 'Other than paying attention while I'm driving – and I'm doing my best – I've done everything I can.' She sees that dwelling on judgemental ruminative thoughts won't help. She gently turns her attention to whatever she's doing in the moment.

Steps to Follow When You Catch Yourself Ruminating

Step 1 – Labelling

As soon as you recognize that you've fallen into the trap of rumination, label it by saying to yourself, 'This is rumination,' or 'Ruminative thoughts have come to my mind,' or 'The ruminating guests are here again.' If you notice judgemental thoughts, such as 'I'm such an idiot,' or 'This is really stupid,' notice that these are judgements. Practise labelling the rumination in a gentle, matter-of-fact tone and letting go of the judgements, as best you can.

Step 2 – Redirecting your attention

Rumination often arises when we're doing something without paying attention, such as walking, driving or washing the dishes. If this happens, continue with what you're doing, but see if you can focus your attention on it more mindfully. If you're driving, feel the steering wheel in your hands and see the road in front of you. If you're washing the dishes, feel the sensations of your hands in the water, see the suds and the light glinting off the dishes, hear the sounds as you work, smell the washing-up soap. If you're walking the dog, notice the movements of the dog's legs, nose or tail, hear the panting, feel the pull on the leash and your feet on the ground, observe the smells in the air and the colours of your surroundings.

Step 3 – Choosing a new activity (if possible)

If you were doing something unconstructive when the rumination arose, like moping in bed, choose something else to do. If you're ruminating about a specific problem and something constructive could be done about it, take steps in that direction. Otherwise, choose something enjoyable, such as reading an engaging book, calling a friend, or watching something funny on TV. Or, do something that will give you a feeling of accomplishment, such as paying bills, working in the garden, or cooking an interesting dish. It might be helpful to make a list of activities to have on hand. If you don't feel like doing anything when rumination crosses your threshold, gently coax yourself to do something anyway, just as you might with a reluctant child. If one activity is not helpful, try another one. As best you can, focus your attention on what you're doing.

When the ruminative thoughts come up again, politely say hello to them and carry on with your activity, as if the thoughts were guests passing by in the corridor of your B&B. You might continue to hear them, but you don't have to participate in their conversation. Keep shifting your attention back to what you're doing – gently, and without giving yourself a hard time.

If the guest house metaphor feels unnatural, unrealistic or too difficult at this point, that's understandable. It's a new way of thinking that may seem quite foreign. See if you can keep an open mind about it, remembering the spirit of exploration and friendly curiosity. And remember that the journey has just begun. As you continue, you'll learn many more skills that help with rumination.

Even as your mindfulness skills improve, you'll occasionally have thoughts and feelings that are so threatening or unpleasant that you'll want to get rid of them. Trying to suppress or avoid particular thoughts and feelings is another trap. In the next chapter, we'll explore the avoidance trap and how mindfulness skills can help us stay out of it.

Chapter Summary

- Rumination, also known as brooding about or dwelling on things, is an unhelpful form of negative repetitive thinking. When we're ruminating, negative thoughts swirl persistently in our minds, intensifying negative moods without solving anything.

- Rumination has many unhealthy consequences. It reduces motivation and interferes with concentration and memory. It increases the risk of depression, anxiety, alcohol abuse, binge eating and post-traumatic stress.

- Observing your own thinking processes will help you learn to recognize rumination and distinguish it from constructive problem-solving.

- The guest house metaphor is a helpful way to cultivate a mindful attitude toward unpleasant thoughts and feelings. Allowing them to come and go, as if they were guests in a B&B, and turning our attention to other aspects of the present moment, helps us escape from the rumination trap.

4 Avoidance

'Try to pose for yourself this task: not to think of a polar bear, and you will see that the cursed thing will come to mind every minute.'

Fyodor Dostoyevsky

The famous Russian writer Dostoyevsky suggests an interesting paradox: the more we try *not* to think about something, the more we think about it. Psychologists began studying this paradox in the 1980s. In a famous experiment, university students were asked to sit alone in a room for five minutes, with no books or electronic devices, and to try not to think of a white bear. If thoughts of white bears came to mind, despite their efforts, they rang a bell. On average, participants rang the bell six times, or just more than once per minute. Before the experiment started, they probably were not thinking of white bears so often. They only started thinking of them every minute when asked *not* to think about them.

The experiment continued for another five minutes. Now the students were asked to think about white bears. They had many white-bear thoughts. In fact, they had significantly *more* white-bear thoughts than students who were asked to think about white bears from the beginning, but were never told *not* to think about them. This pattern was labelled the 'rebound effect'. Suppressing thoughts of white bears for five minutes caused the thoughts to bounce back at a higher rate than if they were never suppressed.

Thought suppression, or deliberately trying *not* to think about something, is a common psychological trap. On the surface, it looks like a sensible way of dealing with unwanted thoughts. But it often backfires and makes the thoughts more frequent. The same thing happens with unwanted emotions and urges. The more we try to avoid or suppress them, the stronger they become. In this chapter, we'll consider how this trap works, why we fall into it and how mindfulness skills can lead us out.

Suppressing Unwanted Thoughts and Feelings

Most of us have thoughts we'd like to avoid. We have painful memories of moments we'd prefer to forget. We worry about upcoming stressors, like giving a speech, even when we'd rather not think about it. People trying to cut back on smoking, drinking or overeating are often troubled by persistent, unwanted thoughts about cigarettes, alcohol or food. People suffering from post-traumatic stress, depression and anxiety often have intrusive, negative thoughts that are very upsetting. Nearly everyone has the occasional unwanted thought that seems bizarre or even shameful – thoughts of jumping off a tall building, shouting something nasty during a gathering, or attacking someone.

Thought suppression seems an obvious way to help ourselves feel better when we're preoccupied with something troubling. Conventional wisdom suggests that we should put such things out of our minds. However, since the original white-bear experiments, many studies have confirmed that trying to suppress upsetting thoughts has paradoxical effects: the thoughts come to mind more often and emotional distress gets worse.

In one experiment, smokers trying to quit were asked to sit alone in a room for five minutes. Half were told to avoid all thoughts of smoking. The others were told that they could think about anything that came to mind, including smoking. Those told *not* to think about smoking reported *more* smoking-related thoughts. Other studies show similar patterns in heavy drinkers trying not to think about alcohol and in people trying to suppress memories of stressful or traumatic events. The pattern is clear: for people with troubling thoughts, trying to get rid of the thoughts can make matters worse.

Theo's Story – Part 1

A year ago, Theo lost a high-paying job. After eight months of searching, he found a position paying a third of his former salary. He and his wife sold their heavily mortgaged house and rented an apartment. He traded his expensive car for an economical one. Instead of flying to the Caribbean for a vacation, they walked to the nearby park every day with their three-year-old son.

Theo tells himself how lucky he is. It's hard to get a new job and sell a house in today's economy. He knows people who've been unemployed for longer than he was. And yet, he finds it hard to stop longing for the life he used to have: the big home with the landscaped garden, eating out on a whim, the expensive private school where they had planned to send their son. 'How did I lose all that?' he keeps asking himself. Feelings of guilt and regret wash over him.

'Don't think about it,' he tells himself repeatedly. 'Don't dwell on the past.' But daily life is full of reminders. Every time he sees an expensive car, he remembers that he used to drive one. Walking into his small apartment triggers thoughts of being a poor provider. 'I have no right to feel bad,' he tells himself. 'Many people are worse off. I should appreciate what I have.' But the more Theo criticizes himself for his inability to control his thoughts and emotions, the worse he feels.

Theo is caught in the suppression trap. He has set himself an unrealistic goal: to keep certain thoughts, images and emotions out of his mind. This won't work. Troubling thoughts and feelings come to mind whether we want them to or not. Trying to suppress them makes them worse.

Mindfulness skills will help Theo with this problem. Later in the chapter, we'll see how. First, let's consider other types of unhealthy avoidance.

Other Forms of Avoidance

Sometimes we try to avoid uncomfortable thoughts and feelings by staying away from the people, places and activities that bring them up. This has appealing short-term benefits: we feel better if we don't put ourselves in awkward or stressful situations. In the long run, however, problems get worse and life becomes less satisfying and meaningful. The following stories illustrate the short-term benefits and long-term costs of avoiding situations and activities.

Andrew

Andrew suffers from severe social anxiety. He'd like to have friends and social connections, but he avoids situations where he might feel shy and uncomfortable about not knowing what to say. He comes to work very early in the morning so that he won't have to chat with co-workers on the way in from the parking lot. He brings his lunch and eats at his desk instead of joining his co-workers in the cafeteria. He works late and waits until the hallway is quiet before leaving.

Andrew enjoys cycling and goes for long rides alone at the weekends. He hasn't joined the local cycling club because of fears that the other members won't like or accept him. As a teenager, he enjoyed the youth group at his church. He tried going to church where he lives now, but couldn't summon the courage to talk to anyone and left feeling disappointed in himself and resentful of church members for not being friendlier.

Andrew hopes that someday he'll meet someone who understands him and with whom he feels at ease. He'd like to have a family, but he avoids the situations and activities that could lead him toward these goals. The short-term pay-off for avoidance is that he doesn't have to feel unpleasant sensations – pounding heart, sweaty palms, dry mouth. He doesn't have to experience the flood of negative thoughts that arise in social situations (*I never know what to say ... people must think I'm a loser*). On the other hand, his loneliness is getting worse. He is making no progress toward his long-term goal of having a family.

Roger

Roger doesn't like helping his children with their homework. As a child, Roger was unmotivated in school and got below-average grades, despite above-average intelligence. Later, he earned a certificate in electrical technology and now makes a good living as an electrician. But he still feels incompetent with academic tasks.

Every evening after dinner, Roger does the dishes and thoroughly cleans the kitchen. Then he pays bills, does laundry and makes household repairs while his kids do their homework. As soon as they've finished, he plays games or watches TV with them before bedtime.

Roger is a single parent. No one else is available to help the kids with their homework. Roger tells himself that he's encouraging his children's academic independence while taking good care of the house. But his children need more supervision with their homework. They're becoming lazier about it and not learning as much as they could. Roger avoids the homework because he's afraid of looking foolish if he doesn't understand their assignments.

Kate

Kate would like to be promoted at work, but she's afraid of criticism and disapproval. She works hard on every assignment and rarely makes mistakes. Her presentations and reports are highly polished. On the other hand, she spends much longer on these tasks than most of her colleagues. She barely meets her deadlines, completes only the tasks assigned to her, and never volunteers for anything else because she doesn't have time.

Kate's boss has not offered her a promotion because she perceives Kate as competent but slow. The boss would prefer less perfectionism and more initiative. Kate tells herself that her primary goal is to do excellent work. However, her over-preparation is driven by avoidance. She's avoiding the sinking feeling and thoughts of inadequacy that are triggered when she makes even the smallest mistake. As a result, her career has stalled.

These stories illustrate several important points about avoidance:

- It's easy to fool ourselves into thinking that avoidance behaviour is helpful. We tell ourselves something that sounds convincing: 'My reports need to be as good as I can possibly make them,' or 'My children need to be independent about doing their homework,' or 'I need to stay away from social activities until I get control of my anxiety.' If we act in accordance with these thoughts, we feel better in the short term. In the long run, problems get worse.

- Depending on the motivation, the same behaviour can be constructive or avoidant. Doing the laundry so that the children have clean clothes is constructive. Doing the laundry to avoid helping the children with their homework is problematic. Taking the stairs to get more exercise strengthens your body. Taking the stairs to avoid your co-workers in the lift contributes to loneliness.

- The same behaviour might be constructive and avoidant at the same time. For example, you might go to a friend's birthday party to make your friend happy *and* to avoid an assignment for work or school. If this is true, then a non-avoidant approach might require a compromise, such as going to the party for an hour and then working on your assignment.

Most of us try to suppress our thoughts and feelings now and then. We stay away from uncomfortable situations or activities. If it works and does no harm, then it isn't a problem. On the other hand, if it happens often and in many situations, it may be interfering with our happiness and quality of life. The following self-test will help you determine whether you're susceptible to these types of avoidance.

SELF-TEST: TWO TYPES OF AVOIDANCE

1	2	3	4
Rarely	Sometimes	Often	Very often

Suppression of thoughts and feelings:

_____ When something upsetting comes to mind, I try very hard to stop thinking about it.

_____ When negative thoughts come up, I try to put them out of my mind.

_____ I try to distract myself when I feel something uncomfortable.

_____ I work hard to get rid of upsetting feelings.

_____ When distressing memories come up, I try to push them out of my mind.

Avoidance of situations, behaviours or activities:

_____ I won't do something if I think it will make me uncomfortable.

_____ I tend to put off unpleasant things that need to get done.

_____ I go out of my way to avoid stressful situations.

_____ I'm quick to leave any situation that makes me feel uneasy.

_____ I avoid doing things that might bring up uncomfortable thoughts and feelings.

If you scored between 11–14 on either section, you may have a moderate tendency for unhelpful suppression or avoidance. If you scored 15–20 on either section (or between 30–40 in total), your suppression and avoidance may be more seriously problematic. You may be struggling fruitlessly to keep unpleasant thoughts, memories or feelings out of your mind. Or you may be procrastinating about important tasks or avoiding situations or activities that would help you reach valued goals.

Why We Fall into the Avoidance Trap

If avoidance is so harmful, why do we do it? There are several good reasons.

1 – Avoidance is useful in many situations

Avoiding dark streets in dangerous parts of town reduces the chance of being robbed. Avoiding a colleague who came to work with the flu reduces the likelihood of getting sick. Vicious dogs, tornadoes, touching hot stoves – many things should be avoided. It's part of human nature to feel fear, anxiety, nervousness or reluctance in situations that might be dangerous. These feelings motivate us to stay away from harm.

2 – Short-term distraction is sometimes helpful

How do you feel about dental work? If you have an appointment coming up in a few days, would you rather not think about it? Computer games, books, TV and other absorbing activities may keep your mind occupied temporarily. In this case, avoidance has short-term benefits (less anxiety about the dental work), but probably no significant long-term harm.

What about violent movies, or having a blood test? Do you cover your eyes or look away? If so, you're avoiding short-term discomfort. In the long run, you won't adapt to these experiences, but this may not be a problem. Your quality of life probably won't suffer.

3 – We think we should be able to get rid of unpleasant thoughts and feelings

As children, we may have been told not to be sad, angry or nervous, not to worry, or not to cry, even when these were normal reactions to situations. Such directives from adults are often well intentioned, but they lead children to believe that mature people have their thoughts and feelings under complete voluntary control. This assumption may persist into adulthood.

It's an illusion. Many people who look calm and happy on the outside are struggling on the inside. Even the happiest, most well-adjusted people don't completely control their thoughts and feelings.

4 – We're susceptible to short-term effects of our own behaviour

It's part of human nature to be strongly influenced by the immediate effects of our behaviour. When avoidance reduces distress and makes us more comfortable, we're encouraged to keep using it, even when it's inconsistent with important, long-term goals, stops us from solving our problems, and makes us feel worse over time.

Understanding Your Own Patterns of Suppression and Avoidance

We all have our own ways of suppressing and avoiding. The following worksheet will help you observe and understand your patterns. Remember that avoidance behaviour is a natural reaction to unpleasant thoughts, feelings and situations. Sometimes it's automatic and unplanned.

Occasionally, it looks like constructive behaviour. It can be difficult to discern whether a specific behaviour is a form of avoidance. Looking closely at the short-term and long-term effects helps us clarify what's happening. This worksheet will help you learn to recognize various forms of avoidance and respond to them in skilful ways.

As you become more familiar with your avoidance patterns, you may find that you're criticizing yourself for avoiding. Remember that mindfulness of your own mental processes means observing them with friendly curiosity rather than judgement. The purpose of filling out this avoidance worksheet is not to criticize yourself, but to develop self-awareness and insight that will make it easier to deal with stress in the future.

Worksheet: Understanding your patterns of avoidance

Remember to maintain an attitude of friendly curiosity

Day and time	Event or situation	Avoidance behaviour: What did you say or do?	What were you avoiding? (Thoughts, feelings, urges, people, places, activities)	Short-term benefits of avoidance	Long-term harm of avoidance
When did this avoidance behaviour occur? Writing down the day and time helps you be specific and reveals patterns.	What triggered your avoidance behaviour? Where were you? What was going on? Were other people involved? Common situations for avoidance: • relationships • work, school • household tasks • money, finances • personal wellbeing	Describe your behaviour in the situation. Be specific about what you did that helped you avoid something. Examples: • suppressed thoughts or feelings • distracted yourself with activities (TV, eating, shopping) • did something useful (exercise, work, chores) to avoid something else • turned down an opportunity in order to avoid stress, discomfort	Did you stay away from particular people, situations or activities? If so, what thoughts, memories, images, emotions, sensations, urges or temptations were you avoiding?	The short-term effects are often positive or desirable. You didn't have to: • put yourself in a difficult situation • do or think about something unpleasant • feel unwanted sensations, emotions or urges	The long-term effects are often harmful: • you feel worse • a problem gets worse in the long run • avoiding stops you from making progress towards an important goal

The next page shows how Andrew filled in this worksheet. Andrew was the lonely man we met earlier who avoids his co-workers. He used to believe that staying away from stressful situations would help him feel better, and that after he felt better he could start working toward his goals.

By completing this worksheet, Andrew is beginning to understand that trying to avoid his thoughts and feelings backfires. The more he tries to avoid feeling anxious, the more he feels lonely and unfulfilled.

On page 64 is a blank version of the worksheet. Make multiple copies of it. You'll be better able to see patterns in your behaviour if you write down several examples.

How Mindfulness Helps with Avoidance

Avoidance of unpleasant thoughts and feelings often backfires. But we learned in chapter 2 that ruminating about them also backfires. If we shouldn't avoid them and shouldn't dwell on them, what can we do?

Mindfulness of thoughts and feelings is the healthy path between avoidance and rumination.

Theo's Story – Part 2

Theo is at the playground with his little boy. A passing car, just like the one he used to drive, catches his eye. He feels a sharp pang of envy and regret. Images of his former life flash through his mind. 'I can't believe I lost all that,' he thinks. Then he feels guilty for dwelling on the past.

But now he knows the mindfulness skills taught in this book. 'OK,' he says to himself. 'Those are thoughts and feelings about the past. They're visitors who come along now and then. They can come and go as they please. I can't really control them. Let me focus on what I'm doing right now.' He digs his bare feet into the sandbox where his son is playing, feeling the gritty texture, noticing that the sand is warm near the surface, cooler below. He takes a deep breath and feels the air flowing through his nose. He looks at his son, seeing the sun glint off his hair, watching

Worksheet: Understanding your patterns of avoidance

Your name: <u>Andrew</u>

Remember to maintain an attitude of friendly curiosity

Day and time	Event or situation	Avoidance behaviour: What did you say or do?	What were you avoiding? (Thoughts, feelings, urges, people, places, activities)	Short-term benefits of avoidance	Long-term harm of avoidance
Saturday 9.00a.m.	Riding my bike, saw 2 cyclists at side of road, repairing flat tyre.	Could have stopped to see if they needed help, but I just gave a little wave and rode on.	Awkwardness of talking to people I don't know.	Didn't have to face up to feeling awkward talking to new people.	Felt guilty about not checking if they needed help. Missed opportunity to meet other cyclists.
Tuesday lunchtime	Co-worker stopped by my office, asked me to go to lunch in cafeteria.	I said no, too much work to do.	Feeling awkward and embarrassed if I can't keep conversation going through lunch.	Got a little work done over lunch. Didn't have to talk to co-worker, could have been awkward.	I feel lonely at work. People will ignore me if I'm never sociable.
Wednesday 3.00p.m.	Goodbye party at work for someone who's moving away.	Came late, sat off to one side, only talked to one person, left early.	Having to make small talk. Feeling awkward and nervous.	Didn't have to worry about what to say, keeping conversations going.	Felt like a loser. I barely know my co-workers.

Worksheet: Understanding your patterns of avoidance

Your name: _____

*****Remember to maintain an attitude of friendly curiosity*****

Day and time	Event or situation	Avoidance behaviour: What did you say or do?	What were you avoiding? (Thoughts, feelings, urges, people, places, activities)	Short–term benefits of avoidance	Long–term harm of avoidance

his body move and the concentration on his face as he digs in the sand. 'What are you building now?' Theo asks. 'Can I help?'

Theo is using the guest house metaphor discussed in the previous chapter, allowing his thoughts and feelings to come and go at their own pace, as if they were guests in his B&B, while turning his attention to what he's doing in the present: playing with his son. This is not a form of avoidance. He's not suppressing his painful thoughts and feelings; he's completely aware of them. But he's also not ruminating about them. He's accepting them as visitors to his mind while continuing with an activity he values and finding contentment in the present moment.

Another Helpful Metaphor: Passengers on the Bus

The passengers-on-the-bus metaphor, in the next box, is an alternative to the guest house metaphor. It provides another way of understanding the mindful approach to thoughts and feelings. Read it through carefully with your own difficult thoughts and feelings in mind – the ones you'd most like to suppress or avoid.

PASSENGERS ON THE BUS

Imagine that you're a shy, lonely person and your goal is to have more friends and a satisfying social life. To work toward this goal, you're trying to be more sociable: initiating conversations, going to parties, and inviting people to lunch and the movies.

It's difficult because of the thoughts and feelings that come up. Socializing makes you feel sweaty, tense, and anxious. Your thoughts are like intimidating people in your head. 'You are an awkward misfit,' they say. 'You're the type who never fits in. This won't work. People don't want to spend time with you.'

Now picture yourself driving a bus. Your destination is **A Better Social**

Life, and you're steering in this direction. Imagine that your thoughts and feelings are the passengers on the bus. They sit in the back, shouting at you. 'Turn around,' they say. 'There's no point in going this way. You'll never have friends.' They're loud and persistent.

You have a sinking feeling that the passengers might be right, but you're determined to try. 'I have to do something about these nasty passengers,' you say to yourself. 'I'll never get anywhere with them interfering like this. They're dragging me down.'

So you stop the bus and walk to the back. 'You have to be quiet,' you say to the passengers. 'This is important to me. To have any hope of improving my social life, I need to stay calm. I can't have you shouting at me.' But the passengers are stubborn and won't change their minds.

'Well if that's your attitude, you can't ride on my bus,' you say. 'Out you go.' But they won't leave, and they're too heavy to push out the door.

You realize that your bus isn't going anywhere.

'OK,' you say in frustration. 'What will you do to me if I keep driving towards my goal?'

'We'll tell you where you should go,' they reply.

'But what if I don't?' you ask. They stare at you blankly.

You realize an important fact about the passengers. They have loud ugly voices and discouraging things to say, but they can't literally hurt you. You don't have to believe them or follow their orders. With this new insight in mind, you return to the driver's seat and resume driving the bus in your chosen direction.

The passengers continue to talk. They tell you why you'll never succeed and shouldn't try. It's unpleasant and you wish you could be rid of them. With practice, however, you become more skilful at driving in the direction you want to go, despite what the passengers say. Their voices begin to fade. You find them less upsetting. You begin to understand: your passengers are the voices of previous experiences that can't be changed. You develop nonjudgemental acceptance of your passengers and allow them to be who they are.

And you don't let them drive the bus.

Notice what you're *not* doing when you take this mindful attitude towards your unpleasant thoughts and feelings.

- You're not suppressing or avoiding them. You're allowing them to ride on your bus.

- You're not ruminating about them. You can hear them, but most of your attention is devoted to driving in your chosen direction.

- You're not trying to change them. You're accepting them for what they are.

- You're not allowing them to control your behaviour. You're deciding for yourself where to drive.

Andrew's Use of Mindfulness Skills

Andrew wrote on his worksheet that he avoided going to lunch with a co-worker because he felt awkward and shy. But he wants to have more friends at work. So let's picture the same situation after Andrew works his way through this book.

1 – Andrew is now more aware of what's happening in each moment

When his co-worker asks him to lunch, Andrew observes that he's tempted to decline because he feels anxious – his heart is beating faster and he's afraid of not having enough to talk about. But he remembers that he'd like to have more friends at work. Being mindful of the moment gives him a chance to choose thoughtfully, rather than automatically declining the invitation and then criticizing himself.

2 – Andrew's thoughts and feelings are less scary

Andrew still has occasional negative thoughts (*I'm boring . . . this will be awkward . . . what if I don't have enough to talk about?*) and unpleasant feelings (pounding heart, sweaty hands), but now he thinks of them as passengers on his bus and he allows them to come and go. He realizes several important facts about the passengers:

- they're unpleasant but not harmful

- he has little control over which passengers get on, where they get off, or what they say

- no matter what they say, the passengers don't have to control his behaviour

3 – Andrew pursues important goals even when he's having unpleasant thoughts and feelings

When his co-worker asks him to lunch, Andrew accepts the invitation, despite his trepidation. Of course, there's no guarantee that lunch will go well. But there's a good chance it will be fine, and he'll be pleased that he took a step that's consistent with his goals.

In time, as he takes these steps regularly, Andrew's anxiety will diminish as his social life improves. Even if anxiety is still present on some occasions, Andrew now understands that he can pursue a satisfying social life whether he feels anxious or not. He's much happier, not because his anxiety has completely disappeared, but because he's relating to it differently. He's able to make room for it without being controlled by it. He understands that avoiding social situations makes things worse.

Steps for Working with Your Own Avoidance Patterns

1. Use the worksheet to become more familiar with your patterns.

2. When you catch yourself trying to avoid your thoughts and feelings, remind yourself that they're passengers on your bus.

3. See if you can find a way to drive the bus in the direction you'd like to go: towards something that's consistent with your important, long-term goals. This may require that you allow the passengers to be themselves, rather than fighting with them.

4. Be kind to yourself about the unpleasant passengers on your bus. Everyone has them. They're part of being alive.

5. Continue with this book. Later chapters will provide more mindfulness exercises that help with suppression and avoidance.

Even skilful drivers find that strong emotions occasionally take control and send the bus off course. This is *emotion-driven behaviour,* another trap. In the next chapter, we'll consider this trap and how mindfulness skills can lead us out of it.

Chapter Summary

*   Avoidance of unpleasant thoughts and feelings often backfires. If we try to suppress them or get rid of them, there's a good chance they'll get stronger.

*   Avoidance of difficult situations or activities reduces anxiety temporarily, but in the long run it interferes with progress towards important goals.

*   Mindful observation of our own avoidance patterns helps us stay out of this trap. We learn to recognize when we're tempted to avoid something and make a wise decision about how to proceed.

*   When the pursuit of important goals requires that we do something uncomfortable, like socialize when feeling shy and nervous, mindfulness reminds us that thoughts and feelings don't have to control our behaviour. Like passengers on a bus, they might be unpleasant and unkind, but we don't have to obey them. We can allow them to come and go while continuing with behaviour that's consistent with our goals.

5 Emotion–driven Behaviour

'Cherish your own emotions and never undervalue them.'

Robert Henri

Mari's Story

Mari had a stressful day at work. During a staff meeting, her boss criticized a report she'd written. Then he assigned her two more projects with impossible deadlines. After work, Mari played tennis with a friend. Although she normally enjoys tennis, Mari was preoccupied with work and couldn't concentrate. After missing several shots, she felt so frustrated that she shouted an obscenity and slammed her racket on the ground. Her tennis partner didn't say anything, but looked disgusted and turned down Mari's invitation to go for a drink afterwards.

On the way home, Mari became irritated at a slow driver. She hooted several times and then passed the other car so fast that a police officer pulled her over and warned her to be more careful.

Once home, Mari didn't feel like making dinner. She drank several beers while watching TV and fell asleep on the couch. She woke up at 3.00a.m. and went to bed, but couldn't sleep. She tortured herself with recriminations about her lack of self-control. Embarrassing images of slamming her racket on the ground in front of her tennis partner and speeding past the slow driver replayed in her mind. She got up at 6.30 a.m. and went to work feeling exhausted and angry with herself.

When we're upset or under stress, we often do things that we later regret. Psychologists call this 'emotion-driven behaviour'. We usually know that we're behaving unwisely, but we lose control and do it anyway because it relieves the intensity of our feelings. Unfortunately, the relief is temporary and the behaviour is usually inconsistent with our long-term goals. When Mari slammed her tennis racket on the ground, it reduced her frustration for a moment, but she doesn't like herself when she behaves this way, and she fears that her friend now thinks less of her. Speeding past the slow driver was exhilarating and relieved her impatience, but she knows she deserved a ticket and was lucky to get off with a warning. Drinking beer all evening dulled her negative emotions, but made her less able to work the next day. Mari admires people who keep their cool under stress. She'd like to be one of them.

The following self-test will help you determine whether you're susceptible to unconstructive emotion-driven behaviour.

SELF-TEST: EMOTION-DRIVEN BEHAVIOUR

1	2	3	4
Rarely true	Sometimes true	Often true	Very often true

_____ When I'm feeling upset, I do things that have bad consequences.

_____ When I'm unhappy, I make matters worse by acting without thinking.

_____ When I'm under stress, I have trouble resisting temptations.

_____ When I'm feeling annoyed with someone, I say things I later regret.

_____ When I'm in a bad mood, I do things that make me feel better temporarily but cause problems in the long run.

If you scored between 11–14, you may have a moderate tendency for emotion-driven behaviour when you're feeling upset. If you scored between 15–20, your emotion-driven behaviour may be causing you more serious problems. You're probably aware of the consequences, yet find it difficult to maintain your self-control under stress. In the rest of this chapter, we'll explore why this happens and how mindfulness skills can help.

What is an Emotion?

In order to understand emotion-driven behaviour, we need to understand emotions. We often experience emotions as subjective, internal feelings that are hard to describe. In order to communicate about emotions, we learn to label them: sadness, anger, fear, embarrassment, envy, happiness, disappointment, boredom. The English language includes more than 500 such words. Although some have similar meanings (such as fury, rage and wrath), the existence of so many different terms shows that we're capable of a huge variety of emotional experiences. Each has its own subtle qualities of feeling, tone and intensity. In the next box are some lists of emotion terms, grouped into general categories of emotion.

EMOTION TERMS

Sadness: anguished, dejected, depressed, disappointed, dismayed, gloomy, glum, hopeless, hurt, melancholy, sorrowful

Fear: afraid, apprehensive, anxious, edgy, frightened, jumpy, nervous, panicked, tense, terrified, uneasy, worried

Anger: aggravated, annoyed, bitter, furious, grouchy, hostile, irritated, outraged, resentful, spiteful, vengeful

Shame and guilt: ashamed, chagrined, contrite, embarrassed, guilty, humiliated, mortified, regretful, remorseful, repentant

Happiness: blissful, cheerful, content, delighted, elated, enthusiastic, excited, glad, gleeful, joyful, satisfied, thrilled

---

Love: adoring, affectionate, caring, compassionate, friendly, infatuated, passionate, sympathetic, tender, warm

Surprise: amazed, astonished, shocked

Disgust: contemptuous, disdainful, revolted, scornful

Other: bashful, bored, calm, interested, proud, reluctant, sceptical, suspicious

Most emotions come and go like waves in the ocean. When allowed to run their natural course, emotions usually last a few seconds or minutes. Repeated or ongoing events and circumstances, such as the loss of a loved one, can prolong them. So can ruminating, as we saw in chapter 2. Longer-lasting emotions are called moods. Moods are usually less intense than emotions. A grumpy mood may last all day, but the full heat of rage only for short periods.

Everyone has their own emotional style. Some people have very intense emotions, both positive and negative. Others have mostly mild or moderate emotions. Some people have strong positive emotions and mild negative ones; others have the opposite pattern. Many people tend to feel one dominant emotion in a variety of situations. For example, if you often feel anxious, you may think of yourself as a nervous person, or a 'worrywart'. If you're usually cheerful, others may think of you as a happy person, although you have your share of negative emotions.

The Three Components of Emotion

Whatever your emotional style, you may have noticed that when you're feeling an emotion, several things are happening in your body and mind. Single words, such as 'happy' or 'sad', may not fully capture the complexity of an emotional experience. We can understand our emotions more easily if we break them down into three components: (1) sensations in the body; (2) thoughts in the mind; and (3) urges to act in certain ways.

1 – Sensations in the body

If you're fearful or anxious, you may feel your heart racing, your palms sweating and your muscles tensing. If you're angry, your face may feel hot and your fists tight. Sadness often brings sensations of heaviness or slowness, while happiness can make us feel energetic and light. Some sensations are common to more than one emotion. For example, a flushed face could reflect anger, embarrassment or excitement. Feeling energized could reflect anger or elation – two quite different emotions.

2 – Thoughts in the mind

Thoughts often take the form of phrases or sentences. If you're anxious or fearful you may have thoughts such as 'I need to get out of here', 'This is going to be a disaster', or 'What if something terrible happens?' If you're feeling regretful, you might think, 'I wish I had (or hadn't) . . . ' or 'If only . . . ' If you're disappointed, you may be thinking, 'Things never work out for me'. Anger usually includes thoughts like 'This isn't fair', 'I hate this', or 'How could she . . . ?'

Many people have images in their minds while they feel an emotion. As you joyfully anticipate your wedding day, you might envision exchanging rings with your loved one, your friends and family gathered around. If you're anxious about a presentation, you might picture the audience looking inattentive and bored.

3 – Urges

Urges (also known as action tendencies) are desires or impulses to behave in particular ways. Sometimes we act on these urges – that's emotion-driven behaviour. At other times, we restrain ourselves. Most emotions include urges to do specific things. If you're feeling depressed, you may have an urge to stay in bed all day. If you're angry, you might have impulses to yell, curse, throw things or slam doors. If you're feeling anxious, you'll probably have an urge to get away from the situation. For example, if you're afraid of crowds but a friend persuades you to go to a movie, you might feel an impulse to leave when you see that the theatre is nearly full. Positive emotions also include urges to clap your hands when you're happy, or to hug someone you love.

The table below shows components of Mari's emotions.

COMPONENTS OF MARI'S EMOTIONS

Emotion and situation	Body sensations	Thoughts	Urges
Frustration while playing tennis.	Heart pounding Hands tight	What's wrong with me? Why can't I hit the ball? I'm such an idiot!	Curse Slam racket on ground
Irritation at slow driver.	Heat in face Tension in hands Clenched jaw	What's wrong with you? Don't you know how to drive?	Pound steering wheel Sound the horn Accelerate rapidly
Dejection after getting home.	Fatigue Hollowness in abdomen Eyes near tears	I don't feel like doing anything. Nothing's going right for me.	Lie around Drink beer Watch TV

Why Do We Have Emotions?

Research shows that basic emotions, including happiness, sadness, anger, fear, disgust and surprise, are expressed with distinct facial expressions that are similar all over the world. Even people who've been blind since birth smile when they're happy, frown when they're sad, and clench their teeth when they're angry, despite having never seen these expressions on other people's faces. Scientists believe that these emotions are universal aspects of human nature that evolved because they're necessary for survival. Although emotions can be difficult and painful, we have them because they're helpful to us. Emotions serve several purposes.

1 – Emotions tell us important information

Fear is a signal that something in the environment may pose a threat. Sadness alerts us to a significant loss or personal setback. Anger is a message that we've been wronged. Guilt suggests that we've wronged someone else.

2 – Emotions motivate and prepare us to take constructive actions

Some emotion-driven behaviour is helpful. If a car speeds toward you while you're crossing the street, fear provides the energy to jump out of the way. If you have an important presentation coming up, anxiety can motivate you to research your topic thoroughly, practise your presentation and anticipate likely questions from the audience. When you've suffered a major loss, sadness reduces your energy level and encourages you to withdraw from normal activities. This is helpful for a while because it allows time to accept the loss and adapt to your new circumstances.

Anger provides energy to make changes in unfair situations. It can motivate you to stand up for your rights or the rights of others. Guilt pushes you to apologize and make amends if you've wronged someone. Love motivates caring for others. Passion provides the energy for creative achievements. In general, emotions can protect us from harm, energize us to accomplish important goals and help us maintain our relationships, if we handle them constructively.

3 – Emotions communicate to others

Facial expression, behaviour, tone of voice and body language communicate to others how we're feeling. This allows them to help if they can. Sadness lets others know that we need support; anger tells them that we're feeling mistreated; fear communicates a need for protection.

The non-verbal communication of emotion is especially useful for children too young to speak or comprehend language. Imagine a young child who is reaching for a sharp knife that has fallen to the floor. A frightened gasp and horrified look from the nearest adult communicates effectively that the knife is dangerous. And, of course, if hunger, pain and unfamiliar situations did not cause noticeable distress in babies, adults would be less likely to attend to their needs, and fewer babies would survive.

Emotion-driven Behaviour Can Be a Trap

Emotions evolved to be useful, yet they often cause trouble. How does this happen? Emotions are often triggered quickly. Bodily reactions and impulses arise before we have time to think. Sometimes these instantaneous responses are necessary for survival. If a wild animal is attacking, it's safer to fight or flee immediately than to consider the pros and cons of doing either.

Unfortunately, our spontaneous reactions are not always well suited to modern life. When fear arises, blood flows to the legs to make it easier to run away. Hormones that circulate in the bloodstream prepare the body for physical action. This is great if you're being chased by an assailant. It's less useful if you're about to give a speech, attend an interview for a job or ask someone for a date. The body perceives a threat and it prepares to fight or flee, even when you wish it would stay calm.

Anger presents similar problems. The body is flooded with hormones that create energy. The face may take on a threatening expression. Urges arise to speak loudly and behave aggressively. This is helpful if you need to fight an attacker, but less so when you're angered by a co-worker during a staff meeting or a driver on a crowded motorway.

Given these difficulties, it's understandable that some of our emotion-driven behaviour is unconstructive or even harmful. We get trapped in several ways:

- We're trapped by our genetic heritage to feel emotions that evolved for conditions that predate modern times. To behave according to contemporary social norms, sometimes we have to suppress or override our emotions. This is difficult and creates tension.

- We're also trapped by the short-term effects of emotion-driven behaviour, which often feels satisfying in the moment but causes trouble in the long run.

- We're trapped by a uniquely human characteristic: the ability to feel emotions about our own emotions. These are called 'secondary emotions'.

Secondary Emotions

A secondary emotion occurs *in response* to another emotion. Consider Mari, from the beginning of the chapter. She felt angry when her boss criticized her work. Then she told herself she shouldn't be so sensitive and felt ashamed of being angry. Anger was the *primary emotion* – a natural response to being criticized. Shame was the *secondary emotion* – a reaction to the anger.

When thinking about secondary emotions, it's important to remember several points:

- Secondary emotions are common. We can feel angry about feeling anxious, embarrassed about feeling sad, anxious about feeling depressed, and many other combinations. We can also feel guilty about being happy, embarrassed about how much we love something, or worried about when contentment will end.

- Secondary emotions are learned from experience. If a child is consistently shamed for expressing anger, the child may learn that anger is bad or wrong. Feeling shame whenever anger arises then becomes a lifelong pattern.

- Secondary emotions are brought on by negative judgements about primary emotions. If you tell yourself that you're overreacting, that your primary emotion is wrong, bad, silly, crazy, weak, stupid or immature, you'll get upset with yourself for having the primary emotion. This is unfortunate, because primary emotions are natural responses to events or situations. Criticizing ourselves for having them makes matters worse – emotions get stronger, longer-lasting and more complicated.

- Once secondary emotions have complicated the situation, unhealthy emotion-driven behaviour becomes more likely. Examples of primary emotions, judgements about them, secondary emotions and unhealthy behaviours are shown in the next box.

Primary emotion	Judgement about primary emotion	Secondary emotion	Unhealthy behaviour
Sadness about death of a pet.	It's silly to feel sad about this.	Embarrassment about feeling sad.	Avoid supportive friends who would understand your sadness and help you feel better.
Anger at a friend who cancelled a date.	I shouldn't feel angry. I'm overreacting.	Shame or disappointment in self for feeling angry.	Drink or eat too much to stifle anger and shame; avoid friend.
Anxiety about giving a talk.	Feeling anxious is a sign of weakness, shows I'm incompetent.	Anger at self for feeling anxious.	Lose temper with others; avoid working on talk.

'But What If I Really Am Overreacting?'

'I'm overreacting,' is a judgemental thought about an emotion you're feeling. This thought is likely to come to mind if your emotional reaction is:

- more intense than the average person would experience in this situation.

- stronger than your usual emotions.

- more intense than someone else thinks it should be.

- puzzling or confusing – you don't understand why you're feeling this way.

When you tell yourself that you're overreacting, you're implying that the intensity of your emotion doesn't make sense or isn't justified. In reality, intense emotions occur for several reasons:

1. The tendency to have strong emotions can be inherited. Some people naturally have intense emotions because of their brain and body chemistry, whereas others have calmer temperaments.

2. Strong emotional reactions to seemingly minor events may be related to previous experiences. For example, you may feel deeply sad about a TV show if it reminds you of a sad experience in your past. Others may wonder why the show has affected you so strongly.

3. Normal conditioning processes can cause apparently neutral aspects of the environment to trigger emotions, for reasons that we don't always recognize. For example, an unfamiliar parking lot can make you feel nostalgic if it resembles the one where you found the stray kitten that brought you years of companionship. You may not realize why the parking lot has triggered this feeling, but it makes sense in its own way.

4. Temporary conditions in your mind and body also influence your emotions. If you're tired, hungry, sick or stressed, minor events can trigger surprisingly intense feelings. This is normal.

If you're telling yourself you're overreacting because your emotion is intense or unexpected, remember that emotions happen for reasons. Even if you don't see how they make sense, they do. They may seem odd, or stronger than you'd like, but if you criticize yourself for feeling what you feel, there's a good chance you'll feel worse. This will increase the risk of unhelpful, emotion-driven behaviour. You'll be less able to make wise decisions about what to do.

Understanding Your Own Emotional Experiences

To handle our emotions skilfully, we have to understand them. The following worksheet will help you observe your emotional experiences and respond to them with wisdom and insight. If you're not accustomed to paying attention to your emotions, it may feel awkward at first, but it becomes easier with practice.

As you become more aware of your emotions, you may find that you're criticizing yourself for having particular feelings, or for the intensity of your feelings. See if you can let go of the criticism. Remember that being mindful of our emotions means observing them with friendly curiosity, not judging ourselves for having them.

On the next page is a worksheet with instructions, followed by one completed by Jim, who just got a new job after being fired a few months ago. He's worried about getting fired again.

Worksheet: Understanding an emotional experience

Remember to maintain an attitude of friendly curiosity

Day and time: When did this happen?	*Writing down the day and time helps you to be specific about which emotional experience you are working with and helps you see patterns over time.*
Describe the situation: What happened that triggered your emotion?	*This might be an event that happened in the external world, such as learning that a friend was in a car accident. It could be an internal experience, such as remembering that your friend is having surgery tomorrow. If you're unsure of the trigger, leave this blank for now. Over time, you'll become more skilful at identifying the triggering event.*
What emotions did you feel? (underline the strongest)	*Look back at the list shown earlier in this chapter for help with emotion names. If you felt more than one emotion, write them all down. Underline the strongest emotion and use it for the rest of the worksheet. You can do more worksheets for the other emotions that you felt.*
Intensity of the strongest emotion: (1–10)	*1 = mildest possible, 10 = most intense possible.*
What thoughts or images were going through your mind?	*Your thoughts might include interpretations or assumptions about the situation or predictions about what will happen. If you had images in your mind, describe them.*
What sensations did you notice in your body?	*Did you notice a change in your heart rate or breathing? Any muscle tension or trembling? Did you feel hot, cold, or sweaty? Heavy or light? Any sensations in your chest, stomach, face, eyes, head, hands, or anywhere else?*
What did you feel like saying or doing (urges)?	*Did you feel like escaping or avoiding a person or situation? Shouting or throwing things? Staying in bed? Eating or drinking too much? Talking to someone?*
What did you say or do (behaviour)?	*You may not have acted on all of your urges. If you restrained yourself in any way, write that down too.*
Secondary emotions	*Did this emotion trigger other emotions? For example, did you get angry with yourself for feeling sad? Did you feel ashamed of yourself for getting angry?*

Worksheet: Understanding an emotional experience

Your name: <u>Jim</u>

Remember to maintain an attitude of friendly curiosity

Day and time: When did this happen?	*Thursday morning around 10.15.*
Describe the situation: What happened that triggered your emotion?	*I was sitting at my desk at work. My boss walked by and gave me an angry look.*
What emotions did you feel? (underline the strongest)	*nervousness, <u>fear</u>*
Intensity of the strongest emotion (1–10)	*7*
What thoughts or images were going through your mind?	*He's going to fire me. He's not happy with my work. I knew this job would never last. I'm going to be unemployed again. I'll never get another job as good as this one.*
What sensations did you notice in your body?	*My heart was beating fast, breathing was shallow. I had a sinking feeling in my chest.*
What did you feel like saying or doing (urges)?	*I had an urge to just give up and go home. I also wanted to go into my boss's office and make him tell me what I've been doing wrong and give me another chance.*
What did you say or do (behaviour)?	*I made myself stay at my desk and keep working, though I couldn't concentrate. Later I told my co-worker about it. He told me not to worry – the boss was in a bad mood all day because his son wrecked his car.*
Secondary emotions	*I got mad at myself and told myself I was an idiot for jumping to conclusions and getting scared for no good reason. I felt embarrassed about it.*

Now use the blank version following to practise being mindful of your own emotional experiences. Again, make copies so that you can do this exercise more than once. The more you practise, the more skilful you'll become. Consider doing this exercise three times over the next week, or even daily if you have more frequent emotions.

Each time you complete the worksheet, choose one specific occasion to write about: an emotional experience that occurred on a particular day at a specific time. Remember that a perfect record is not your goal. The purpose of the exercise is to practise being *observant, curious, open-minded* and *non-judgemental* about your own emotions. In time, you'll become less susceptible to unhealthy, emotion-driven behaviour.

How Mindfulness Helps with Emotion-driven Behaviour

If you have strong emotions, you may already be very much aware of them. Increasing your emotional awareness by practising mindfulness may seem like an unhelpful thing to do. The key is to remember the difference between *problem-solving mode* and *mindful acceptance.* In problem-solving mode, we may be acutely aware of negative emotions, but we think of them as problems that need solving. We have negative judgements about them and try to escape or get rid of them. We forget that unpleasant emotions are normal in many situations and may be sending important messages.

The alternative is to observe our emotions mindfully, accepting them as visitors to the guest house or passengers on the bus. See if you can watch them unfold moment by moment and observe the sensations with interest and curiosity. Notice the associated thoughts. Recognize that thoughts like 'It's stupid to feel this way' and 'I'm overreacting' are judgements, rather than truth or reality. Acknowledge the urges to behave in particular ways, without necessarily acting on them. Over time, emotions will become less scary and their complexity easier to understand.

Worksheet: Understanding an emotional experience

Your name: _____

*** Remember to maintain an attitude of friendly curiosity ***

Day and time: When did this happen?	
Describe the situation: What happened that triggered your emotion?	
What emotions did you feel? (underline the strongest)	
Intensity of the strongest emotion (1–10)	
What thoughts or images were going through your mind?	
What sensations did you notice in your body?	
What did you feel like saying or doing (urges)?	
What did you say or do (behaviour)?	
Secondary emotions	

For some people, the most troubling aspect of negative emotions is the emotion-driven behaviour: overeating when they're sad, yelling and throwing things when they're angry. Practising mindfulness skills is an excellent way to address this problem. Over time, observing our emotions without judgement creates a space between the emotion and the corresponding behaviour. This gap provides an opportunity to choose what to do.

For example, Mari will learn to observe when she's feeling an urge to slam her tennis racket on the ground. She'll recognize the feelings of frustration, the self-critical thoughts and the tension in her body, and she'll have a moment to choose: she could either slam her racket or refrain from doing so. This does not mean that she's suppressing her feelings. Instead, she's learning to make room for them without letting them drive her behaviour.

The exercises in the next box will help you develop a mindful approach to mild, commonplace urges. These exercises are designed to be easier to work with than the urges caused by intense, negative emotions. Practising these introductory exercises is a good way to get started on reducing the emotion-driven behaviour that causes problems in your life. Try doing one of these exercises three times over the next week, and continue practising whenever urges arise. A later chapter in this book will provide detailed descriptions of exercises that help with more intense urges triggered by strong emotions.

INTRODUCTORY EXERCISES: MINDFULNESS OF URGES

1 – Observe naturally occurring urges in daily life

- When you brush your teeth, observe the process carefully. Notice when you feel the urge to spit. Observe the urge without spitting. Notice the nature of the urge and how you feel while having the urge. You will have to spit eventually, so make a deliberate decision about when to spit. Practise not being controlled by the urge.

- The next time your nose itches, observe the urge to rub it. Notice what the urge feels like, without acting on it. Keep observing and see if the urge gets stronger or subsides. Decide for yourself if and when to rub your nose. If you rub your nose, do so mindfully. Observe the movements and sensations.

- If you get itchy insect bites, try this exercise with urges to scratch.

- As you go through your day, practise with other urges that arise.

2 – Observe self-induced urges

- Set a piece of food you like in front of you. Notice if you have an urge to eat it. Observe the urge. Keep observing, and see if the urge gets stronger or subsides. Either way, make a deliberate decision about whether to eat the food.

- Eat something slowly and notice when you have the urge to swallow. For a few moments, observe the urge without swallowing. Decide when to swallow.

- Hold a book or another object at arm's length, in front of you or to one side. Notice the sensations in your arm. Before long, you'll have an urge to set the object down. For a short time, observe the urge without acting on it. Make a mindful decision about when to set the object down. Don't overstrain your arm.

3 – Remember the attitude of friendly curiosity

If you notice critical thoughts about yourself or the urges (*I shouldn't feel this way, this urge is bad*, etc.), notice that these are thoughts. Practise exploring your urges in a friendly way.

As you experiment with these exercises and start paying more attention to your urges in daily life, you may find it difficult to let go of judging and criticizing yourself for having particular urges or for acting on them. Unfortunately, self-criticism usually makes matters worse. It's another psychological trap. In the next chapter, we'll learn more about self-criticism and how mindfulness skills can help us avoid it.

Chapter Summary

- Emotions are complex experiences. They include bodily sensations, thoughts and urges to act in particular ways.

- Although emotions can be painful, we have them because they serve useful purposes. They give us important information, communicate to others, and can motivate us to behave constructively, if we handle them in healthy ways.

- Unfortunately, we often do things we regret when we're feeling negative emotions. Unconstructive, emotion-driven behaviour is a trap – we do it because it temporarily relieves unpleasant feelings, but it causes problems and makes us feel worse in the long run.

- Mindful observation of emotional experiences helps us recognize their components, including bodily sensations, thoughts and urges. We learn to observe them without judgement and without acting on them in impulsive ways. With practice, mindfulness of urges gives us time to decide wisely how to respond.

6 Self–criticism

'If we treat ourselves harshly, this is the way we are likely to treat other people.'

Karen Armstrong

It's late in the afternoon and you've had a long day at work. You stop in the restroom before heading home and notice a shred of lettuce stuck in your front teeth. It must have been there since lunch. You've seen several people this afternoon, including two new customers, and no one said anything. Which set of thoughts goes through your mind?

A: 'I'm such an idiot. Why didn't I check the mirror after lunch? People must have been laughing at me all afternoon.'

B: 'Oh dear, how embarrassing. Well, this sort of thing happens to everyone now and then.'

Another scenario: You applied for a job that you really wanted. Out of more than fifty applicants, you and two others were invited for interviews. Your interview went very well and you felt optimistic. But this afternoon you learned that you didn't get the job. You're extremely disappointed. All evening you've been sitting on the couch, eating cookies and watching silly TV shows. Now it's time to go to bed. Which set of thoughts goes through your mind?

A: 'It's disgusting how many cookies I ate. I have no self-control. No wonder I didn't get that job. I really didn't deserve it.'

B: 'I've had a big disappointment. I was really qualified for that job and it's a shame I didn't get it. Cookies and TV are OK for a little while, but I need to take care of myself. Tomorrow, I'll ask my friend to go for a walk with me.'

Your thoughts might fall somewhere in between, but if they're closer to option A than to option B, you may be falling prey to self-criticism. It's quite common. Most of us criticize ourselves frequently, often harshly. Self-criticism feels like an inner voice. Depending on the situation, it says things like, 'I'm an idiot . . . I'm a loser . . . I'm not good enough . . . I made a total mess of that . . . I'll never amount to anything . . . I'm disgusting, stupid, lazy, ugly, useless, crazy . . . ' and so on. Sometimes it calls you by name, as if you were a separate person: 'Ruth, you're hopeless, you can't do anything right.' The inner critic can be brutal.

Criticism from Others

When we want to develop our skills or learn new ones, *constructive* criticism is valuable, even essential. It's part of good teaching and provides the information we need to do better. Constructive criticism from others is most helpful when it has the following characteristics:

- It provides specific information about what went wrong and what to do differently.

- It has a considerate, respectful tone.

- It judges the work rather than the person.

- It points out strengths as well as weaknesses.

The table on the next page provides examples of constructive and unconstructive criticism provided by two cooking teachers.

To learn about cooking in a helpful and supportive atmosphere, most people would prefer to join Teacher A's class. Notice that constructive criticism is clear about mistakes and weaknesses – it doesn't say that everything is excellent when it isn't.

Research confirms the benefits of constructive criticism. When university students receive constructive criticism (rather than vague, insulting, personal or one-sided criticism), they feel less angry and tense. They're more willing to collaborate with the person providing the criticism. They set higher goals and feel more confidence in their ability to reach them. A study with employees of a large company found that criticism from supervisors that embarrassed or blamed the recipients, without helping them improve, was a major cause of conflict in their workplace.

Teacher A: Constructive criticism	Teacher B: Unconstructive criticism
Specific: *The oven wasn't hot enough when you put the chicken in to roast. That's why it didn't turn brown and crispy on the outside.*	**Vague:** *This chicken looks awful.*
Considerate: *That's a common mistake.*	**Inconsiderate:** *How could you be so careless?*
Directed at the work: *These muffins are a little dense and tough and didn't rise very well. That shows the batter was mixed too much.*	**Directed at the person:** *You did a terrible job with these muffins.*
Balanced: *The fish is nice and tender but the vegetables were simmered for too long.*	**Unbalanced:** *You overcooked the vegetables. The meal is ruined.*

The same principles apply to self-criticism. If we're going to criticize ourselves, we should do so in the style of Teacher A from the cooking class. But much of the time, we behave like Teacher B. We don't think specifically about what went wrong, how we might improve, or how to get help if we need it. Instead, we're vague (*I did a terrible job*), inconsiderate (*My ideas are really stupid*), judgemental of ourselves rather than our behaviour or our work (*I'm incompetent*), and unbalanced (*I can't do anything right*). Sometimes we threaten ourselves with future misfortunes (*If I go on like this, I'll never accomplish anything*).

Facing our mistakes and weaknesses in a helpful way is already diffi-cult enough. Insulting ourselves with harsh self-criticism makes us feel worse. It interferes with the ability to improve when improvement is needed. It also keeps us from accepting aspects of ourselves that can't be changed or are fine the way they are.

The following self-test will help you determine whether unconstructive self-criticism is a problem for you.

SELF−TEST: SELF−CRITICISM

1	2	3	4
Rarely	Sometimes	Often	Very often

_____ I criticize myself harshly for things I've said or done.

_____ I put myself down or call myself names whenever anything goes wrong.

_____ I blame myself for my failures without taking credit for my successes.

_____ I'm intolerant of my own flaws and weaknesses.

_____ I tell myself I'm an idiot or not good enough.

If your score was greater than 10, you may be criticizing yourself exces-sively. If you scored between 15–20, your self-criticism may be causing you significant problems, especially if you're attacking and condemn-ing yourself, rather than taking a constructive, balanced view of your strengths and weaknesses.

Isabel's Story

Isabel is an intelligent and hard-working student who was raised in a critical family. Her parents, who hadn't gone beyond high school, were determined that their only child would go further. They closely supervised Isabel's school work and criticized anything less than outstanding grades.

Isabel did well in school and was admitted to a large university, where she found the work much more difficult. She worried that she had only come this far because of her parents' relentless pressure and that she wasn't bright enough for university work. She coped by adopting a highly self-critical style – constantly telling herself that she wasn't very competent and could avoid failure only by working extremely hard.

For two years, Isabel earned good grades despite her shaky confidence. In her third year, she was invited to work with a faculty adviser on a research project. Although she doubted her ability to succeed, her parents were thrilled and Isabel felt she couldn't say no.

After several meetings to discuss the topic for her project, Isabel's adviser, Dr Haley, gave her a deadline for writing a rough draft of the first section of the paper. For the first time in her life, Isabel found that she couldn't complete her assigned work. She didn't understand how to organize her ideas or what the first section should include. Every time she tried to work on it, she was overwhelmed with self-critical thoughts: 'This isn't good enough. I'm incapable of doing this. I'm going to fail.' She sent an email to Dr Haley requesting a one-week extension, which he granted. Isabel criticized herself further. 'It's stupid of me to need an extension. Dr Haley will think I'm an idiot. I'm obviously hopeless at this.'

Filled with uncertainty about how to continue, Isabel began to procrastinate. Then she criticized herself for not working. 'What's wrong with me?' she wondered, as her anxiety intensified. 'Why can't I just do it? I have no discipline at all. I'm not cut out for this.' Ashamed of her lack of progress, Isabel didn't mention the problem to anyone.

The week's extension passed. Dr Haley sent emails expressing concern; Isabel didn't reply. She avoided the building where Dr Haley's office was located. After two weeks of constant rumination about her uncompleted assignment, Isabel unexpectedly saw Dr Haley in a coffee shop. 'Hi, Isabel,' said Dr Haley. 'Nice to see you!'

'Hi,' said Isabel, hoping he wouldn't mention the paper.

'What's going on with your paper?' Dr Haley asked. Isabel burst into tears and said she was giving up the research project.

Dr Haley insisted on meeting with Isabel the next day. He reminded her that the adviser's job is to provide guidance, that the purpose of the first draft is to get constructive feedback, and that the student's job is to bring up questions and concerns during regular meetings. He helped her outline the first section. Isabel promised to meet weekly and to bring a draft, no matter how rough, to their next session.

The Consequences of Harsh Self-criticism

Isabel's story illustrates an interesting paradox about unconstructive self-criticism: Most of us do it for the purpose of self-discipline or self-correction, yet many studies show that harsh self-criticism actually interferes with progress toward our goals.

In one study, 180 overweight adults signed up for a weight-loss programme. Before the programme started, they completed a questionnaire measuring unconstructive self-criticism (similar to the one in the box on page 92). Then they were weighed. After six months of working on diet and exercise, they were weighed again. Those who were *more* harshly self-critical at the beginning of the programme had lost *less* weight six months later.

University athletes in swimming or track and field showed a similar pattern. At the beginning of the athletics season, they completed a self-criticism questionnaire and identified their most important goal for the season, such as improving their time in the 100-metre backstroke or learning to do a triple jump. At the end of the season, the more self-critical athletes had made less progress toward their goals.

Why do highly self-critical people make less progress than those who don't judge themselves so harshly? Instead of motivating and energizing us to pursue our goals, self-criticism triggers feelings of shame, guilt, sadness, anger, frustration, embarrassment, disappointment and hopelessness. It saps our energy, morale, motivation and confidence, making it hard to keep going in the face of difficulties. We're likely to procrastinate and avoid, as Isabel found. We're less likely to seek help when we need it. Progress slows down, which leads to more self-criticism. A vicious cycle is created.

Unconstructive self-criticism has many other negative effects. People who criticize themselves severely are more likely to become depressed, anxious and lonely. They're more likely to have trouble in their romantic relationships, perhaps because they expect their partners to judge them as harshly as they judge themselves and are therefore less open. Self-critical people are more likely to binge-eat, especially if they grew up in critical or emotionally abusive families. People who've experienced an extremely stressful event, like a serious accident or an assault, are more likely to develop symptoms of post-traumatic stress if they're highly self-critical.

Why Do We Criticize Ourselves So Harshly?

When asked why they criticize themselves, most people say that it's for their own good. Many believe that self-criticism prevents laziness, complacency and self-indulgence. We think it helps us meet responsibilities, maintain self-discipline and prevent mistakes. We probably learned it in childhood, perhaps from parents or teachers who didn't understand the difference between constructive and unconstructive criticism. When children are harshly criticized, but rarely praised, encouraged or given constructive feedback, they may learn that criticism is the only way to motivate good behaviour.

Shame and Fear of Rejection

Self-criticism is closely connected with shame, an intensely unpleasant emotion that includes feelings of inferiority and a desire to hide or conceal oneself. As we saw in the previous chapter, emotions evolved because they help us survive: Fear helps us escape danger; anger helps us defend ourselves. Experts believe that shame may have a similar purpose.

Most people feel a strong need to belong to a group – a family, circle of friends or other community. Most groups have rules of behaviour. When a group member violates these rules, the group or its leaders may try to shame the wrongdoer as a way of controlling this person's behaviour. The wrongdoer who expresses shame may be treated more leniently and allowed to stay in the group. If the wrongdoer expresses no shame, the group may inflict severe punishment, such as rejection and isolation. Shame, therefore, appears to exist for a reason: it can help us avoid conflict and ostracism.

Unfortunately, most of us are so sensitive to rejection that we've learned to internalize this process and we inflict it on ourselves. If we've done something that we fear others won't like, we use harsh self-criticism to punish ourselves. Then we submit to our own self-criticism by feeling ashamed. This may be useful if it helps us avoid getting thrown out of our family, school or workplace, or being sent to prison. But if the self-criticism is excessive, vague, demeaning and unbalanced, it interferes with the ability to improve. It also interferes with mental health.

Is Shame the Same as Guilt?

Shame and guilt are similar but not exactly the same. Shame is focused on the whole person and creates feelings of overall worthlessness (*I am a bad person*) and the desire to hide or disappear. Shame is so painful that we often try to escape it by shifting blame to others, lashing out in anger, or denying responsibility for misdeeds. Guilt is also painful, but it's focused on specific behaviours and creates the desire to confess, apologize and make amends.

Imagine spilling a bowl of spaghetti sauce on a friend's new carpet. If you're telling yourself you're an awful person and wishing you could disappear, that's shame. If you're focused on your friend's feelings, regretting the distress you've caused, apologizing, trying to clean up the mess and offering to pay for professional carpet cleaning, that's guilt. You might be feeling both emotions at once. Excessive, harmful self-criticism is more likely to stem from shame, and to intensify shame, in a vicious cycle that makes it harder to handle the situation as you'd like to.

Harsh Self-criticism is a Psychological Trap

We get caught in the trap of unconstructive self-criticism for several reasons. We learn it in childhood, we believe it should keep us on track, and sometimes it does, at least for a while. But many of us are so sensitive to failure and rejection that we use it too harshly on ourselves, forgetting that constructive suggestions usually work better when improvement is required, and that kindness is more helpful than cruelty whether improvement is needed or not.

This point may be clearer if you imagine giving harsh criticism to someone you care about. If a good friend tells you that he had spinach in his teeth all afternoon and is feeling a little foolish, what would you say?

A: 'You're such an idiot. Why didn't you check the mirror after lunch? People must have been laughing at you all afternoon.'

B: 'Oh dear, how embarrassing. Well, this sort of thing happens to everyone now and then. I once gave a presentation with mustard on my shirt. And I know a lawyer who walked out of the restroom and into the courtroom with the back of her skirt caught in her underwear.'

Now imagine that a friend says that she didn't get the job she really wanted and watched stupid TV shows all evening while eating a whole bag of cookies. What would you say?

A: 'I can't believe how many cookies you ate. That's disgusting. You have no self-control. No wonder you didn't get that job. You really didn't deserve it.'

B: 'You've had a big disappointment. You were really qualified for that job and it's a shame you didn't get it. Cookies and TV are OK for a little while, but it's good to take care of yourself at times like this. Let's go for a walk tomorrow.'

If option A makes you cringe, that's probably because you would never be so unkind to someone you care about. Most of us can easily imagine saying such things to ourselves but not to loved ones. Why is this? We know that we wouldn't reject our friends for such minor things. We understand that it won't help; in fact, it will hurt the friend and damage the friendship. Yet we're so sensitive to rejection and failure that when we make mistakes or fall short of our usual standards, we fear the worst. We think we're deteriorating into hopeless messes, that we'll be laughed at, or even shunned. We get caught in the self-criticism trap. It's bad for our mental health to treat ourselves this way.

Understanding Your Own Patterns of Self-criticism

If you've been criticizing yourself for a long time, it may have become a habit. You may be doing it automatically, without realizing what's happening. To change this habit, it's important to observe and understand your own patterns of self-criticism. The following worksheet will help. It may be painful to take a close look at your self-critical thoughts, but it has important advantages. Putting your thoughts on paper makes them seem less like the absolute truth. Seeing them written down will help you take a more balanced perspective on your self-critical thoughts – you'll realize when they're unfair, unreasonable, unconstructive and even cruel.

See if you can bring the same attitude of friendly curiosity and interest to this task that you practised with the other psychological traps. Remember that self-criticism is very common in Western society. Most of us have been trained to be self-critical. It's important not to chastise yourself for it.

Like the other worksheets in this book, this one is most helpful if you use it repeatedly. Keep copies of it handy, and fill one out as soon as possible after each episode of self-criticism. The longer you wait, the harder it is to remember the thoughts that went through your mind.

Worksheet: Understanding self-criticism

Remember to maintain an attitude of friendly curiosity

Day & time	Triggering event: What started the self-criticism?	What self-critical thoughts were in your mind?	After-effects and consequences	What would you say to a friend in this situation?
When did this example of self-criticism occur?	What situation or circumstance started the self-critical thoughts? • Where were you? • What was going on? • Were other people involved? What were you criticizing yourself for? • Behaviour • Thoughts • Feelings • Urges	What were you saying to yourself? • Write down the self-critical thoughts exactly as they appeared in your mind. • If you had mental images, describe them.	What did you notice after criticizing yourself? • Thoughts • Emotions • Body sensations • Urges Note any effects on your behaviour. Did you do anything self-defeating, like avoid people or situations?	Imagine that someone you care about experienced the same triggering event. What would you say to this person?

The next page shows how Isabel completed this worksheet. Look at her responses and then try this out for yourself, using the blank worksheet on page 102. Remember to use it several times. See if you observe any patterns. What do you criticize yourself about? Could you talk to yourself more constructively?

How Mindfulness Helps with Self-criticism

Most self-criticism is a form of *thinking*. 'I'm _____' (a loser, weak, immature, silly, ugly, stupid, etc.) are all thoughts. Much of the time, when thoughts like this appear, we believe they're completely true. Psychologists call this 'fusion'. When we're fused with our thoughts, we take them seriously because we assume that they're facts, that they reflect important realities. So when we think, 'I'm a complete idiot and I'll never amount to anything,' it feels like we've realized something significant about the way things truly are. Fusion with thoughts leads to negative emotions, such as disappointment, anger and sadness, along with unhelpful behaviour.

Practising mindfulness teaches us to understand thoughts in a different way. We learn that we're constantly thinking, that numerous thoughts appear and disappear, that they aren't necessarily realistic, important or meaningful. We don't have to believe them or act on them. Instead, we can allow them to come and go in their own time while continuing to behave in ways that are consistent with our goals. We can *choose* to act on our thoughts when it's helpful to do so, but we don't have to be ruled by them. This attitude towards thoughts is called 'defusion'.

Suppose you make a mistake at work and 'I'm so incompetent' pops into your head. If you're fused with this thought, you believe it unquestioningly. It feels like the truth – like an important fact. The *thought* triggers *emotions*: you feel embarrassed, ashamed, disappointed and angry at yourself. The emotions trigger *urges*: to curse, throw something, quit your job, get drunk.

If you're being mindful, you recognize that 'I'm so incompetent' is a thought. Moreover, it's a judgemental, unbalanced, unkind thought. You observe the emotions that it triggers and the urges that follow. 'OK,' you say to yourself, 'I made a mistake, and now I'm feeling embarrassed and frustrated and I'm tempted to give up and go home.'

Worksheet: Understanding self-criticism

Your name: Isabel

Remember to maintain an attitude of friendly curiosity

Day & time	Triggering event: What started the self-criticism?	What self-critical thoughts were in your mind?	After-effects and consequences	What would you say to a friend in this situation?
Thursday evening around 8.00p.m.	I was working on my research paper. I got stuck and didn't know how to continue.	I'm incompetent. I shouldn't be doing this project. I'm not smart enough.	I felt anger and disappointment at myself, and discouraged about my lack of progress. I gave up on the paper and watched TV. Then I couldn't sleep. The next day I felt hopeless and unmotivated.	Of course this is difficult. You've never done a research paper before. You wouldn't have been invited to do this if you weren't capable of succeeding. Don't beat yourself up. Make a list of your questions and go see your adviser tomorrow.

Worksheet: Understanding self-criticism

Your name: _____

*** Remember to maintain an attitude of friendly curiosity ***

Day & time	Triggering event: What started the self-criticism?	What self-critical thoughts were in your mind?	After-effects and consequences	What would you say to a friend in this situation?

Now you're in a position to choose what to do. You might curse, throw your coffee mug at the wall and storm out, or you might take a short break to allow yourself time to settle down. Then you might think constructively about how to remedy the situation, remembering to treat yourself with respect while you do so, as you would a friend who had made the same mistake.

Mindfulness of thoughts does NOT mean making thoughts go away. We saw in a previous chapter that trying to suppress our thoughts often backfires. The same is true of self-critical thoughts. Mindfulness is simply observing the thoughts, without judging yourself for having them, and without necessarily believing them, taking them seriously, or doing what they tell you to do. This is a difficult skill to learn, but not impossible. The exercises in the box below will help you develop a mindful approach to self-critical thoughts, rather than trying to get rid of them or being controlled by them.

EXERCISES: DEFUSING FROM SELF–CRITICAL THOUGHTS

1 – Label your thoughts as thoughts

When you notice a self-critical thought like 'I'm an idiot', say it again to yourself with the following phrase in front of it: 'I'm having the thought that . . . ' or 'I'm noticing the thought that . . . ' If you're having numerous self-critical thoughts at once, label them as a group. If you notice a repeating pattern of thoughts, label them as a tape that plays in your mind. Here are some examples:

Thought	Labelled Thought
I can't do anything right.	I'm having the thought that I can't do anything right.
I'm an idiot.	I'm noticing the thought that I'm an idiot.
I'm stupid, useless and ugly.	I'm noticing a lot of self-critical thoughts right now.
No one likes me.	The 'No one likes me' tape is playing again.

2 – Greet your thoughts as if they were people passing by

Imagine that the self-critical thoughts are guests in your guest house, passengers on your bus, or people passing by on the street. When they criticize you, greet them politely, without getting into a discussion of what they're saying. Then continue on your way.

Thought	Greeting
You'll never amount to anything.	*Good morning, Mrs Criticism, have a nice day!*
You're hopeless.	*Hello, Mr Judgement, lovely weather we're having!*

3 – Notice the radio in your mind

When you notice unconstructive self-critical thoughts, imagine they're coming from a radio in your mind. It's stuck on a station that features criticism of you. For example, imagine the announcer saying:

- *'Our latest bulletin: New research confirms that Ruth is a lazy good-for-nothing! Experts report they've suspected it all along – details at 11.00!*

- *'News flash! Ruth is acting like an idiot again. You won't believe what she did this time. Stay tuned for this developing story!'*

When you hear these things, remind yourself that it's the radio in your mind. You can't turn it off, but you don't have to get caught up in it or believe everything that it broadcasts.

A Two-day Experiment

Are you still concerned that if you don't take your harsh self-criticism seriously you'll get lazy? Try this two-day experiment. On the first day, criticize yourself in your usual way. Notice all your mistakes, faults and weaknesses, and scold yourself for them. On the second day, practise the exercises in the box opposite and give yourself only constructive criticism.

Throughout each day, carefully observe how you feel. How does this compare to a typical day? How motivated are you to pursue your goals? Also notice your behaviour. Are you achieving more or less than usual? Is your behaviour constructive and consistent with your goals?

Carefully observe the differences between the two days. There's a good chance you'll discover that you're happier and more effective when you're kind and constructive with yourself.

Final Thoughts about Psychological Traps

In this group of chapters, we've explored several important psychological traps: rumination, avoidance, emotion-driven behaviour and self-criticism. Although each trap had its own chapter, you may have realized by now that they're not completely separate. We can easily fall into several traps in quick succession. Unpleasant thoughts and feelings arise and we try to avoid or suppress them. This works temporarily but, in time, the thoughts and feelings get worse. Then we ruminate about our problems, hoping to find a more effective way of getting rid of them, but rumination intensifies the difficulties. We get so upset that we lash out, or over-indulge in food, alcohol, shopping and other distractions. Then we criticize ourselves for our behaviour, calling ourselves weak, immature, stupid and worse. This makes us feel even more stressed, anxious and unhappy. We try to suppress or avoid these feelings, or the situations that bring them on, and the vicious cycles repeat.

Why Are These Traps so Difficult to Avoid?

There are several reasons why it's very difficult to stay out of these traps.

1 – Each trap is an unhelpful version of a useful human strategy

When they're constructive, persistent thinking, avoidance of difficulties, emotion-driven behaviour and self-criticism help us learn, solve problems and survive. Unfortunately, each has an unhelpful version that isn't constructive; instead, it's a trap. Unless we're paying very close attention to our behaviour and its consequences, it can be hard to tell the difference between the helpful and unhelpful versions of these strategies. A summary is provided in the next box.

2 – The behaviours that lead us into the traps seem reasonable on the surface

In the short term, when we use the unhealthy versions of these strategies, we feel better (avoidance, emotion-driven behaviour), or we think we're doing something useful, like working on a problem (rumination) or preventing laziness (self-criticism). As a result, we feel encouraged to continue using these strategies.

3 – These behaviours create vicious cycles over the long term

Over time, the traps intensify the problems we're trying to solve. This makes us think we need to try harder. But using the same strategies with increased effort gets us even more stuck in the traps. It's difficult to see this pattern, unless we're mindfully observing.

USEFUL STRATEGY	UNHELPFUL VERSION OF STRATEGY
Persistent thinking • problem-solving • planning • reflection	Rumination • depressive rumination • anger rumination • worrying
Avoiding true dangers in the external world • harmful objects • dangerous situations • risky activities	Avoiding/suppressing internal experiences • thoughts, memories, images • emotions, sensations • temptations, urges
Constructive, emotion-driven behaviour • protection of self, others (fear) • correction of injustices (anger) • creative achievements (passion) • care of others (love)	Harmful, emotion-driven behaviour • temper outbursts, lashing out at others • overeating • misuse of alcohol or drugs • excessive shopping or other distractions
Constructive self-criticism • specific • considerate • balanced	Harmful self-criticism • vague • demeaning • unbalanced

Looking Ahead

If you've read this far, you've learned a huge amount about how psychological traps work in general. If you've completed the self-tests and worksheets, you have important new insights about how they work *for you*. If you've practised the exercises, you've made an excellent start on learning the mindfulness skills that will help you out of the traps.

Getting this far in the book is like climbing a mountain up to base camp. Take a moment to rest and congratulate yourself on your progress. If you're not entirely confident that you've adapted to the altitude, go back and re-read previous chapters, use the worksheets, and practise the exercises a few more times before moving on.

When you're ready to forge ahead, the rest of this book provides detailed descriptions of numerous additional exercises, with instructions on how to practise them and apply them to your own life.

First, however, let's recall the 'passengers-on-the-bus' exercise from chapter 4. The bus is your life, and you're trying to drive it in the direction you want to go. Falling into psychological traps makes your bus go off course. Struggling with stress, anxiety and unhappiness makes you lose sight of your chosen directions. Do you know where you want to drive your bus? The next chapter will help you clarify your thoughts on this important question.

Chapter Summary

- Unconstructive self-criticism is vague, inconsiderate, judgemental and unbalanced.

- We often criticize ourselves harshly because we think it's necessary to prevent mistakes and laziness and to maintain our self-discipline. In reality, unconstructive self-criticism triggers negative emotions, reduces motivation and energy, and encourages procrastination and avoidance. It can lead to depression, anxiety, stress and unhealthy behaviour.

- Mindfulness of our own self-critical thoughts helps us see these patterns. It teaches us to recognize harshly self-critical thoughts and allow them to pass through the mind, without getting caught up in them or believing everything they say.

- If we've made mistakes or our behaviour needs improvement, mindfulness helps us respond wisely to the situation.

Part 3

Mindfulness Skills

7 Why it Matters: Values and Goals

'Our souls are hungry for meaning, for the sense that we have figured out how to live so that our lives matter.'

Harold Kushner

Ryan's Story

Ryan is a high-school science teacher. His parents work in the medical field and wanted him to become a doctor. As a teenager and young adult, Ryan was unsure of what he wanted from life. At his parents' urging, he pursued pre-medical studies at university. He liked the science classes, worked hard and earned excellent grades. In his free time, he volunteered as a tutor for a high school in a low-income neighbourhood. He enjoyed helping the students with their homework and supporting them in the struggles of adolescence. He decided that, as a doctor, he would specialize in adolescent medicine.

In his senior year, Ryan was accepted to medical school. At this point, to his surprise, he began to feel depressed. The prospect of years of medical training was exhausting. Ryan saw a psychologist at the student health centre who encouraged him to join a mindfulness group. He learned to observe his thoughts, feelings and emotional reactions in a non-judgemental and open-minded way. In time, he realized that his motivation for success in pre-medical studies depended on his parents' approval and the praise and respect of his classmates and teachers. He doubted whether these rewards could sustain him through the rigours of medical school. He loved teenagers and wanted to make a career of working with them. He also loved science. But he was much more interested in education than in medicine.

Ryan met with an adviser to discuss becoming a high-school science teacher. He told his parents that he had decided not to go to medical school and was pursuing a teaching degree. They were disappointed and puzzled. Why would he give up a prestigious and lucrative career? Ryan acknowledged that he would earn less money, but felt lighter and happier than he had in a long time. He had found a purpose that was truly his own.

Where do you want to drive your bus? What do you really care about, deep down? What would you like to be remembered for? What path are you on? Practising mindfulness can help you answer these questions and build a life that feels meaningful, satisfying and rich.

Happiness

Many people say that happiness is their primary goal in life. But what do we mean by happiness? One definition equates happiness with pleasure or feeling good. According to this view, a happy person experiences mostly positive emotions and relatively little pain.

Another definition emphasizes the satisfaction that comes from being true to oneself, finding one's inner strengths, and using them in ways that give meaning and direction to life, even when doing so is difficult and stressful.

Research shows that both ways of defining happiness are useful. People who have more positive emotions report higher levels of overall satisfaction with life. In fact, studies show that positive emotions are more than merely enjoyable – they also motivate and energize us for healthy behaviour. Just as fear creates the urge to escape and anger the urge to attack, feelings like love, joy, contentment, interest and pride create urges to explore the environment, take in new information, savour the present moment, share feelings with others, play, be creative and plan future achievements. These behaviours build social bonds, cultivate new skills, and encourage the development of long-term goals and purposes. All of this contributes to happiness and wellbeing.

Does this mean that you should pursue whatever feels best in the moment? Probably not. Pursuit of positive feelings for their own sake can become a trap. For example, some drugs create intensely positive feelings, but regular use can ruin careers and relationships. TV, computer games and surfing the Internet can be quite enjoyable, even almost addictive, without contributing to quality of life in a meaningful way. There's nothing wrong with TV and computer games in moderation. But if you're thinking seriously about where to drive your bus, you'll find more satisfaction by identifying your most important values and goals and using them to guide your behaviour.

Values and Goals

The word 'values' has many meanings. In the context of mindfulness and mental health, values are your personal choices about what matters most to you in life. They're the important principles that guide your actions. Here are some examples of values:

- Being a kind and caring friend.

- Being a loving and supportive parent.

- Being competent, productive, helpful or creative in your work.

- Contributing to your community or other worthy causes.

- Taking good care of your health.

Values are like compass points; they provide a direction, but not a final destination. Values-consistent behaviour is a journey that never ends. Being a supportive friend, for example, is a lifelong process.

In order to live in a values-consistent way, it's helpful to set specific, realistic goals. Goals are like milestones along the journey. If you value competence and helpfulness in your work, you might set goals for learning a new software programme, adopting it for your daily tasks, and teaching your co-workers to use it. Each goal can be completed and crossed off your to-do list, but the underlying values of competence and helpfulness continue. New goals will arise that reflect them.

Values help us choose goals that feel worthwhile. They also make it easier to persist when the pursuit of long-term goals is not going well. If you're writing a book, running a business, raising a child, or learning to swim, you'll experience frustration, disappointment, pain and anxiety along the way. Your underlying values (creativity, contributing to the community, caring for others, challenging yourself) provide the energy to persevere and the wisdom to choose a new goal if a previous one becomes unattainable.

Don's Story

Don is an avid runner who values physical fitness, his relationship with his father, and contributing to worthy causes. When his father was diagnosed with leukaemia, Don signed up with an organization that raises money for cancer research by training amateur athletes to run marathons. Don requested donations from his friends, colleagues and acquaintances, attended frequent coaching sessions and gradually increased his running speed and distance. After a few months of training, he injured an ankle and had to withdraw from the marathon. Though terribly disappointed, he took comfort in having raised several hundred dollars for cancer research. He continued to serve the organization by helping to coordinate the annual one-mile walk – another fundraising event.

Don's situation illustrates several important points. His goals – to run the marathon and raise money for cancer research in honour of his father – were realistic, though ambitious, and consistent with his values. Training for a marathon and asking people for money can be uncomfortable; Don persevered because of the importance of the values these behaviours served. When the marathon became impossible, his values helped him find a new goal that was satisfying in a different way.

Traps We Fall into When Pursuing Values and Goals

Many studies have confirmed that people who consistently work towards valued goals feel happier, more fulfilled and more satisfied with their lives. But it's important to choose our values and goals carefully. We can fall into traps while pursuing them.

1 – Adopting other people's values and goals instead of finding our own

Research shows that *autonomy* is a basic psychological need and contributes to happiness and wellbeing. Autonomy is the ability to make your own decisions about how to think and behave, rather than relying excessively on others' opinions or approval. Autonomous people resist social pressures that are inconsistent with their inner standards or preferences. People who pursue freely chosen goals that they genuinely value make better progress and feel happier than people whose goals are based on others' wishes and the avoidance of disapproval.

The desire to avoid disapproval is completely understandable. Disapproval makes us feel anxious, resentful and insecure. However, avoiding such feelings is often a trap that makes matters worse in the long run. Before realizing that he wanted to be a science teacher, Ryan had fallen into this trap. He was motivated primarily by the approval of others. To find his own values and goals, he had to recognize his inner strengths and interests: teaching, science, working with teenagers. Then he had to pursue these interests despite others' opinions.

2 – Focusing on what you'd like to avoid instead of what you want to pursue

Some people say that their primary goal is never to be depressed again, never to have another panic attack, never to get drunk, over-eat, or say the wrong thing, never to be as badly hurt, disappointed or embarrassed as they've been before. Unfortunately, it's impossible to live a rewarding life without the risk of emotional and physical pain. When people try to avoid anything that might hurt, their lives become severely constricted. Happiness and vitality dry up. This causes its own type of pain: dissatisfaction, boredom and the regret of lost opportunities.

When thinking about what you really want from life, ask yourself, 'Is this goal focused on avoiding something?' If the answer is yes, try stating your goals and values in a different way. Instead of 'My goal is never to feel depressed again,' consider, 'I value caring for my mind and body so that I can face life's challenges more effectively.' Think about what you'd do if you were less susceptible to depression. Spend more time with your family? Work on your career? Develop new skills? Volunteer for a worthy cause? Enjoy your leisure time? State these as your values and set goals that are consistent with them.

3 – Expecting the road always to be clear, straight and enjoyable

It's easy to assume that once you've found your true path, you'll always enjoy travelling along it. This is a fallacy. While often deeply rewarding, values-consistent behaviour can be scary, painful, annoying, confusing or dull. We encounter obstacles, take wrong turns, even crash occasionally. Ryan found some of his education classes exciting and inspiring, but others were frustrating and tedious. He failed a required foreign language class at his first attempt and barely passed the second time. He had to remind himself repeatedly that these classes were necessary to realize his long-term plans.

Ryan has now taught science in a poverty-stricken, inner-city high school for several years. He's warm, accepting and generous with his time, providing extra help with academic and personal problems. He's made a huge difference to the lives of many of his students and finds this deeply satisfying. Despite his best efforts, a few of his students have dropped out of school and are now unemployed, abusing drugs and alcohol, or committing crimes. Ryan feels a great sense of failure and regret about these students. Occasionally, he's tempted to find a job with less stress and disappointment. Most of the time, however, he realizes that he genuinely values working with disadvantaged teenagers, even if he's unsuccessful in some cases. He finds meaning and purpose in doing the best he can.

Identifying Your Own Values and Goals

If identifying your values feels daunting, it may help to consider the types of values that provide meaning and satisfaction to others, even if you don't share all of them. The following domains of life are commonly considered by people thinking seriously about what matters most to them.

1 – Relationships

Most people feel a strong need for personal connections and would not be happy or satisfied without trusting and supportive relationships. The specific nature of the desired relationships varies considerably. For many people, a marital or long-term relationship with a partner is very important; others prefer the single life. Many people wish to raise children; others choose to remain childless. Extroverted people enjoy a large circle of friends and an active social life; introverts prefer a small number of friends seen less often. Some people like to work closely with colleagues or co-workers; others prefer to work more independently.

To identify your values in the relationship domain, think beyond the relationships you'd like to have. Getting married and having children are goals rather than values. The underlying question is how you'd like to *be* in these relationships. Loving, attentive, kind? Open, honest, communicative? Assertive, independent, strong?

2 – Work (including education and household management)

Most people are happier if they have knowledge, skills and competencies and can use them to solve problems and accomplish worthwhile tasks. Work, school and household management provide rich opportunities for skilful, competent behaviour. Whether your work is complex or straight-forward, interesting or dull, pleasant or unpleasant, it can also provide a sense of purpose – a way to contribute to something that matters to you.

To identify your values in this domain, think beyond the jobs you'd like to have. Getting a job is a goal. The underlying question is what matters to you about doing the work. What types of contributions would you like to make? What sort of employee, student or household manager would you like to be? Productive, competent, dependable? A good problem-solver? A supportive colleague? A helpful service provider? An innovator?

3 – Community involvement

This domain includes contributing to causes or organizations that are consistent with your ideals. Depending on what you value, you might volunteer with an animal welfare group, an environmental organization, a political campaign, a homeless shelter, a literacy programme. The list of possibilities is virtually endless. What kinds of contributions would you like to make?

4 – Self-care, personal growth, recreation, leisure activity

Many people value their physical and mental health, for their own sake and because good health makes it easier to participate in other domains of life. Diet, exercise and sleep nurture our bodies and minds. Leisure activities reduce stress and re-energize us for important work. Some people value religion or spirituality as a way of caring for themselves and others or expanding their understanding of life. Some find value in appreciating beauty through nature and the arts; they spend time outdoors, play an instrument or sing, attend concerts, plays, art exhibits.

Many valued activities fall in more than one category. Parenting is a relationship, but it also requires numerous skills and competencies, like changing nappies, helping with homework, and communicating with teenagers. Volunteering with community organizations may be a way of developing friendships and building skills as well as contributing to worthy causes. Church involvement can be a form of self-care or personal growth, a way to make friends and a way to contribute to others.

What about Wealth and Fame?

When asked what they most want from life, some people think of being rich, famous or attractive. Psychologists call these 'extrinsic' goals because they depend on the judgements, attitudes or behaviour of other people. Wealth depends on others paying you a salary, leaving you an inheritance, or buying something that you sell. Fame and attractiveness depend on the recognition and admiration of others.

There's nothing wrong with aspiring to be rich, famous or attractive, or with enjoying these conditions if you have them. However, research shows that people who emphasize these goals are less happy and satisfied with their lives than people who focus on 'intrinsic' values such as relationships, health, meaningful work and community involvement. If extrinsic goals are important to you, look for underlying values by asking what they make possible. For example, wealth may allow you to provide financial security for yourself and your family or contribute to causes you believe in. In this case, acquiring wealth is a goal, whereas caring for yourself, your family and your community are values.

Exercise for Clarifying Your Values

The worksheet on page 124 will help you think about your most important values. As you complete the worksheet, remember these points:

1. If you're thinking of something that can be completed or obtained and checked off a list (such as 'getting a master's degree'), that's a goal, not a value. Write down the value that the goal will serve, such as 'developing my professional skills'.

2. If you're thinking of a way you'd like to feel (for example, 'confident'), remember that feelings are not completely under your control and that values-consistent behaviour sometimes feels unpleasant. What would you be *doing* if you felt more confident? Inviting people over for dinner? Sharing your poetry with others? Then your values might be 'cultivating relationships' or 'sharing the fruits of my creativity'.

3. If you're uncertain of your values in some domains, leave them blank for now. Start paying attention to how you feel in various situations and your values may become clearer. Some domains may be unimportant to you; not everyone values everything. But consider whether you're fooling yourself because you find certain areas painful and would rather not think about them. Do you *really* value spending your weekends alone, or are you avoiding the discomfort of finding ways to socialize?

4. Values can conflict with each other, usually because of the time required to pursue them. If you value working hard at your job and spending time with your children, you may find it difficult to do both to your satisfaction. Often there is no easy solution to this problem and you have to find a compromise.

5. Reflecting on values can be painful. You may realize that your behaviour has not been consistent with your true priorities. Feelings of disappointment, resentment and sadness may arise, along with self-critical, pessimistic and hopeless thoughts (*I'll only be disappointed . . .*

I'll never achieve my goals). These thoughts and feelings are natural. They're passengers on your bus. You don't have to let them control your behaviour. Remember that values-consistent behaviour can start anytime, regardless of the thoughts and feelings that may be present.

Samantha's Story

On the next page is a copy of the worksheet completed by Samantha, a freelance writer in her mid-thirties. Samantha is interested in the environment and writes articles for newspapers and magazines about climate change, wildlife conservation and ecotourism. She has a happy and stable relationship with a boyfriend, but is unsure whether she wants to get married and is confident she doesn't want children. She loves animals, has two dogs, and volunteers with the Humane Society. She lives in a small, economical house so that she can afford to travel. She visits other countries once or twice each year to learn about environmental issues and to volunteer for conservation projects and wildlife sanctuaries. She writes about her experiences in her articles.

Samantha has an uneasy relationship with her parents. They wish she would marry her boyfriend, start a family before it's too late, and join their business, a successful paint and wallpaper shop. They'd like her to take over the shop when they retire in five years. Samantha is not interested in doing so, but she hasn't discussed this with her parents and helps in the shop whenever an employee is ill or away. She would prefer to limit her time there to focus on her writing and travel, but hasn't found a way to say 'no' to her parents' frequent requests. She's their only child and is fearful of disappointing them.

Worksheet: Describing your values

Your name: <u>Samantha</u>

In this domain	I value
Spouse, partner	*being open and honest with my boyfriend.*
Parenting	*not applicable, don't plan to have children.*
Other family	*being assertive with my parents, standing up for myself, also being loving, caring and respectful.*
Friends	*feeling connected, sharing about myself in addition to listening to others.*
Work	*spending my time on meaningful projects, being productive, enjoying my work.*
Education, training	*occasional writing workshops, seminars about environment & climate change, learning while travelling (wildlife conservation).*
Household management	*being clean and organized enough to be productive & comfortable, avoiding perfectionism about appearance and neatness.*
Community	*volunteering with the Humane Society (helping stray cats & dogs), teaching an occasional writing class, volunteering while travelling.*
Personal wellbeing	*eating, sleeping and exercising to be healthy and strong.*
Personal growth	*travel to other countries to work on environmental projects.*
Recreation, leisure	*taking the dogs on walks, going to movies with my boyfriend, seeing friends.*
Spirituality	*not very religious, but travel helps me feel in touch with the larger world, connected with others in different cultures.*
Appreciation of beauty	*travel (mostly scenery and wildlife), photography and painting, walking the dogs in the arboretum.*
Other	*staying in touch with people I meet on my travels, taking care of my dogs.*

On the next page is a blank version of the worksheet for your own use. Make several copies, so that you can clarify your thoughts as you work with it over time. There are no right or wrong answers.

Worksheet: Describing your values

Your name: _____

In this domain	I value
Spouse, partner	
Parenting	
Other family	
Friends	
Work	
Education, training	
Household management	
Community	
Personal wellbeing	
Personal growth	
Recreation, leisure	
Spirituality	
Appreciation of beauty	
Other	

The next worksheet provides a way to examine whether your behaviour is consistent with what matters most to you. Confronting discrepancies between values and behaviour can be uncomfortable, but it illuminates priorities and helps you set goals for being true to them. Samantha's is on the next page.

Worksheet: Rating your values and behaviour

Your name: <u>Samantha</u>

Use the scale from 1–10 below to rate your values and behaviour:

IMPORTANCE: How important is this domain at this point in your life?
1: not at all important   5: moderately important   10: extremely important

ACTION: How active have you been with this domain in the last few weeks?
1: not at all active   5: moderately active   10: extremely active

SATISFACTION WITH ACTION: How satisfied are you with your recent action in this area?
1: not at all satisfied   5: moderately satisfied   10: extremely satisfied

Domain	Importance (1–10)	Action (1–10)	Satisfaction with Action (1–10)	Notes
Spouse/partner	9	7	5	Arguing with boyfriend about time I spend in parents' shop.
Parenting	1	1	10	Not an issue.
Other family	8	4	4	Parents ask me to work in the shop a lot, I give in too much.
Friends	9	8	8	Doing well here (they also think I should assert myself with parents).

Work	9	5	2	Too little time writing, too much in parents' shop.
Education, training	5	4	9	Writing workshop coming up this summer.
Household management	5	3	9	No major concerns here.
Community involvement	7	6	9	Volunteering with Humane Society, teaching at writing centre.
Personal wellbeing	6	6	8	No major concerns here.
Personal growth	8	5	2	Agreed to work in shop during employee's maternity leave, had to cancel a wildlife trip.
Recreation, leisure	7	5	6	Doing OK here.
Spirituality	5	5	4	Wildlife trips are spiritual for me, cancelled one to help in shop.
Appreciation of beauty	7	5	5	Enjoying walking the dogs but regret missing wildlife trip.
Other (dogs, contact with distant friends)	9	8	8	Doing well here.

Samantha's worksheet shows that her behaviour is consistent with her values in many domains. However, she is dissatisfied with her response to her parents' requests for help in the shop and their repeated suggestions that she take over the shop when they retire. She regrets having agreed to work full time for three months while a regular employee is on maternity leave and wishes she had been more assertive about saying 'no'. This issue is affecting her relationship with her boyfriend, who urges her to talk more openly with her parents about it. She's finding it difficult to complete writing assignments and she cancelled a week-long stay at a wildlife sanctuary in Costa Rica.

If you find discrepancies between your values and your behaviour, it's important to set goals for change. Samantha realized that she needed to have a serious talk with her parents about her goals for the future and her involvement in their shop. Though nervous about it, she explained herself as lovingly and respectfully as she could. She offered to help them find a new employee and explore options for selling their business when they're ready to retire. They were sad and disappointed, though not surprised. They also supported Samantha's values and goals and agreed to ask her to work in the shop less often.

On pages 130–1 is a blank copy of this worksheet for your own use.

How Mindfulness Helps with Values and Goals

Practising mindfulness helps with values and goals in several important ways. It enables us to recognize our values and persist in values-consistent behaviour when it's difficult and stressful to do so. It also helps us find a balance between working for the future and living in the present.

Mindfulness and Recognizing Your Values

If you've been suffering from anxiety, depression, anger, guilt or other difficulties, you may think that nothing really matters to you except feeling better. This is completely understandable – stress and unhappiness often demand most of our attention. However, we all have values that go beyond feeling better, even if we're not fully aware of them. If you're not sure what you truly care about, practising mindfulness will help you recognize your values. If you pay attention to your daily experiences, in an open-minded, friendly and curious way, you'll begin to notice things. Small moments of meaning and satisfaction will arise; perhaps when you're talking with someone, working on a particular problem or task, or reading about something. These moments are important indicators of what matters most to you.

Practising mindfulness will also help you observe when you're acting in accordance with other people's standards and values rather than your own. You may begin to notice feelings of discomfort about it. It's important to be open to these moments without judging yourself harshly. Think about what you'd like to be doing instead and set goals for small changes in your behaviour that will lead you in that direction. Over time, your self-understanding and autonomy will increase.

Mindfulness and Persistence with Values-Consistent Behaviour

Even when we know what we'd like to do and why it's important to do it, unpleasant emotions and thoughts (*I'll never succeed . . . this is a waste of time . . . people will disapprove*) can undermine motivation. Instead of taking constructive action, we fall into the traps discussed in the preceding chapters. We try to avoid the unpleasant thoughts and feelings, or the situations that bring them up. We ruminate about our problems, which makes it harder to solve them. We behave impulsively, in ways we later regret. We criticize ourselves, which creates more negative emotions and reduces our motivation to act.

Research shows that mindfulness helps us persist with difficult or stressful tasks. In one study, students completed a mindfulness questionnaire and then were asked to solve some difficult scrambled word puzzles. Those who were generally more mindful (according to the questionnaire

Worksheet: Rating your values and behaviour

Your name: _____

Use the scale from 1–10 below to rate your values and behaviour.

IMPORTANCE: How important is this domain at this point in your life?
1: not at all important   5: moderately important   10: extremely important

ACTION: How active have you been with this domain in the last few weeks?
1: not at all active   5: moderately active   10: extremely active

SATISFACTION WITH ACTION: How satisfied are you with your recent action in this area?
1: not at all satisfied   5: moderately satisfied   10: extremely satisfied

Domain	Importance (1–10)	Action (1–10)	Satisfaction with Action (1–10)	Notes
Spouse/partner				
Parenting				
Other family				
Friends				

Work	Education, training	Household management	Community involvement	Personal wellbeing	Personal growth	Recreation, leisure	Spirituality	Appreciation of beauty

persisted longer in trying to solve the puzzles. In another study, people with emotional problems who were in an angry mood were asked either to ruminate about their mood or to practise mindfulness for a few minutes. Then they worked on a stressful, computerized maths task. Those who practised mindfulness felt less angry afterwards and persisted much longer on the stressful task.

Studies like these are a little artificial. For most people, solving arithmetic problems and word puzzles isn't an important value in life. Even so, the studies suggest that mindfulness increases goal-directed behaviour.

Mindfulness and Appreciating the Journey

Imagine that you have a young child. One day, to your surprise, a wizard appears at your door. 'I can grant you one wish,' he says. 'What is your deepest desire for the future?'

'I want my child to become a happy, healthy and independent adult,' you reply.

'Done!' says the wizard, waving his wand. Your child is instantly transformed into a cheerful thirty-year-old with a lovely family, a rewarding career and a nice house a few miles away.

Is this what you wanted? Perhaps not. It has deprived you of the chance to live in the present with your child and to watch him/her grow into adulthood. Most people who value caring for a child want to take this journey, even if it's scary and painful at times and doesn't turn out exactly as they'd imagined. They want the shared experiences, the memories and the intimate knowledge of how their child developed over the years. They want the sense of accomplishment that long-term engagement brings.

Your goals for the future guide your behaviour in the present, but the real goal is to participate in the journey. Practising mindfulness helps you appreciate the countless moments that make up the journey. When it's joyful, fascinating, peaceful or exciting, you fully feel it. When it's scary, painful, infuriating or dull, you feel that, too. At difficult moments, you may wish for the wizard to fast-forward you to your goal. This is entirely understandable. If no wizard appears, mindful observation of the present moment helps you understand what's happening and choose values-consistent behaviour. It reminds you of the enduring sense of wellbeing that comes from doing the best you can with something you care about, even when it's stressful.

Mindfulness keeps you from missing large chunks of your life. In the following chapters, we'll explore in detail the nature of mindfulness and how to cultivate it by practising skills and exercises. At the heart of mindfulness is *observation* – seeing what's happening in the present moment. In the next chapter, we'll consider how to develop mindful observation skills.

Chapter Summary

- Most people find life happier and more satisfying if they recognize what matters most to them and behave consistently with their values and goals.

- Although pursuing our deepest values and goals can be very rewarding, it's also stressful and uncomfortable at times. Difficult thoughts and feelings may arise when we're engaged in important pursuits.

- Mindfulness helps us identify our values and goals, persist when pursuing them is unpleasant or even painful, and appreciate the journey.

8 Mindful Observation

'Mindfulness means paying attention in a particular way: on purpose, in the present moment, and non-judgementally.'

Jon Kabat-Zinn

At any moment in time, we have many choices about where to focus our attention. The outer world is full of sights and sounds. The inner world is full of thoughts and feelings. When we're mindful, we notice more of them.

Mindful observation has several characteristics:

1 – We can choose what to pay attention to

Imagine that you're in a classroom, listening to a lecture. You hear a bird singing through an open window. For a moment, your attention is drawn to the bird. If you're being mindful, you'll notice that your attention has shifted. If you choose, you can redirect it to the lecture.

2 – Mindful observation focuses on the present

Imagine that you're confused by the lecture. You feel discouraged and frustrated. Then you start thinking, 'I'm such an idiot, I'll never understand this. I'll fail this course and then I won't be able to get the kind of job I want. That will be terrible.' If you're being mindful, you'll realize that you've become absorbed in an imagined future. If you choose, you can come back to the present.

3 – Mindful observation is non-judgemental

If you're being mindful, you'll recognize that 'I'm an idiot' and 'That will be terrible' are judgemental thoughts. You'll remind yourself to let go of judging and simply observe.

Mindful observation helps you see what's actually happening right now. If your present situation is difficult and stressful, you'll make wiser decisions about what to do. If it's pleasant and enjoyable, you'll appreciate it more. Mindful observation is the key to escaping the psychological traps described in earlier chapters: rumination, avoidance, emotion-driven behaviour and self-criticism. People who are mindful of the present moment, whether it's pleasant, unpleasant or neutral, are less susceptible to depression, anxiety, stress, anger, overeating, alcohol abuse and many other problems. They're better able to meet daily demands, more autonomous and purposeful, happier and more satisfied with life.

Remember that being mindful does NOT mean you never get distracted, you never get absorbed in the future or the past, or you never have judgemental thoughts. Such experiences are common and normal, even for people who've practised mindfulness for many years. Mindful observation means that when these things occur, you notice them, without judging yourself. Then you can return your attention to what's happening in the present, if you choose.

In this chapter, we'll focus on exercises that cultivate mindful observation skills. First, let's consider an example of non-mindful observation.

Jill's Story – Part 1

Jill is twenty-two years old and has been frightened of thunderstorms since she was five. She was in a park with her parents one day when a storm came up suddenly. As they ran to their car, an old tree was struck by lightning and fell on to the playground, knocking over the swings where Jill had been playing moments before.

Ever since, Jill has been anxious about stormy weather. Even gentle rain scares her because she fears that a storm might develop. If she's at home, she stays in her basement when it rains. If she's anywhere else when the rain begins, she races home as quickly as possible, driving dangerously fast and disregarding traffic lights and stop signs. When storms are predicted, she cancels appointments and social activities. She's most concerned about the craft fairs where she sells her pottery. If the weather looks threatening, she leaves early or doesn't show up at all.

Much of the time, Jill is extremely observant of the weather. She notices the shapes and sizes of the clouds, the colours of the sky, the temperature and humidity of the air, the speed and direction of the wind. But this is not mindful observation. It's unmindful in several ways:

1. **Her attention is controlled by the weather.** When she's worried about storms, Jill has trouble thinking of anything else. At work, she gets little done because she's constantly looking out of the window, checking the forecast on her computer, and thinking of excuses to leave early. At craft fairs, she finds it hard to converse with customers because she's preoccupied with getting home.

2. **She tries to escape rather than staying present.** Jill has intense reactions to threatening weather. Her heart pounds; she feels sweaty, breathless and shaky. Rather than mindfully observing the storm and her reactions to it, Jill gets absorbed in thoughts about getting home as fast as possible. Her desire to escape is understandable – intense anxiety is very unpleasant. But her behaviour is making matters worse.

3. **She's judgemental.** Jill judges the weather as 'good' or 'bad', based solely on how it makes her feel. She judges her reactions as 'good' (staying calm) or 'bad' (feeling anxious). She judges herself as stupid, crazy and weak for getting upset about conditions that are usually harmless. This makes her more upset and less able to think clearly.

Jill has fallen into all of the psychological traps described in earlier chapters. She *ruminates* about the weather and how she'll cope with it. She *avoids* activities and responsibilities when the weather seems threatening.

Her frantic driving during storms is *emotion-driven behaviour*. She *criticizes* herself harshly for her feelings, thoughts and actions.

Jill is working on the mindful observation skills described in this chapter. With practice, she'll learn to observe the weather in a mindful way. She'll begin to appreciate the interesting sights, sounds, scents and sensations that it creates. When necessary, she'll take reasonable precautions during rainy weather, such as closing windows and bringing her cat indoors. She'll learn to stay present with her emotional reactions – noticing them as they happen without taking drastic steps to escape them. She'll see that the sensations of anxiety are unpleasant but not dangerous, that they pass in time, and that she can behave constructively even while feeling anxious. In time, the intensity of her fear will decrease. Even when she's scared, she'll be able to control her behaviour.

Mindful Observation – Introductory Exercises

Mindful observation is easier when the present moment is pleasant or neutral than when it's scary, painful and stressful. The following exercises will help you practise mindful observation of ordinary, non-threatening experiences. Some of these exercises were introduced in an earlier chapter; here, you'll have a chance to refine your skills. Later in this chapter, we'll consider how to apply the skills to more difficult situations.

1 – Hand on a surface

Put one of your hands on a nearby surface, such as a table, desk or the arm of a chair. Observe the sensations in your hand as it rests on this surface. Take a few moments to notice each of your fingers, your thumb, the back of your hand, the palm. Notice the feel of the air on your skin and the points of contact with the surface. Continue for about a minute. Experiment with keeping your eyes open or closed – either way is fine.

Your mind will wander at some point. When you realize that you're thinking of something else, gently bring your attention back to the sensations in your hand. If you criticize yourself for letting your mind wander, remember that it's normal. Everyone's mind wanders. See if you can let go of the criticism and return to observing the sensations in your hand with an attitude of interest and curiosity.

2 – Hand on your head

Put one hand on top of your head. Observe the sensations for a minute or so. See if you can observe the sensations in your hand and your head. Notice texture, temperature, points of contact. Then shift your attention to your arm, as it works to keep your hand on your head. Notice what you feel in your arm. If you start thinking, analysing or judging (*my hair is so thin . . . why does my shoulder ache? . . . this is silly*), notice that these are thoughts. As best you can, and without criticizing, return your attention to observing the sensations in your hand, head or arm.

3 – Mindful observation of sounds

Turn your attention to any sounds you can hear. Listen closely for a minute or two. Be open to all sounds, whatever their source. Observe the qualities of the sounds. How long do they last? Are they loud or soft? Is the pitch high or low? Notice periods of silence between sounds. If you notice a tendency to think about or analyse the sounds (*that's a bird . . . that's the fridge humming . . . what could be making that sound?*), gently redirect your attention to hearing the sounds.

Does a sound create an urge to do something, such as investigate what's making the sound? If so, notice the urge. Decide mindfully whether to act on it. Return your attention to observing the sounds. When your mind wanders off, bring it back gently.

4 – Mindful observation of sights

Now turn your attention to whatever you see around you. Observe the colours, shapes, textures or movements of what you see. Notice any tendency to label it (*that's a light switch ... that's a clock ... I see a tree through the window*). If possible, allow the labelling to fade away and focus on the experience of seeing. Look closely. Notice if you judge what you see as good or bad, pretty or ugly, desirable or undesirable. If possible, let go of the judgements and focus on seeing what's actually there.

If you have thoughts (*it's getting late ... I should make dinner ... that window really needs cleaning*), notice that these are thoughts and return your attention to seeing. If you feel an emotion, such as delight when seeing a bird, or disgust when seeing an insect, observe that for a moment, allow the emotion to be as it is, and then return your attention to seeing.

5 – Mindful observation of daily activities

Mindful observation can be practised with many things that we experience in daily life. Janet, a new mother, practised mindful observation of feeding her baby and wrote a short description of what she noticed:

> 'My husband and I are both full-time students and we're always worrying about getting our work done and having enough money. We have a three-month-old daughter, Abby. Whenever I'm away from Abby, I worry about whether she's OK and I feel guilty about the time I spend apart from her. But then when I'm with her, I worry about all the work I have to do.

> 'This week I decided to practise mindful observation while feeding Abby. At first, I couldn't stop obsessing about how far behind I am in my studies and the money we had to spend when our roof was leaking last week. But one day, I was able gradually to bring my attention to the feeding experience and I started noticing some amazing things – the feeling of the gentle, soft touch of Abby's tiny hand on my stomach, the way her long eyelashes curve up at the very tips, the narrow blue vein that runs from her ear to the back of her skull, the way her breathing changed and her body relaxed as she drifted off to sleep. All of these things might have escaped my attention had I been thinking of other things.

'I found that my anxiety about being away from her most of the day was quickly replaced by a calm, happy, peaceful feeling. I sat with her for quite a while after she fell asleep, enjoying the experience of mindfully observing her. When thoughts about work and money came up, I was able to let them pass and just observe Abby.'

For Janet, mindful observation while feeding Abby made her more aware of a pleasant activity. Although it was difficult at first to disengage from rumination and worry, once she had turned her attention to Abby, she enjoyed observing her.

Mindful observation is less enjoyable, though very useful, if the present moment is unpleasant and stressful. Wendy, another new mother, also practised mindful observation with her baby, but her experience was quite different.

'My baby Kevin is very emotional. He has crying spells all the time. He seems so desperate, won't take a bottle, and nothing soothes him. I try so hard to comfort him but nothing really works except waiting it out. Normally, I struggle really hard to stay calm. I tell myself over and over that if I get upset it only makes things worse. When Kevin finally calms down, I feel drained and exhausted.

'One day this week, I tried mindful observation. I tried to have a non-judgemental attitude. I observed Kevin's arms and legs flailing and his little red, scowling face. I listened to his cries. I noticed the feeling of his body as I tried holding him different ways and setting him on the bed. I also observed my own thoughts and feelings. The whole experience was really hard. I felt frustrated, worried, sad and resentful about having such a fussy baby. But I didn't fight with the feelings. I just noticed them and kept observing Kevin. I tried to let things take their natural course and stay present without criticizing.

'After Kevin calmed down, I was much less exhausted than usual, I think because I wasn't trying to stifle my feelings. I felt more accepting of having a fussy baby and compassion for both of us having to get through this difficult phase.'

For Wendy, mindful observation of Kevin's crying spell was difficult, but less stressful than her usual approach of trying to suppress her own thoughts and feelings. Mindful observation did not transform Kevin into an easy baby, but it helped Wendy manage his crying spell and feel compassion for both of them.

Mindful Observation of Breathing

Mindful breathing is an excellent tool for bringing attention into the present, especially when the moment is difficult and stressful. For centuries, ancient meditation traditions have used mindful breathing to cultivate awareness, insight and wisdom. Why is this?

- Breathing is continuous. You don't have to think back to the last time you breathed or look ahead to future breaths. You're breathing now. If you focus on it, you're in the present. With practice, you can learn to attend to your breathing at any moment you choose.

- Breathing creates sensations and movements: feelings in the nose and throat as the air passes through; rising and falling, expanding and contracting in the chest or abdomen. Something observable is always happening.

- We don't have to control our breathing; the body breathes on its own. We can use mindful breathing to practise observing something while allowing it to be how it is, rather than trying to change it. Of course, you can change your breathing to some extent if you choose; singers, actors, swimmers and wind-instrument players learn to control their breath in particular ways. But most of the time, breathing is automatic.

- Breathing is sensitive to thoughts, emotions and physical states. When we feel angry, anxious, tired, interested or excited, breathing becomes slower or faster, deeper or shallower, regular or uneven. If we consistently observe our breathing, we learn about our internal patterns of thinking, feeling and reacting. Self-understanding and insight improve.

Mindful Breathing as a Meditation Exercise

Mindful breathing can be practised in two ways: as a meditation exercise and in ordinary daily life. It's helpful to practise the meditation exercise first. Sitting in a quiet place with few distractions makes it easier to focus your attention on your breathing. Once you're familiar with awareness of breathing, you can use this skill in daily life. Here are instructions for the mindful breathing meditation. Later, we'll consider mindful breathing in daily life.

How to sit for mindful breathing meditation

Find a posture that's comfortable, relaxed and alert. If you sit in a chair, rest your feet comfortably on the floor, about hip-width apart. Don't cross your legs. Sit up straight (don't slouch or slump), but remember that the spine is naturally curved. Don't try to straighten it completely – this will create stiffness and tension. If possible, sit a bit forward, without leaning against the back of the chair. Align your head and neck with your spine. Rest your hands on your thighs.

If you prefer to sit cross-legged on the floor, use a meditation cushion or a pillow, so that your hips are a little higher than your knees. Gently rest your hands on your thighs, or bring them together in your lap, whichever is more comfortable.

Where do you feel the breath?

Next, explore where you can most easily feel the breath going in and out of your body. Some people focus their attention on the nostrils. Often the air feels cooler going into the nostrils and warmer coming out. Others prefer to focus on the chest or abdomen and to feel the sensations of rising and falling, expanding and contracting, or stretching and deflating. Choose one spot for your first practice; you can try different spots at other times.

How much to practise

Start with five minutes; set a timer so that you don't have to keep track. For the next week, see if you can practise for five minutes every day. Twice a day is even better. If you're willing, increase the time to ten minutes. Eventually, experiment with twenty minutes or even longer.

Now you're ready to start. The rest of the instructions are in the next box. Read them carefully, then set the book aside, set the timer for five minutes, and begin. If you prefer, you can practise with the recording on the website for this book.

MINDFUL BREATHING MEDITATION

1. Settle into your sitting posture. Gently close your eyes or gaze downwards at the floor in front of you.

2. Focus your attention on the spot you chose for observing the breath (nostrils, chest or abdomen).

3. Observe the sensations and movements as the breath goes in and out of your body. As best you can, follow the breath all the way in and all the way out.

4. Allow the breath to go at its own pace and rhythm without trying to change it.

5. Your mind will wander off. When this happens, notice briefly where it went. You might say to yourself, 'Ah, thinking . . . ' and then gently return your attention to the breath, observing whether it's going in or out when you come back to it.

6. Don't try to clear your mind: this is not the goal. Instead, notice when your mind wanders to thoughts, images, memories, fantasies, plans or anything else. Gently turn your attention back to your breath, without giving yourself a hard time.

---

7. Your mind will continue to drift away. This is normal and may happen repeatedly. Notice if you criticize yourself and see if you can let go of the criticism. Instead, congratulate yourself for coming back to the breath. Practise patience and kindness.

8. Continue to bring your attention back to the breath, gently and kindly, every time the mind wanders.

9. When the timer sounds, notice where your mind is. If it's not on the breath, return to the breath for a moment before stopping the exercise.

What Did You Notice?

Everyone's experience is different. Some people find this exercise relaxing and enjoyable, others find it difficult and unpleasant, and experiences can vary from day to day. Here are some typical concerns about the mindful breathing exercise:

1 – Concerns about how you were breathing

You may have wondered if your breathing was too slow or fast, too shallow or deep, or too uneven. Perhaps you noticed a tendency to control or change your breathing pattern. These are common reactions. However, there's no right or wrong way to breathe while doing this exercise. The goal is only to observe whatever the breath is doing. The next time you practise, see if you can focus on the sensations of the breath without trying to change its pace, depth or rhythm. Practise friendly interest rather than criticism.

2 – Concerns about how you felt

If you're not accustomed to observing your breath, you may have felt awkward or uncomfortable. Perhaps you felt nervous, impatient, bored, restless or sleepy. Five minutes may have felt like an eternity; urges to check the timer may have come up. Or it may have passed by in a flash. Did you criticize yourself for having such feelings? They're all normal and common. They don't mean you're doing it wrong or that the exercise isn't working. The next time you practise, see if you can let go of the criticism. The goal is only to notice whatever is happening.

3 – Concerns about your mind wandering

Many people assume that if they do the exercise correctly, their minds will become clear and won't wander. This is a common misunderstanding. It's normal for our minds to wander. The goal of practising mindfulness is not to shut off your mind but to notice when it wanders and where it goes, and then gently to return to observing your breath. The more often you come back, the more you're strengthening your mindfulness skills.

4 – Thoughts about the exercise

Many people have thoughts such as 'This is silly', 'I don't see the point of this', 'It isn't working', or 'This won't help me'. It's perfectly OK to have such thoughts. As best you can, notice the thoughts as they go through your mind and continue with the exercise. Remind yourself that they're only thoughts. As in previous chapters, imagine your thoughts as people passing by on the street, guests in your B&B, or passengers coming and going from your bus. Say to yourself, 'Ah, there's another one,' and then return your attention to observing your breath.

The same applies to positive thoughts, such as 'This is wonderful', 'It's exactly what I need', 'This will be a great help'. Over time, relating to our thoughts in this way, whether they're positive or negative, helps us remember that we don't have to be controlled by any of our thoughts, unless we choose to be.

Mindful Breathing with Other Sensations

Now that you're familiar with mindful breathing, you can combine it with awareness of other sensations. Let's go back to the introductory exercises and add mindful breathing. This creates an exercise called 'breathing with'. You've been breathing with the rest of your experiences all your life, but perhaps you've never been mindfully aware of it.

These exercises may seem odd and artificial at first. Please be patient. 'Breathing with' is a skill that requires practice. With experience, you'll see that it's worth the effort.

1 – Breathing with the sensations in your hand

Put your hand on a surface and observe the sensations, as you did before. Notice the feelings in each of your fingers, the palm and the back of your hand. Take your time.

Now expand your awareness so that it includes your hand and your breath. Your attention may shift back and forth between your hand and your breath. This is OK. If it's helpful, think of your attention as a spotlight. It can be narrowly focused on just your hand or just your breath, or it can be expanded to include both. Experiment and observe what happens. If your mind wanders off, gently bring it back. Practise patience and open-mindedness.

After you've practised this a few times, try putting your hand in other locations and breathing with the sensations: on your head, on your abdomen, under running water, inside a glove.

2 – Breathing with sounds and sights

Take a few moments to become aware of sounds. Settle into a non-judgemental, curious attitude about sounds, as best you can. Notice their qualities. Observe the silences between sounds.

Now expand your awareness to include your breath. Practise breathing with the sounds. Your attention may shift back and forth between breathing and sounds – this is OK. If your focus narrows to only sounds or only breathing, see if you can expand it to include both.

Now try breathing with sights. Choose something to look at, perhaps a tree outside your window. Observe the leaves and branches. Notice their colours, shapes, movements in the breeze. Expand your attention to include your breath. Continue to observe the tree while also noticing your breathing.

3 – Breathing with routine experiences in daily life

Try breathing with the sensations you feel while sitting at your desk, waiting on the phone, riding in a lift, walking down the hall. During meetings, conversations or household chores, see if you can notice your breath in the background without tuning out or ignoring the task at hand.

4 – Breathing with stressful circumstances

Mindful breathing is especially useful for coping with the stresses of daily life. Ethan is an accountant who spends many hours working at a computer and is susceptible to tension headaches. Here's his description of mindful breathing while having a headache:

> 'I had a tension headache this week while sitting in my office at work. My head, neck and shoulders were really hurting. I was upset and kept thinking about why I get headaches and how much they interfere with everything.

> 'Then I realized this wasn't helping. I closed my door, turned off the light, set the timer in my phone for ten minutes, and sat quietly. First I focused on my breathing and tried to ignore the headache. That didn't work. The headache was too strong to ignore.

'Then I tried focusing directly on the headache, but that felt worse. I got caught up in thinking about how bad it was. So then I focused on my breathing without trying to ignore the headache. I was aware of both. When thoughts came along, I noticed them but didn't obsess as much.

'I noticed my breathing was faster at first and slowed down after a while. I could feel myself getting more relaxed even though my head still hurt. I was less bothered by having a headache.

'After ten minutes the headache was a little better. I did some stretches my doctor showed me, took a pain killer, and went on with my work. The headache gradually faded away.'

At first, Ethan found it difficult to balance his attention. Focusing only on the headache was not helpful; neither was trying to ignore it. Expanding his attention to include his breath and the headache helped him stop ruminating and choose constructive behaviour (stretching, pain killer) for dealing with his headache.

Ethan's experience illustrates important points about the 'breathing with' exercise. It's not a method of suppressing or avoiding an unpleasant experience. It helps us stay present with difficult circumstances in a constructive way.

Jill's Story – Part 2

Let's return to Jill, the young woman with the phobia of thunderstorms. Jill practised the mindful observation exercises described in this chapter. She started with mindful breathing for five minutes each day while sitting in a chair. At first, it made her nervous and uncomfortable. She felt strangely breathless, as if she couldn't get enough air. She cut back to two minutes each day.

Over the course of two weeks, she became accustomed to observing her breath and extended the time to ten minutes per day. During rainy weather, she practised on the sofa in her basement. When her heart raced and her stomach tightened, she practised breathing with these sensations. Her breath began to feel familiar and comforting.

Then she began observing rainy weather through a closed window. She observed the rain falling and forming puddles, watched the trees blow and listened to the wind. When she noticed her heart pounding, she breathed with these sensations for a few moments, and then resumed looking out of the window. In time, she was able to watch through an open window, noticing the feel and smell of the air and hearing the raindrops hit the ground. Later, she ventured on to her front porch to observe the rain.

For several weeks, there were no thunderstorms. Then a storm arose suddenly in the middle of the night. Jill awoke in a panic and hurried downstairs to the basement. In her usual way, she turned on the TV, wrapped herself in a blanket and huddled on the sofa. After a few minutes, she realized that this might be a good opportunity to practise mindful observation. 'No,' she told herself. 'That would be too difficult.'

Then she realized that 'That would be too difficult' is a thought. She remembered her long-term goal: to participate in craft fairs, rain or shine. She turned down the volume on the TV, just enough to hear the thunder. Her heart pounded. She observed the sensations and breathed with them.

After a few minutes, she turned off the TV and continued to listen to the thunder. She felt anxious and shaky but realized she could observe the sensations in her body while continuing to listen and breathe. After a few minutes, she slowly walked up the stairs, keeping the blanket wrapped around her for comfort. At the top of the stairs, she saw a flash of lightning through a window. A loud boom sounded. She turned quickly and started back down, but stopped herself after five or six steps. She sat on a step for a few minutes, observing her breathing and her body sensations while gazing into the basement.

As the storm continued, Jill slowly made her way into the living room and watched through a window. She checked in regularly with her breathing. She noticed urges to return to the basement but didn't act on them, although several times she put the blanket over her head for a few moments. As the storm subsided, she went out to her front porch and listened to the fading thunder and the gentle rain. Her body felt weak and tired, yet she was excited about her progress. She went inside and rewarded herself with a snack before going back to bed.

Jill realized that breathing with her anxiety symptoms (racing heart, shaky sensations) helped her see that she could tolerate them while working towards her goal of not avoiding the storm. Knowing that her behaviour did not have to be controlled by the weather gave her a feeling of strength and helped her let go of self-criticism.

Jill continues to practise mindful observation during storms. At night, she lies in bed and listens. During the day, she watches through a window, or she carries on with whatever she's doing. She's begun to practise mindful observation of the weather while driving and no longer speeds during storms.

Keeping Track of Your Practice

The following worksheet will help you keep a record of your practice of mindful observation. First is Jill's, followed by a blank one for your own use. Remember to make copies so that you can practise for several weeks. Start by using the mindful breathing recording on the website for this book: www.practising-happiness.co.uk. Then see if you can incorporate mindfulness of breathing and body sensations into normal daily life.

Practice record form: Mindful observation

Your name: <u>Jill</u>

Day/Date	Exercises practised	Comments
Thursday	10 minutes mindful breathing with recording.	Felt relaxing, getting used to it.
Friday	Observed blue skies, sunshine.	Felt fine, nice weather today.
Saturday	Observed rain from living room window, breathing with nervous feeling.	Felt nervous but didn't go to basement.
Sunday	Observed neighbour's two puppies playing in back garden.	Very enjoyable.
Monday	10 minutes mindful breathing, observed cloudy sky while driving.	Driving was hard, tempted to race home but didn't.
Tuesday	Observed rain through open window for 20 minutes, mindful breathing at the same time.	Breathing while watching rain is getting easier. Heart doesn't race as fast.
Wednesday	Mindful breathing in staff meeting, nervous about possible storm that afternoon.	Worried about getting home before storm starts. Breathing helped me concentrate during meeting.

Practice record form: Mindful observation

Your name: _____

Day/Date	Exercises practised	Comments

Chapter Summary

- Mindful observation will help free you from the psychological traps described in previous chapters: rumination, avoidance, emotion-driven behaviour and self-criticism.

- Mindful observation means looking closely at present-moment experiences, both internal to the body and mind (thoughts, emotions, sensations) and in the external world.

- Mindful observation means letting go of judgements and criticism, as best you can, and staying present with whatever you observe.

- Mindful breathing is a useful tool for keeping your attention focused on the present moment. It prevents rumination and avoidance and helps with choosing constructive behaviour in stressful circumstances.

9 Mindful Observation with Labelling

'We can become aware of judgement . . . Start by simply noting "judging" when it arises – and noting it softly, like a whisper, not like a baseball bat.'

Joseph Goldstein and Jack Kornfield

Imagine that you wake up one morning with a runny nose, sore throat, headache and fatigue. 'Oh no!' you think, 'I'm getting a cold. It feels like a bad one. I don't have time to be sick now. I have too much work to do. This is terrible!' You're tempted to stay in bed, but you dread the consequences of taking the day off: meetings you'll miss, money you won't earn, people you'll inconvenience. You tell yourself you'll have to carry on as usual, but then you realize how exhausted you'll be by the end of the day. You worry about getting even sicker. Your stress and anxiety increase. All of these thoughts and feelings occur within a minute or two of waking up.

The inner world of thoughts and feelings is a busy place. We all have constant streams of sensations, emotions, thoughts and urges passing through our minds and bodies. If we're not mindfully aware of them, we may act on them in unhealthy ways. We ruminate and criticize: *Why do I always get sick at such bad times? It must be stress. I should be able to handle things better.* Or we ignore our symptoms and press on at full speed, making ourselves sicker and spreading germs among family, friends and co-workers. We avoid constructive actions, such as going to the doctor or rescheduling some of our commitments. Malaise and stress make us short-tempered in ways we regret.

Mindful observation is the key to handling situations like this, but it's very difficult when the inner world is swarming with unpleasant thoughts, emotions, sensations and urges. Learning a new skill, 'mindful labelling', can help. Labelling is simply the act of naming what you're observing. In this chapter, we'll explore how to use labelling to enhance the ability to be mindful of the present moment and respond to it constructively.

One-word Labelling

Let's consider four labels for things that happen in the body and mind: *sensation*, *thought*, *urge* and *emotion*.

- A **sensation** is a physical feeling in the body, such as aching, tingling, tension or the pounding of your heart.

- A **thought** is a string of words that passes through the mind, such as 'I can't do anything right', 'That went well', 'Something bad is going to happen', or 'What's the weather like today?' (For this exercise, we'll also include mental images and memories in the *thought* category.)

- An **urge** is an impulse, temptation or desire to do something, such as scratch your nose, have a drink or shout at someone.

- An **emotion**, as we learned previously, is a combination of sensations, thoughts and urges. Emotions are complex, but they can be labelled with a single word, such as *anger*, *happiness* or *sadness*.

Use the worksheet in the following box to practise using these labels. The first few are filled in as examples.

ONE-WORD LABELLING: SENSATIONS, THOUGHTS, EMOTIONS AND URGES

In each blank, write whether each item is a **Sensation (S)**, **Thought (T)**, **Urge (U)**, or **Emotion (E)**. The first few are filled in as examples. Answers are provided at the end of this chapter.

1. Why is he being so rude? __T__	9. Sadness ____	17. I have too much work to do ____
2. Anger __E__	10. Temptation to stay in bed ____	18. Temptation to quit ____
3. Pounding heart __S__	11. Heaviness in chest ____	19. Churning in stomach ____
4. Temptation to yell __U__	12. I shouldn't feel like this ____	20. Anxiety ____
5. I hope no one saw me ____	13. Trembling in legs ____	21. Frustration ____
6. Heat in face ____	14. I'm making a mess of things ____	22. Why hasn't she called? ____
7. Embarrassment ____	15. Impulse to leave ____	23. Impulse to check messages ____
8. Impulse to hide ____	16. Dread ____	24. Disappointment ____

Now that you're familiar with the labels, let's try using them in a meditation exercise. This exercise is a variation of the mindful breathing meditation in the previous chapter. Just as before, sit in a relaxed but alert posture. If you prefer, lie on a comfortable surface. Instructions are in the next box. Read them carefully, then set a timer for five or ten minutes and begin. If you like, use the recording on the website for this book (www. practising-happiness.co.uk).

MINDFUL BREATHING MEDITATION WITH
ONE-WORD LABELLING

1. Settle into a posture that's relaxed yet awake. Gently close your eyes or gaze at a neutral spot. Focus your attention on the movements and sensations of your breath. Allow it to go at its own pace and rhythm, without trying to change it.

2. When you're ready, expand your attention to include whatever you notice within your mind and body. Use these words to label what you observe: *thought, emotion, sensation* or *urge*. Say the word silently to yourself. Here are some examples:

What you observe	What you say to yourself
• Itching, aching, heat, cold, pressure, tension . . .	*sensation*
• Desire to scratch, stretch, move, quit . . .	*urge*
• Boredom, irritation, sadness, contentment . . .	*emotion*
• *This is silly, I can't do this, what's the point . . .*	*thought*
• *This is great, very interesting, I love these exercises . . .*	*thought*
• *What's for lunch? What time is it? I need a nap . . .*	*thought*
• *Memory, image, daydream, fantasy . . .*	*thought*
• Something from the outer world, like a sound or scent . . .	*sound* or *scent*
• Something that's hard to label	*hmm*

3.   Don't try to force anything, just label whatever appears. As best you can, use a gentle tone for your mental labelling.

4.   Use the plural (sensations, thoughts) if you notice several at once.

5.   After you've said the label silently to yourself, continue with mindful observation. Breathe with whatever you observe.

6.   If you get confused about what to do, focus on your breath. Label it by saying 'in' and 'out' as you inhale and exhale. When you feel ready, resume labelling your thoughts, emotions, etc.

7.   Remember the attitude of friendly curiosity. Practise patience, kindness and interest. Let go of judgements and criticism as best you can.

What Did You Notice?

Like all meditation exercises, this one can be relaxing and enjoyable, challenging and unpleasant, or relatively straightforward. The goal is not to feel a particular way; the goal is to observe and label the happenings in the inner world, whether they're pleasant, unpleasant or neutral. Here are some common concerns that come up during this exercise:

1 – What to do about urges

Many people feel inhibited about acting on urges that arise, as if it would be unmindful to scratch an itch or stretch an achy muscle. Acting on urges can be part of the exercise. After you've labelled the urge, observe it closely and with interest. If you act on it, observe how it feels to do so. Notice the sensations afterwards.

If you have an urge to stop the exercise, perhaps because you find it boring, silly or a waste of time, remember that boredom is an emotion and 'This is silly' (or 'a waste of time') is a thought. The purpose of the exercise is to observe emotions and thoughts as they come and go. See if you can refrain from acting on the urge to stop the exercise until the timer sounds. Instead, observe the urge to quit. Notice what it feels like, where you feel it in your body, if it changes over time. As best you can, refrain from judging yourself for having this urge.

If you're in severe discomfort or distress, and it would be unkind to yourself to continue, stop the exercise and do what you need to do to take care of yourself. Don't give up – return to the exercise another time.

2 – Uncertainty about the labels

It's easy, but unhelpful, to get overly involved in thinking about the labels themselves. You may have felt unsure of what label to use. Perhaps you observed something that didn't seem to fit one of the labels. The next time you practise, just say, 'Hmm,' to yourself when this happens and return to observing. 'Hmm' is shorthand for 'I don't know what this is' or 'Doesn't seem to fit'. If you get caught up in thinking about the labels, notice that you're having thoughts. Silently say, 'Thoughts . . . ' and gently return to observing.

3 – Wanting different labels

The four words used here are helpful but not required. If you notice mental images or pictures, try using 'Image' as one of your labels. If you'd like to distinguish memories from other experiences, use 'Memory' as one of your labels. You could use more than four labels, although more than five or six might make the task too complex. Experiment with different labels to find the ones that work best for you.

One-sentence Labelling

Much of the time, we assume that our thoughts and feelings are true and important. We think we should take them seriously and act on them. Sometimes this is helpful. If you wake up feeling anxious and thinking,

'I have an important meeting at 2.00p.m. and I'm not prepared. I should spend the morning getting organized,' these thoughts and feelings may guide your behaviour in useful ways. On the other hand, if you wake up feeling anxious and thinking, 'The meeting is going to be a disaster. There's no point in trying,' these thoughts and feelings may guide you to do something you'll regret later, like calling in sick or avoiding constructive preparation.

The purpose of mindfully labelling thoughts and feelings is to recognize that they're distinct from the person who's having them. You are not your thoughts and feelings – they're the guests in your guest house or the passengers on your bus. They come and go, while you remain yourself. You don't have to believe them or do what they say, unless you choose to.

A short sentence is sometimes more effective than a single word for reminding us to take this perspective. A particular type of sentence works best. Examples are in the next box:

ONE–SENTENCE LABELLING: EXAMPLES

- I'm having feelings of anxiety.

- Here is a memory.

- A feeling of sadness has come up.

- I'm having thoughts about being incompetent.

- This is a sensation.

- I'm feeling an urge to eat.

- An angry feeling is here.

- I'm noticing butterflies in my stomach.

- I'm having shaky sensations in my legs.

- Troubling thoughts are in my mind.

- A feeling of embarrassment has arisen within me.

- I'm noticing worries about my health.

- I'm feeling a temptation to leave work early.

- I have an urge to yell at my spouse.

These sentences may seem odd or unnatural to you, but there's a good reason for constructing them this way. It helps us remember that we *have* thoughts, emotions, sensations and urges, but they come and go – they're visitors. They don't have to define or control us. We can choose what to do while these visitors are swirling around in our minds. So when you catch yourself using sentences such as 'I'm an idiot . . . I can't stand this', try rephrasing them in this way: 'The thought that I'm an idiot has come to my mind . . . I'm feeling a strong urge to get out of here.'

With practice, it will become more natural.

Meditation with One-sentence Labelling

To practise using sentences like this to label your experience, repeat the meditation exercise in the previous box. This time, label whatever you observe with a mindful sentence:

> *I'm noticing an ache in my knee.*
>
> *I'm feeling an urge to stretch my neck.*
>
> *I'm having thoughts about tomorrow.*
>
> *A feeling of boredom has come up.*

Remember to use a gentle, friendly, non-judgemental tone. Do this exercise several times over the next week or two.

Mindful Labelling in Daily Life

When you're comfortable with mindful labelling using words or sentences, try practising in daily life. Here are two examples.

Dan's experience with mindful labelling

Dan enjoys indoor rock climbing at a fitness centre with a climbing wall. After learning about mindful labelling, he wrote this account of a session.

> 'Yesterday during my climbing session I decided to attempt a harder route than usual. I tried twice and fell. As I got ready to try again, the thought "I can't do this" came into my head. I felt discouraged and almost gave up. Then I remembered the labelling exercise and said to myself, "A feeling of doubt has come up." I took a good look at the route and considered whether it's really too advanced for me. I decided to try again, even though I felt a bit doubtful. I fell a couple more times but eventually was able to finish the route. That felt great.

> 'I learned that it makes difficult tasks easier if I allow thoughts to be thoughts and don't let them stop me from persevering. Using the labelling skill helped me realize that I didn't have to give up even though I had doubts.'

Michelle's experience with mindful labelling

> 'I was doing my statistics homework and I thought, "I'm never going to understand this." I felt anxious about failing my statistics class. My friends were going out and I was really tempted to join them. I remembered to label all of this: "thought", "emotion", "urge". I kept working until I finished my homework but I wasn't sure I really understood it.

> 'I was about to go out and join my friends, but I felt uneasy. I observed the feeling. It helped to put it into words. I actually said out loud, "I

still have worries about statistics." So I emailed the teaching assistant to make an appointment. Then I felt a lot better and went to find my friends.'

Both Dan and Michelle found that mindful labelling helped them become aware of their thoughts and feelings and take constructive action. Without mindful labelling, Dan would have followed his urge to give up on the challenging rock climb. Michelle wouldn't have taken steps to clear up her confusion about statistics.

More about Emotion Labelling

Emotions can be particularly difficult to label. They're complex experiences with several components (thoughts, sensations, urges). We're capable of feeling a wide variety of different emotions, and sometimes we feel several at once. If you're ever uncertain about which emotion you're feeling, you're not alone.

The next box provides general information about the most common categories of emotion and the typical thoughts, sensations and urges that go with them. Your emotions may fit these descriptions, but remember that everyone has their own emotional style. Your genetics, background and learning experiences have influenced how you feel your emotions.

If you find it difficult to label your emotions, start with the general categories as your labels (happy, sad, angry, fearful or anxious, ashamed or guilty). Focus on the specific thoughts, sensations and urges you're feeling. In time, you'll become more familiar with emotion labels.

Emotion category	Specific emotions	Typical thoughts	Typical sensations	Typical urges
Sadness	Depression Disappointment Grief Hurt Sorrow	This is awful I'm so sad I really miss . . . This is hopeless Things never work out	Heaviness Fatigue Hollowness Emptiness Lump in throat	Withdraw Isolate self Give up Lie around Ruminate
Anger	Annoyance Frustration Irritation Rage Resentment	I hate . . . I can't stand . . . How dare they . . . It shouldn't be this way This isn't fair	Face flushing Jaw clenching Fists clenching Heart pounding Neck tense	Yell, curse Attack Pound fist Slam door Throw things
Fear	Anxiety Dread Nervousness Panic Terror	This will go badly I'm going to get hurt I won't manage I'm in danger I'll be rejected, criticized	Racing heart Sweaty hands Trembling Tension Jitteriness	Get away Avoid Freeze Pace Plea for help
Shame, guilt	Embarrassment Humiliation Regret Remorse Self-disgust	I'm inferior, a loser I made a terrible mistake I shouldn't have . . . I'm stupid, silly, crazy I've disappointed people	Blushing Sinking feeling Ache in stomach Tension Heaviness	Hide, withdraw Criticize self Avoid Apologize Make amends
Happiness	Cheeriness Contentment Delight Elation Gladness	This is wonderful I'm so excited I love . . . I'm really pleased Couldn't be better	Lightness Energy Flushing Bubbly feeling Bouncy feeling	Jump for joy Shout, laugh Talk, hug Raise arms Clap hands

Tina's Story

Tina, aged twenty-eight, is learning mindfulness skills to help with her problems with angry behaviour. When Tina was growing up, her parents spent most evenings drinking in bars and were hung over most mornings. By the time she was nine years old, Tina was trying to prepare meals, wash clothes and get herself and her younger brother to school on time.

Her parents showed no appreciation for Tina's efforts, but criticized her severely for minor shortcomings such as leaving dirty dishes in the sink. When she showed any signs of distress, they told her to stop complaining.

Tina learned to criticize herself and to expect criticism from others. She never learned to label her emotions – she just says she's 'upset' whenever anything is bothering her. As an adult, she thinks she should be able to control her feelings, but she's easily angered, loses her temper, and then berates herself. She works as a waitress and gets irritable when the restaurant is crowded. She's lost two jobs because of angry outbursts with customers or co-workers.

Tina worked hard on mindful observation and labelling of thoughts, sensations, emotions and urges. She realized that in any situation where she might be criticized, her strongest emotion is fear. For example, if the kitchen at her restaurant is slow, she fears that her customers will be angry with her for providing poor service. She ruminates about how unfair this is; it's not her fault that the cooks are slow. Rumination leads to feelings of anger and urges to lash out. If her customers ask when their dinners will arrive, she snaps at them and then feels disgusted with herself.

Mindful observation with labelling is helping Tina understand what she's thinking and feeling. The labels she uses the most are:

Feeling nervous.

I'm worried that customer is getting angry.

I'm annoyed with the kitchen.

Fear of getting blamed.

I have an urge to yell at someone.

As a result of learning to recognize when she's expecting criticism, fearful that others will be angry with her, and having urges to snap at people, Tina is much better able to keep her temper. Mindful observation with labelling gives her a moment to decide what to do. She was recently complimented by her boss for politely handling a frustrated customer whose dinner arrived later than he desired.

Tina's emotions are completely understandable, given her childhood experiences. But she's extremely judgemental of them, telling herself that her thoughts and feelings are wrong, bad and inappropriate, and that she's weak and immature for feeling them. We'll return to Tina's story after we consider how to work with judgements of our own thoughts and feelings.

Working with Judgements

Do you say things like this to yourself?

- It's stupid of me to be so anxious.

- It's ridiculous that I'm still sad – I should be over it by now.

- It's idiotic of me to get so angry.

- It's crazy how my heart is pounding.

- It's silly of me to worry about such a trivial thing.

- I'm such a failure – I can't speak in a meeting without shaking.

- It's wrong of me to feel this way.

- I can't believe I'm jealous – it's so immature.

- I shouldn't be thinking about this – it's a sign of weakness.

- I'm too emotional – I shouldn't get so worked up.

If these statements sound familiar, you're observing and labelling your thoughts and feelings but you're also judging them – and yourself – as bad or wrong in some way. This is harmful, for two reasons:

1 – Judgement of thoughts and feelings increases emotional suffering

It's painful and difficult to feel scared, sad or embarrassed, to have unpleasant memories or worries in your mind, or to feel urges to do things you know you'll regret. If you tell yourself you shouldn't be having those thoughts and feelings – that it's bad, wrong, silly, crazy or immature – you create more negative emotion.

2 – Judgement of thoughts and feelings makes it harder to act wisely

As we learned in an earlier chapter, emotions occur for reasons and serve useful purposes. They tell us important information and motivate us to take action to solve problems. If you tell yourself that your emotions are a sign of weakness or failure, you miss the messages they're trying to send and you're less able to respond in a helpful way.

Mindful Labelling of Judgements

It's impossible to get rid of judgemental thoughts completely – they will always pop into our minds. As we learned in a previous chapter, suppressing unwanted thoughts often backfires. But we can learn to work with judgements effectively. If you practise the following skills you may have fewer judgemental thoughts. When they come up, you won't take them so seriously and they'll have less power over you.

1 – Observing judgements during the mindful breathing exercise

Continue to practise mindful breathing with one-word labelling. Include 'Judgement' as one of your labels. Every time you notice criticism or disapproval of your thoughts or feelings, label it by saying 'Judgement'. Remember to use a friendly tone.

2 – Observing judgements in daily life

Watch for judgements that come up during ordinary activities. When you spot one, label it by saying, 'Ah, judging,' or 'There's a judgemental thought.' If you notice many judgements in a short period, say, 'I'm noticing a lot of judgements,' or 'Judgemental thoughts are in my mind.' Use a gentle tone.

3 – Beware of judging your judgements

Once you start paying attention to judgements, it's easy to criticize yourself for having judgemental thoughts. Within a few seconds, you might notice an emotion, judge the emotion, judge the judgement, and judge yourself for making judgements, as in the following sequence:

I'm noticing a feeling of anger.

Well that's ridiculous! It's stupid to get angry about such a trivial thing.

Oops, that was a judgement. I shouldn't be making judgements.

This is terrible! I'm hopeless. I'll never learn this.

If you notice a sequence of thoughts like this, adopt a patient attitude with yourself. Take a few mindful breaths. Then practise mindful observation and labelling of whatever the judgement was about. If you were judging an emotion, thought, sensation or urge, observe and label it, as you did before.

OK, lots of judgemental thoughts . . .

Let me take a few breaths (in . . . out . . . in . . . out . . .)

What do I notice now?

Warm face, tense hands . . .

Keep observing and breathing.

4 – Creative labelling for judgements

In previous chapters, we've already touched on whimsical ways to label your judgemental thoughts. See the next box for a review.

CREATIVE LABELLING OF JUDGEMENTS

Label your judgements as:

1. People passing by

Oh, there's Mrs Judgement.

Mr Criticism is making his morning rounds.

2. Tapes playing in your mind

The 'I'm too emotional' tape is playing again.

This is the 'I can't do anything right' tape.

3. A radio playing in your mind

Ah, I'm tuned into the 'I'm a loser' station again.

4. Guests in your B&B

The critical guests have returned for another visit.

5. Passengers on your bus

It seems I've picked up some very judgemental passengers today.

6. Other

Think of your own creative ways of labelling your judgemental thoughts.

5 – Don't confuse judgements with preferences

When we observe our inner workings, we often notice feelings of aversion and dislike. These feelings are not judgements, they're preferences. Adopting a non-judgemental attitude does NOT mean that you have to stop disliking things. It's perfectly OK to have preferences, even strong ones. Don't try to get rid of your likes and dislikes; instead, observe them.

When you read, eat or do anything else, notice what you find enjoyable or unpleasant. Observe any tendency to judge your reactions. Practise accepting the preferences and letting go of the judgements.

> Preference: *I like mysteries better than biographies.*
> Judgement: *I have poor taste in books.*

> Preference: *I really don't like sushi.*
> Judgement: *I must be crazy – people rave about it.*

> Preference: *I don't like horror movies. They make me tense and give me insomnia.*
> Judgement: *I shouldn't be such a wimp.*

Sometimes preferences are difficult to manage. If you prefer high-fat, sugary foods over fruits and vegetables but you'd like to lose weight, you may need to eat in ways that are inconsistent with your preferences. Judging yourself for your likes and dislikes probably won't help. Instead, acknowledge the difficulty (it's part of being human), be kind to yourself, and eat mindfully (more on mindful eating in the next chapter). In time, you may become more tolerant of fruits and vegetables – perhaps you'll even enjoy them. Even if you don't, your ability to choose foods consistent with your goals is likely to improve.

Tina's Experience: Working with Judgements

Tina practised non-judging with the mindful breathing exercise. She learned to say 'Judgement' or 'That's a judgemental thought' whenever she criticized herself for feeling afraid or angry. She used a worksheet, shown opposite, to practise rephrasing her judgements. As she began to let go of judging, she was better able to think of constructive ways to handle situations in the restaurant, such as checking politely with the kitchen about when a meal would be ready, telling the customer what the kitchen staff said, offering a free dessert to those whose dinners took a long time to arrive.

Worksheet: Restating judgements as mindful labels

*** Remember to maintain an attitude of friendly curiosity***

Day and time	What was the situation?	What thoughts, emotions, sensations or urges did you notice?	What was your judgemental thought?	Restate your judgement as a mindful label in 3 different ways
When did the judgemental thoughts occur?	Where were you? What was going on? Were other people involved?	Briefly note what you observed in your body and mind.	Write it down exactly as it appeared in your mind, or as closely as you can remember.	Examples: 1. That's a judgement. 2. I'm having self-critical thoughts. 3. The 'I'm irrational' tape is playing again.

Worksheet: Restating judgements as mindful labels

Your name Tina

Remember to maintain an attitude of friendly curiosity

Day and time	What was the situation?	What thoughts, emotions, sensations or urges did you notice?	What was your judgemental thought?	Restate your judgement as a mindful label in 3 different ways
Saturday, 9.00p.m.	The restaurant was really crowded. I snapped at my co-worker in the kitchen because my customers' food was taking a long time and they were impatient for their dinner.	Thoughts: It's not fair, not my fault the kitchen is slow. Emotion: Afraid the customers might get angry and walk out. Sensations: Tense neck, shoulders. Urge: To quit this job.	It's ridiculous that I get so worked up. I should be able to stay calm.	1. Judgement 2. Self-critical thoughts are here. 3. The 'I'm out of control' tape is playing again.

A blank copy of the worksheet is provided on the next page. Make multiple copies so that you can practise as many times as you like.

Letting Go of Labelling When It's Not Necessary

As we've seen, mindful labelling has many benefits: it helps us learn to identify thoughts, sensations, emotions and urges; it encourages us to remember that they're visitors to the mind; and reminds us to pause to observe them before deciding whether, and how, to act on them.

In time, as your mindfulness skills develop, you'll realize that labelling is not always necessary. It's a bit like learning to play the piano. At first, it may be helpful to label the notes, chords and beats. Eventually, labelling can be dropped. For skilled players, labelling interrupts the flow of the music. This doesn't mean that they're playing mindlessly, with their attention focused elsewhere. Rather, they're participating with awareness in the ongoing activity of playing the piano.

In daily life, it's often enjoyable or helpful to focus full attention on something we're doing, without labelling. Playing a game or a sport, working on a project, singing a song, or having a conversation can feel satisfying when we're fully engaged, not distracted, and not self-conscious. Labelling can get in the way. In the next chapter, we'll consider exercises that cultivate the ability to participate with awareness in the activities of our lives.

Worksheet: Restating judgements as mindful labels

Your name _____

Remember to maintain an attitude of friendly curiosity

Day and time	What was the situation?	What thoughts, emotions, sensations or urges did you notice?	What was your judgemental thought?	Restate your judgement as a mindful label in 3 different ways

Chapter Summary

- Mindful observation with one-word labelling is helpful for keeping attention focused on the present moment, especially when the moment includes a multitude of sensations, thoughts, emotions and urges swirling around in the mind.

- Labelling with non-judgemental sentences helps us remember that thoughts and feelings are temporary experiences that pass through the mind. We don't always have to believe them, take them seriously or act on them, although we can if we choose to do so.

- Judgemental labelling increases emotional suffering and makes it more difficult to act wisely in difficult situations. Although it's impossible to get rid of judgemental thoughts completely, there are many ways of rephrasing them so that they're less harmful.

- Labelling is not always necessary. Practise enough to be familiar with labelling and its benefits. Then remember that mindful observation can be practised with or without labelling.

ANSWERS FOR THE ONE—WORD LABELLING WORKSHEET

SENSATIONS(S), THOUGHTS(T), EMOTIONS(E) AND URGES(U)

1. Why is he being so rude? __T__	9. Sadness __E__	17. I have too much work to do __T__
2. Anger __E__	10. Temptation to stay in bed __U__	18. Temptation to quit __U__
3. Pounding heart __S__	11. Heaviness in chest __S__	19. Churning in stomach __S__
4. Temptation to yell __U__	12. I shouldn't feel like this __T__	20. Anxiety __E__
5. I hope no one saw me __T__	13. Trembling in legs __S__	21. Frustration __E__
6. Heat in face __S__	14. I'm making a mess of things __T__	22. Why hasn't she called? __T__
7. Embarrassment __E__	15. Impulse to leave __U__	23. Impulse to check messages __U__
8. Impulse to hide __U__	16. Dread __E__	24. Disappointment __E__

10 Acting with Awareness

'While washing the dishes, one should only be washing the dishes.'

Thich Nhat Hanh

Thich Nhat Hanh is a famous Zen master, mindfulness teacher, peace activist and author. He was born in Vietnam in 1926, lives in France, and teaches mindfulness all over the world. In one of his popular books, he describes two ways to wash the dishes. The mindful way is to be completely aware of the process, noticing the sights, scents, sounds, sensations and the movements of your body as you work. The other way is to wash them without paying attention, while thinking of other things.

Mindfulness teachers call the second way 'automatic pilot'. Just as a plane can fly itself while the pilot does something else, our bodies can do many things while our minds are elsewhere. We eat while reading or watching TV. We walk or drive while planning the day or daydreaming. We cook, clean, get the kids ready for bed, all while preoccupied with the future or the past.

Much of the time, this causes no serious harm. The ability to function automatically is often valuable. We can look for road signs or talk to passengers while driving automatically. Planning the day while walking to work might be a constructive use of time. The dishes may get perfectly clean, even if you're daydreaming, listening to music or talking with someone while you wash them.

On the other hand, we can make mistakes on automatic pilot. We forget things we'd intended to do, such as buying groceries on the way home from work. We act on habits, like walking towards the old office after moving to a new one. Sometimes we do serious or even deadly harm: numerous accidents have been caused by people driving on automatic pilot while talking on their phones. And we miss countless moments from our lives, each of which, in its own way, might have been interesting, beautiful, enjoyable, important or meaningful: the sunset as we take out the garbage; the taste of an interesting food; a child's laughter as he splashes in the tub.

Research shows that people who spend less time on autopilot are happier and more satisfied with life. In one famous study, several thousand adults of all ages were contacted by phone at random intervals and asked three questions: (1) What were you doing just now? (2) Were you focused on it or thinking of something else? (3) How happy were you feeling?

Participants were consistently happier when they were focused on what they were doing, regardless of what it was. There are probably several reasons for this. Awareness of the present moment keeps us from falling into the psychological traps discussed earlier: rumination, avoidance, emotion-driven behaviour and self-criticism. It allows us to make wise decisions in difficult situations. It helps us appreciate life's small but precious moments.

This doesn't mean that we should never function on autopilot. That would be an unrealistic goal. With practice, however, we can learn to be more aware of what we're doing in the present. It's well worth the effort. Once we've developed the ability to act with awareness, we can choose when to pay attention and when to go on autopilot.

The following exercises cultivate this ability. We'll begin with mindful eating and walking. Then we'll consider two common ways of operating in modern life: multitasking and rushing.

The Raisin Exercise

This well-known exercise is used by many mindfulness teachers. Its purpose is to practise mindful awareness of eating, a routine activity that we all do every day, often without noticing much about it.

You'll need a few raisins. As you prepare to do this exercise, imagine that you're an explorer from outer space, visiting Earth. Like all explorers, you take a strong interest in everything you encounter. At the moment, you've encountered these small, wrinkly objects. As best you can, adopt an attitude of open-minded interest and curiosity about them.

The rest of the instructions are in the next box.

RAISIN EXERCISE

1. Set a raisin gently in the palm of your hand and look at it closely. Notice its shape, size and colour. Notice how the light reflects off it. Observe the wrinkles and the variations of colour. Roll it around and look at it from different sides. Pick it up with your thumb and forefinger and turn it around slowly, looking at it from all angles. Hold it up to the light. Observe everything there is to see about it.

2. Set it back in the palm of your hand and observe the feel of it sitting there. Notice its weight and the sensations where it touches your palm. Rub it gently with a finger and notice the texture. Pick it up again and observe the feeling of it between your finger and thumb.

3. Hold it under your nose and inhale gently. Notice the aroma. If smelling it leads to sensations in your mouth or stomach, observe them.

4. Associations, memories and thoughts may arise. If so, notice them without judgement, as best you can. If you like, use labels, such as *thoughts, memories* or *images*. Gently return your attention to observing the raisin.

5. Hold the raisin close to your ear. Gently squish it around between your thumb and forefinger, noticing if it makes any sounds.

6. Return to looking at it for a few moments. If you're having thoughts

or feelings about the raisin or the exercise, notice them and return to observing the raisin.

7. Slowly bring the raisin up to your mouth. Notice the sensations in your arm as you do this.

8. Gently touch the raisin to your lips. Observe the sensations. Notice if anything happens in your mouth as you do this.

9. Put the raisin in your mouth, setting it on your tongue. Observe what happens.

10. Experiment with moving the raisin around in your mouth. Put it into one cheek, then the other one. Notice the sensations and texture.

11. Position the raisin between your upper and lower teeth. Slowly bite down on it, observing what happens to its texture. Notice the taste and sensations in your mouth.

12. Slowly chew the raisin, observing the movements, tastes, textures and sensations. Notice how the raisin changes as you chew.

13. Notice when you first feel an urge to swallow. Pause and observe the urge.

14. Observe the movements and sensations when you swallow.

15. Notice what happens next. Observe as any remaining bits are cleared away.

16. When the raisin is gone, notice the after-effects: tastes, sensations, thoughts, images, memories or emotions.

17. Repeat with another raisin.

The raisin exercise illustrates important points about doing routine activities mindfully.

1 – We notice details that we usually overlook

When we pay attention to something we normally do automatically, we notice many things we haven't observed before, even though they've been present all along. Here are some comments by members of a mindfulness-based stress reduction (MBSR) class:

'I never looked closely at a raisin before. It wasn't very appealing. It looked dry and wrinkly and sort of ugly. If I were a Martian I might not think of eating this thing.'

'When I first put it in my mouth it seemed pretty tasteless. But after biting down on it there was a lot of flavour. I was surprised how much flavour one little raisin could have. Usually I eat a handful all at once and don't notice the taste that much.'

'I never tried to listen to a raisin! At first I thought that was ridiculous but then I actually heard some little sounds.'

2 – The mind has a life of its own

It's normal for the mind to wander during this exercise. Memories, plans, thoughts and emotions may arise. Chains of associations can take us on journeys through time. Here are more observations from the MBSR class:

'I remembered making oatmeal raisin cookies with my sister when we were young. That was a pleasant memory and I thought about making some cookies this weekend. Then I started thinking about what I need to buy – raisins, oats, and I wasn't sure what else. I was trying to remember my mother's old recipe and wondering if I have it written down somewhere. Then suddenly I remembered to focus on the raisin.'

'I had a mental image of a vineyard I visited last summer. I was thinking about how the grapes are so juicy on the vine and how they get all dried up and shrivelled when they're turned into raisins.'

'Eating the raisin reminded me that I didn't have time for dinner because my boss wanted me to stay late. I barely got here on time and

I'm hungry and annoyed. I started thinking about all my problems with my job. It was hard to focus on the raisin.'

'I've never liked raisins and I didn't want to eat this one. I ate it anyway. I still don't like them, but it wasn't terrible. I didn't mind it as much as I thought I would.'

'We spent so much time looking at the raisins that I got sort of attached to mine. Then it seemed cruel to eat it. I told myself that was silly.'

3 – Paying attention enhances both pleasant and unpleasant experiences

If you like raisins, you may have noticed that eating them mindfully made the experience more enjoyable than usual. The same thing happens with other pleasant experiences in daily life; they're more vivid, rich and intense if we're paying attention.

What if you don't like raisins? The benefits of mindful attention to unpleasant experiences are less obvious, but just as important. Our usual reactions to unpleasantness often lead us into psychological traps, like the MBSR participant who got caught up in ruminating about her job, or the one who criticized herself for getting attached to her raisin. If we're mindfully aware of unpleasantness, rather than trying to avoid it, we often find that we can tolerate it more easily than we thought. We can choose wisely how to respond.

Variations on the Raisin Exercise

- Mindfully eat a food that you like very much, such as chocolate or ice cream. Practise savouring the pleasant tastes, textures and sensations.

- Mindfully eat a food that you don't like, perhaps one you've avoided for a long time. As best you can, practise non-judgemental observation of the taste, texture and your feelings of aversion. Remember, the point is not to torture yourself, but to practise mindfulness of an unpleasant, though harmless, experience.

- Mindfully eat something that you eat often but isn't very healthy – something with chemicals, artificial ingredients, or high levels of fat, sugar or salt.

- Eat mindfully during your usual meals and snacks.

Here are some descriptions of mindful eating from members of a mindfulness class: Scott works for a landscaping service; Alison is an administrative assistant in a hospital; Jason is a university student; Judy is a retired school teacher.

Scott's experience with a burrito

'After a long morning of planting and trimming trees, I stopped for a steak burrito for lunch. I eat them a lot, but never mindfully. Usually I'm looking over the schedule for my afternoon jobs. First I noticed how large the burrito was and how eager I was to start eating it. Next I smelled it. My mouth watered, my stomach rumbled, and I felt really hungry. Then I took a bite. I noticed all the delicious tastes and textures. The rice was soft and chewy and somewhat sweet. The onions and peppers had strong flavours. They were soft and slid around in my mouth. The salsa was cool, wet and smooth. The chunks of steak were coarse and rough on the outside, but rare and juicy on the inside. I also noticed the heat from the spices. My nose was running and my forehead was sweating.

'I enjoyed this so much that my mind hardly wandered at all. Just once I thought about the work I needed to do after lunch. The most surprising thing was that I got full more quickly than usual and didn't finish the burrito. Normally I eat the whole thing.'

Alison's experience with cookies from the vending machine

'I have a bad habit of eating unhealthy snacks from the vending machine at work. One day this week I bought a packet of cookies. I've

eaten these cookies many times and I thought I liked them. But this time I decided to eat them mindfully and I was very surprised. I didn't like them at all. The first one tasted like chemicals and the texture was unpleasant. At first it was dry and gritty and then, as I chewed, it felt slimy in my mouth. I couldn't believe it. I ate another one to be sure and it was just as bad. I looked closely to see if they were mouldy, but they looked normal. I threw the rest away.

'This was very interesting, so I experimented with mindfully eating other things from the vending machine. I realized most of it tastes like chemicals and isn't very enjoyable. Now I feel much more motivated to bring healthier snacks to work.'

Judy's experience with breakfast and the newspaper

'Normally I read the newspaper while eating breakfast, but this week I tried eating mindfully and reading the paper later. At first, it was interesting to really taste my cereal and toast, but after a couple of days I decided to go back to eating while reading the paper. I don't think I'm missing much. I eat the same thing every morning, and I enjoy reading the paper while I eat.

'I did notice an effect of mindful eating. My attention now seems to switch to my food more often, just for a few moments. I appreciate the flavour of the toast, which is made from very nice bread from a local bakery. So I'm enjoying it a bit more, even though I still read the paper while eating.'

Jason's experience with a dirt-flavoured jellybean

'My friend Thomas had some Harry Potter jellybeans so we experimented with eating nasty flavours mindfully. When I put the dirt-flavoured one in my mouth, I was bracing for an unpleasant experience, but at first it wasn't bad, just smooth and not much taste. Then I bit down on it and the flavour flooded my mouth. I had a strong

reaction of disgust and a powerful urge to spit it out. I grimaced and tried to get my tongue away from it. Then I thought, wait, this won't kill me, let me just notice this. I chewed it mindfully and swallowed it, though much faster than with the raisin. It was definitely unpleasant, but very interesting in a strange way.

'In the end, I decided this was a good way to practise observing things I don't like. In other situations, there's a risk of doing things I'll regret later when I encounter something unpleasant. This taught me I can slow down and think about what to do. I don't have to react right away even when I have a really strong urge to avoid something.'

Scott's experience illustrates two important consequences of mindful eating: appreciating the pleasant flavours and textures, and noticing when he was full. Alison's experience is also quite common – realizing that we often eat things that we wouldn't like if we paid attention to them. Judy's experience shows that we have a choice about when to eat while doing something else, and Jason's experience shows how mindful eating of foods we don't like can be a useful way to practise dealing with unpleasantness.

Mindful Walking

Mindful walking is another way to practise awareness of present-moment behaviour. In the next box are instructions for a meditative walking exercise. You'll need a place where you can walk slowly back and forth without a destination: across a room, yard or garden. Choose a place where you won't be concerned about anyone observing you.

As in the raisin exercise, imagine that you're an explorer from another planet. For your visit to Earth, you've taken on human form. This is your first experience with walking in a human body, so you're very curious about it.

WALKING MEDITATION

1. Begin by standing still. Allow your arms to hang loosely at your sides, or gently clasp your hands in front of your abdomen. Take a few mindful breaths. Observe the sensations in your body.

2. While continuing to stand, see if you can direct your attention to your feet. You don't have to look at them; look softly ahead in the direction you'll be walking. Notice the sensations in your feet as you stand. Feel the weight as they support you. Notice contact with your shoes, socks, the ground or floor.

3. Slowly shift your weight on to one leg. Allow the other knee to bend and the heel to come off the floor. Move this foot slowly forward through the air and set your heel down a short distance in front of you.

4. Slowly shift your weight forward, noticing as your front foot lowers to the ground and the heel of the back foot lifts up. Pause here. Notice how your weight is balanced. Feel the sensations in your feet and legs.

5. Bring the back foot up and slowly move it forward through the air, setting your heel down just in front of you.

6. Continue to walk very slowly across the room. As best you can, notice the sensations in your feet and lower legs as you walk.

7. Experiment with silent labels: *lifting, moving, placing, shifting*. Labelling helps some people stay focused; others find the labels a nuisance. Try it both ways.

8. When you reach the other side of the room or garden, stand still again. Notice your breath and the sensations throughout your body.

9. Slowly turn around. Observe the complex movements involved in turning around. Walk slowly back the other way.

10. When your mind wanders off, gently bring it back to focusing on walking.

11. If you observe judgemental thoughts about this exercise, feeling awkward or silly, losing your balance, mind-wandering or anything else, briefly label them as judgements and return your attention to walking.

Vary the exercise by walking at a normal pace or quickly. Experiment with observing your arms and hands, your body as a whole, or your breath. Try turning your attention outward to the sights and sounds in the environment.

This is a form of meditation, so practise allowing the present moment to be as it is and simply observing it. You don't have to get anywhere. You have no goals, except to observe the experience.

Mindful Walking in Ordinary Life

In daily life we usually have a destination and prefer to walk at a normal pace. We can still walk mindfully. Here are some comments about mindful walking from members of a mindfulness class:

> *'Normally when I'm walking to a meeting in another building I have my phone in hand to check emails and send texts. I decided to walk mindfully, without the phone. I realized how much goes on in that five-minute walk. There were smells I'd never noticed before, like hot concrete, exhaust from cars, and that vague but fresh outdoor smell. 'I also realized how quickly I tend to walk, in a rush and absorbed in my own world. I walked more slowly and noticed how much more relaxed my shoulders and neck felt, as well as my breathing. I had some difficulty letting thoughts pass through, but focusing on my senses helped bring me back to the present moment.'*

'I tried mindfully walking to my car after work. It was difficult. I could only walk about three steps mindfully before I was off in some other world worrying about my day. I got very frustrated with myself and thought I was doing it wrong. Then I realized those were judgements. My mind continued to wander off and I kept bringing it back to focusing on my steps. I tried to let go of the criticism and just refocus on walking.'

'I practised mindfulness while walking my dog. I could feel my feet rolling along and hear the dog making click-click noises with her claws on the pavement. There were so many things to notice, I had trouble deciding what to focus on. I realized it worked best to choose one, like the feel of the breeze on my face. After a while, I switched to hearing the sounds and then went back to feeling my body moving.'

Like any meditation exercise, mindful walking can be pleasant or unpleasant, easy or difficult. Judgemental thoughts and negative emotions may arise. This is all OK. The point is not to feel a particular way, but to observe whatever is happening.

More Exercises: Acting with Awareness

You can do virtually anything mindfully. You already know about eating, walking and washing the dishes. Here's a list of other possibilities. Start by doing one of these mindfully every day. Gradually add more. In time, you'll become skilful at recognizing when you're on automatic pilot, and redirecting your attention to the present moment, *if you choose to do so.*

- Brushing your teeth.
- Taking a bath or shower.
- Petting or brushing your dog or cat.
- Loading or unloading the dishwasher.
- Loading or unloading the washing machine or dryer.

- Folding laundry or ironing.

- Mowing the lawn or weeding the garden.

- Cooking.

- Singing, playing an instrument, dancing, exercising.

- Any craft or hobby (sewing, painting, woodworking, etc.).

Awareness of Multitasking

Consider this example:

> 'Last night I washed the dishes mindfully. I felt the warm water swirling around my hands and heard the dishes clattering. I even heard the bubbles popping, which I'd never noticed before. It was pleasant and peaceful and I enjoyed being in the moment. But there's a radio show I like to listen to while I wash the dinner dishes. It's part of my evening routine. Does this mean I'm not being mindful?'

Not necessarily. It's sometimes possible to be mindful of doing two things at once. Next time you wash the dishes while listening to the radio, observe what's happening with your attention; you'll probably notice that it shifts back and forth. At times, you're absorbed in the radio and washing the dishes automatically. At other times, you attend to the dishes and lose track of the radio. There may be moments when you're aware of both, other moments when you're aware of neither, because you're thinking or daydreaming.

Remember to be non-judgemental of all of these experiences. You may find that washing the dishes on autopilot while listening to the radio is enjoyable and does no harm. Or perhaps you can broaden your attention to include awareness of both. The more you practise mindfulness, the more you'll recognize where your attention goes. Then you can redirect it, as you choose.

Anna's Story

Anna, thirty-six, is married and has nine-year-old twin girls. She and her husband, John, both have full-time jobs: Anna is a social worker and John is a lawyer. Although their marriage and family life are happy, Anna finds it difficult to manage the demands of full-time work and involvement in their children's activities. She's taking a mindfulness class to reduce her stress levels.

After learning the raisin exercise, Anna expressed a desire to do less multitasking and focus on one thing at a time. But she can't see how to meet her responsibilities without doing several things at once. Her teacher encouraged her to practise non-judgemental observation of multitasking over the course of a week, using the worksheet on the next page.

Doing several things at once is very common; Anna filled two sheets on a single day. A blank version is provided for your own use. Remember to make copies.

Worksheet: Awareness of multitasking

*** *Remember to maintain an attitude of friendly curiosity* ***

Day/time	What two or more things were you doing at the same time?	Pleasantness rating from 1–5	Advantages	Disadvantages
When did this example of multitasking occur?	Write down two or more behaviours or activities you were trying to do simultaneously.	Was it pleasant to do these things at the same time? 1: very unpleasant 2: somewhat unpleasant 3: neutral 4: somewhat pleasant 5: very pleasant	What were the advantages of doing these things at the same time?	What were the disadvantages of doing these things at the same time?

Worksheet: Awareness of multitasking

Your name Anna

Remember to maintain an attitude of friendly curiosity

Day/time	What two or more things were you doing at the same time?	Pleasantness rating from 1–5 (1: very unpleasant – 5: very pleasant)	Advantages	Disadvantages
Tuesday 7.00a.m.	Giving the kids their breakfast and talking to John about plans for this evening.	3. Neutral.	Both had to be done, not much time in the morning.	Felt a bit rushed, but no real problems.
Tuesday 7.45a.m.	Driving kids to school and quizzing them on their spelling words for a test today.	5. It was fun, we all enjoyed it.	The girls wanted to review, it made them feel confident about the test.	Have to be careful to pay attention to driving.
Tuesday 8.15a.m.	Walking from car to office, checking email on phone.	2. Stress level rising as I start thinking about the demands of the day.	Getting a head start on what I have to do when I get into my office.	Not watching where I'm going. I don't really accomplish much.
Tuesday 10.30a.m.	Answered a phone call while driving to a home visit with a client.	3. Neutral.	The call was important, something I needed to know for the home visit.	I almost jumped a red light. I know phone calls while driving are dangerous.
Tuesday noon	At work, eating a sandwich while writing a report.	1. Very irritating, constantly stopped typing to pick up sandwich, hard to concentrate.	Report had to get done and I had to eat.	Made me feel grumpy, rushed and disorganized.

Worksheet: Awareness of multitasking

Your name Anna (continued)

Remember to maintain an attitude of friendly curiosity

Day/time	What two or more things were you doing at the same time?	Pleasantness rating from 1–5 (1: very unpleasant – 5: very pleasant)	Advantages	Disadvantages
Tuesday 1.30p.m.	At work, writing a report while helping a new staff member learn her job. She kept coming into my office with questions.	1. I felt annoyed every time she interrupted but it's my job to train her, her questions were good.	Both needed to get done.	I kept losing track of what I was trying to write, felt scattered and inefficient.
Tuesday 6.30p.m	Cooking dinner with John, talking about the day.	5. Nice way to spend time together.	Dinner gets made and we talk to each other.	None that I can think of.
Tuesday 7.30p.m.	Washing dishes while listening to radio.	5. Felt relaxing and I like the radio show.	Enjoyable way to wash the dishes.	I guess I'm not fully present with the dishes but they get clean.
Tuesday 8.00p.m.	At home, trying to catch up on paperwork for work and be available for kids' homework questions.	2. Frustrating. I like helping my kids with homework but felt pulled in two directions.	Both needed to get done.	Never felt really focused, kept losing track of what I was doing with paperwork.
Tuesday 10.00p.m.	John and I folded laundry together while watching TV (kids in bed).	4. Enjoyable, peaceful.	Laundry needed folding, John and I need relaxation time together.	I wish I had time for TV without having to do a chore at the same time.

Worksheet: Awareness of multitasking

Your name _____

Remember to maintain an attitude of friendly curiosity

Day/time	What two or more things were you doing at the same time?	Pleasantness rating from 1–5 (1: very unpleasant – 5: very pleasant)	Advantages	Disadvantages

Anna learned that some forms of multitasking are enjoyable or useful, others neutral or harmless, and some unpleasant or risky. Anna's observations are consistent with research on multitasking. Activities that don't require much mental effort, such as walking, eating, listening to music, watching TV, and simple chores, can often be combined.

When two tasks require concentration, like writing a report and answering a supervisee's questions, it's impossible to do them simultaneously. Instead your attention shifts back and forth. Every time you switch, you lose your train of thought and it's hard to get back on track. It's inefficient and can make us feel stressed and disorganized.

Some forms of multitasking are dangerous. Studies show that driving while using a phone is just as dangerous as driving while intoxicated. Hands-free phones are no better. As you experiment with mindful awareness of multitasking in your daily life, please don't drive while using a phone. It's not worth risking your life or anyone else's.

After observing her experiences with multitasking for a week, Anna decided to change some of her behaviour, starting with working during lunch. She found that taking fifteen minutes just for eating was more productive than trying to eat and work at the same time. She enjoyed her lunch and then could concentrate more efficiently on her work. She also stopped using her phone during the short walk from her car to her office. Instead, she practised mindful observation of her surroundings and felt more refreshed when she entered her building.

Next, she considered her daughters' homework time. Her top priority was to encourage them to work independently but to be available when they had questions. Instead of tasks that required focused concentration, she decided to do less mentally demanding activities during that time, such as household chores or light reading. This made her children's interruptions less stressful.

Multitasking at work was more challenging. Anna scheduled regular meetings with her supervisees and asked them to save their questions for these meetings as much as possible. This gave her a little more uninterrupted time for tasks like report-writing that require sustained concentration.

Final Thoughts on Multitasking

'Multitasking' is a term that originated in the world of computers; it refers to jobs done by central processing units. In daily life, multitasking is hard to define. What counts as a task? When you wash the dishes, you're standing at the sink, keeping your balance, holding a plate with one hand, wiping it with the other, watching the traces of food disappear, discerning when it's clean. Is this multitasking, or are you just washing the dishes?

From the perspective of mindful awareness, it doesn't matter. The point is to practise non-judgemental observation of your behaviour in the moment. We know that some behaviours can be combined, but that trying to do too many things at once can be unpleasant, stressful, inefficient or even dangerous. Observe your own experience, with openness and curiosity, and see for yourself.

Once you understand acting with awareness, you can choose how to direct your attention. If you *choose* to eat your breakfast automatically while reading the newspaper, that's perfectly fine. Try it both ways. Eating your breakfast mindfully and reading the paper later might be more satisfying. Or it might not. Or it might change from day to day. Pay attention, and you'll see what works for you.

Mindful Rushing

Many mindfulness exercises are done slowly, for good reason. It's easier to observe the present moment with openness and interest when we're not rushing. On the other hand, it creates the mistaken impression that we have to be slow to be mindful. People in mindfulness classes often say that they didn't have time to be mindful because they were in a hurry.

In fact, we can practise mindfulness while doing things quickly. If you only have a few minutes to walk to a meeting in a distant building, try walking as quickly and mindfully as you can. Notice the movements of your body as you stride along. Observe your breathing and the air rushing by. Notice your surroundings. Observe your thoughts. Are you criticizing yourself for being late? Ruminating about how you're always late? Worrying about what will happen if you're late? Acknowledge the thoughts briefly by labelling them (*Ah, thoughts and worries are here*) and return your attention to walking quickly, with awareness.

Try this any time you're in a hurry. If you have ten minutes for lunch, eat mindfully and quickly. Notice the sensations, tastes and movements. Acknowledge thoughts and emotions and return your attention to eating mindfully.

Many studies show that immersing yourself in whatever you're doing, so that you're totally focused on it, creates a state called 'flow'. When we're in flow, we feel strong, alert, engaged and in control. Some activities are so enjoyable and absorbing that they naturally lead to flow. But we can experience flow in whatever we're doing, no matter how tedious, if we pay full attention to it. Here's a description by Jon Kabat-Zinn, a leading mindfulness teacher, of mindfully cleaning the stove while listening to jazz:

> 'Cleaning became dancing, the incantations, sounds, and rhythms and the movements of my body merging, blending together, sounds unfolding with motions,
>
> . . . all rising and falling in awareness with the music. One big dance of presence; a celebration of now. And at the end, a clean stove.

The message is clear: acting with awareness provides greater happiness and satisfaction than proceeding on automatic pilot, even when we have to do something potentially tedious or unpleasant, like clean the stove. And mindfully doing two things at once, like listening to music while cleaning, can enhance the experience.

But what if you have to do something that's more challenging, stressful, scary or painful than cleaning the stove? Acting with awareness will help. It's also important to practise another useful skill: *acceptance* of the fact that it's difficult. 'Acceptance' is a tricky term and easily misunderstood. In the next chapter, we'll explore the nature of mindful acceptance and how it helps with difficult experiences.

Chapter Summary

- Acting with awareness, or paying attention to what we're doing while we're doing it, is an important mindfulness skill. It makes us happier and helps us avoid psychological traps.

- Mindful eating and mindful walking cultivate the ability to pay attention to what we're currently doing. We can also practise mindful awareness with most of the routine activities of daily life.

- Sometimes it's useful or enjoyable to do two things at once mindfully, such as washing the dishes while listening to music.

- However, if activities require mental effort and concentration, multitasking can be stressful, inefficient or even dangerous. Practising mindful observation of your own tendency to multi-task will help you make wise decisions about it.

- Rushing is often stressful. Acting with awareness while doing things quickly can reduce the degree of stress.

11 Acceptance and Willingness

'It takes a huge amount of fortitude and motivation to accept what is – expecially when you don't like it – and then work wisely and effectively as best you possibly can with the circumstances you find yourself in.'

Jon Kabat-Zinn

A large group of smokers interested in quitting volunteered for an experiment about coping with cravings. After abstaining from cigarettes for at least twelve hours, they reported to a university classroom. While sitting at a desk, each person opened a pack of cigarettes, took one out, placed it between their lips, and brought a lighter to it without igniting it. This procedure created strong urges to smoke.

Depending on which group they were in, participants practised one of two strategies for coping with the desire to smoke. For about twenty minutes, half practised mindful acceptance of their urges: closely observing their sensations, thoughts and emotions without trying to change or get rid of them; feeling the urges without judgement or self-criticism; and watching the urges ebb and flow like waves, without fighting or giving in to them. The other participants did what they normally do when resisting urges: they tried to ignore them or distracted themselves.

For the next seven days, everyone kept track of their moods, smoking urges and the number of cigarettes they smoked. The groups didn't differ in their moods – they all felt the normal ups and down of daily life. Nor did they differ in urges to smoke – everyone continued to feel urges. But those who'd practised mindful acceptance during the experiment smoked fewer cigarettes. They'd learned to feel their moods and urges without yielding to them by lighting up.

Several other studies have shown a similar pattern:

- Chocolate lovers were asked to carry a transparent box of chocolates with them for 48 hours, without eating any. Those who practised mindful acceptance of urges ate less chocolate than those who tried to distract themselves.

- Patients at a clinic for chronic back pain attempted difficult bending and stretching exercises. Some practised mindful acceptance of the pain; others tried to control or prevent the pain. Both groups found the exercises equally painful, but the mindfulness group completed more of them.

- People with anxiety and depression watched an upsetting scene from the classic film *The Deer Hunter*, in which captured soldiers in Vietnam are forced to play Russian roulette. Everyone found it very distressing. However, those who practised mindful acceptance of their emotions during the film recovered more quickly afterwards than those who tried to suppress and control their emotions.

Acceptance of unpleasant feelings means observing them without judgement and allowing them to take their natural course, rather than trying to change or get rid of them. At first, it doesn't sound like a good idea. In Western society, we're trained to believe that feeling bad is unnecessary, and that we should be able to avoid it if we use the right strategies. But research shows that trying to control or get rid of thoughts and feelings often causes more trouble than allowing them to come and go in their own way and time. Although it seems paradoxical, accepting unpleasant thoughts and feelings has two important advantages over trying to avoid or escape them:

1. It doesn't make them worse, unlike rumination, avoidance, lashing out and self-criticism (as we've learned in previous chapters). In fact, we may recover more quickly after an emotional experience if we accept the feelings as they arise.

2. Acceptance of thoughts and feelings helps us perform important but challenging behaviour, such as refraining from smoking and doing painful but necessary exercises.

Engaging mindfully in goal-consistent behaviour, even when it's stressful and uncomfortable, is called 'willingness'. To pursue our deepest values, such as love and friendship, satisfying work, caring for our health, or contributing to the community, we often have to do uncomfortable things, such as express controversial opinions, allow our work to be evaluated, learn new skills that we perform clumsily at first, tell people how we feel about them, or resist temptations. If we accept the reality that we're going to feel awkward, uncomfortable or tense, and allow these feelings to come and go while focusing on our goals, we'll be more willing to do the things that matter most.

Willingness does not mean forcing yourself to do things while trying to suppress or deny the discomfort and criticizing yourself harshly. 'I'm such a coward, I've got to do these exercises, just ignore the pain . . . ' is not willingness. 'There's no denying these exercises are painful. It's unfortunate that I need to do them. Let me do the best I can, keeping in mind that it will be worth it in the end,' *is* willingness.

In this chapter, we'll consider how to cultivate mindful acceptance of thoughts and feelings, especially the unpleasant and unwanted ones, so that they cause less suffering and less interference with our willingness to do what matters.

Susan's Story

Susan is forty-six years old, married, with two teenage sons and a full-time job as a bookkeeper. She's struggled with intermittent depression since her early twenties. For the last several months, she's had difficulty falling asleep. She lies in bed ruminating about how bad she feels and how little she's contributing to the household. In the morning, she's fatigued, but forces herself to go to work. After work, she feels exhausted and lethargic and spends her evenings watching TV. Her husband cooks dinner and washes the dishes. Susan used to attend her sons' athletic events and band concerts with pride and enthusiasm, but now she's lost interest and makes excuses not to go. Then she feels guilty about not being a good mother.

Susan knows she'd feel better if she exercised regularly. But every time she thinks of going for a walk, she feels tired, fat, discouraged and embarrassed. 'Not today,' she tells herself, 'I really don't have the energy.'

Each evening, as bedtime approaches, she feels regretful and guilty. 'I've got to do better tomorrow,' she thinks, but each day the pattern is the same.

Susan's doctor referred her to a weekly mindfulness class for people with depression. During the first session, the teacher led an exercise called the 'body scan'.

Practising Acceptance with the Body Scan

The body scan is a meditative exercise that cultivates flexible, non-judgemental awareness of bodily sensations. It's used in many mindfulness programmes and involves lying comfortably or sitting in a chair, focusing your attention on different parts of the body, and observing the sensations. Breathing helps you stay in the present and accept the moment as you find it.

Instructions for the body scan are in the box on page 204. Read through them carefully before trying the exercise. Most people find it easier to practise while listening to a recording. A twenty-minute recording for the body scan can be found on the website for this book: www.practising-happiness.co.uk.

It's important to practise the body scan regularly; you won't see much benefit from doing it once or twice. Think about how you could do this exercise every day for a week or two. Some people prefer to practise early in the morning, before the demands of the day have set in. Others prefer the evening. There is no right or wrong time; any time that works for you is fine.

Preparing for the body scan

Find a place where you can lie on your back on a comfortable surface, such as a bed, carpet or mat. If you prefer, practise while sitting in a chair.

Sit with your feet flat on the floor, your back supported, and your hands resting in your lap. Wear loose, comfortable clothes. Use a sweater or a blanket if you like.

It's best to minimize interruptions. If you live with others, ask them not to disturb you. Silence your phone.

Points to consider before beginning

1. You're not trying to achieve any particular state by doing a body scan. You may get relaxed, you may not. You may enjoy it, you may not. You may feel many sensations in your body or only a few. All of these experiences are perfectly OK. Your goal is to focus your attention on each part of the body in turn, bringing your awareness to whatever is happening in each moment and accepting it as it is.

2. See if you can refrain from judgements about whether your body and its sensations are good or bad, right or wrong. You're not trying to change your body or how it feels. You're not trying to create or get rid of sensations. Instead, allow your body to feel just as it feels in each moment. As best you can, adopt an attitude of friendly curiosity and interest about the sensations in your body, as if you were an explorer in new territory. If you notice judgemental thoughts, simply note and label them (*Ah, thinking*) and gently return your attention to observing the sensations.

3. Your mind will wander off; this is normal. The goal is NOT to rid your mind of thoughts. When you notice that your attention has drifted, gently bring it back to observing sensations in the body, without criticizing yourself.

4. You may feel urges to change your position, stretch a muscle, scratch an itch, or rub an ache. Observe the urge closely for a few moments. See if you can adopt a curious and open-minded attitude about the nature of the urge. Where do you feel it exactly? What does it feel like? Are the sensations changing or staying the same? If you decide to act on the urge, do so with mindful awareness. Observe how it

feels to move, stretch, scratch or rub. Notice how your body feels afterwards.

5.   You may feel bored, restless, worried, impatient or anything else. This is normal. It doesn't mean you're doing the exercise wrongly or that it isn't working. As best you can, notice these feelings without judging them, or yourself, as good or bad. Gently return your attention to sensations in the body.

6.   You may also feel relaxed, calm and peaceful. If so, practise mindful observation of the feelings, and remember that they aren't the goal. The goal is simply to observe whatever appears. All feelings come and go. None are right or wrong.

BODY SCAN INSTRUCTIONS

Settle into your position. If you're lying on your back, allow your arms to lie alongside your body, palms up, and let your feet fall away from each other. If you're sitting in a chair, rest your feet comfortably on the floor, hands in your lap. Gently close your eyes and allow the body to become still.

Now bring your attention to the breath going in and out of your body; however that's happening in your body right now. Notice the sensations in your abdomen as you breathe; rising and falling, expanding and contracting. There's no need to change your breathing in any way. Just notice it as it happens, one breath after another. Continue for a few minutes. When your mind wanders off, gently return to observing your breath.

Feet

Now shift your attention down to your feet. Observe them both together or one at a time, whichever you prefer. Notice any sensations. If your feet are warm, cold, itchy or sweaty, observe the feelings. Notice contact with your shoes, socks or the floor. Direct your attention entirely through your feet: toes, heels, soles, skin, muscles. If you don't feel anything in your feet, notice the absence of sensation. Don't try to make your feet feel different; just observe how they feel now. See if you can refrain from judging the sensations as good or bad, right or wrong.

Legs

Now shift your attention to your legs. Slowly move your attention through your ankles, lower legs, knees and thighs. Notice sensations of contact with your clothes, the floor or the chair. Observe sensations on the skin and within the muscles. If you're thinking about your legs (*too fat, too thin, too short*), rather than observing them, let go of the thoughts and return to feeling the sensations as best you can.

Now expand your awareness to include your legs, feet, and breath. Your attention may shift back and forth a bit. This is OK. Observe what happens. If you like, imagine that the breath flows into your legs when you breathe in, all the way down to your feet. Then imagine it flowing all the way back up when you breathe out.

Torso

Now shift your attention to your torso. Move your attention slowly through your hips, pelvis, lower back and lower abdomen. Gradually move up through your back, chest and shoulders. Take your time and notice all the sensations; on the surface and deep inside. If you find yourself thinking about or judging this part of the body (*unattractive, weak, flabby*), gently return to feeling the sensations that are present now.

Expand your awareness to include your torso and your breathing. Observe the sensations in your torso while staying aware of your breathing in the background. If you like, imagine that your breath flows into different parts of the torso: the hips, back or shoulders.

Arms and hands

Slowly move your attention through your arms and hands, noticing all sensations that are present. If you can't feel anything in a particular spot, notice the absence of any sensation there. Let go of judgemental thoughts and simply observe the sensations. If your mind wanders off, gently bring it back.

Expand your awareness to include your breathing. See if you can observe the sensations in your arms and hands while staying aware of your breathing in the background. If you like, imagine that when you breathe in, the breath travels down through your arms and out to your hands. When you breathe out, it comes back the other way.

Neck, head and face

Shift your attention slowly up your neck, feeling all sensations there. Move your awareness into your head. Explore all the regions of your face, taking an interest in any sensations that are present. Allow your attention to include both your breath and your head.

Whole body

Expand your awareness to include your breath and your entire body. Let go of expectations about how your body and breath should be. Accept them as they are right now. When you're ready, resume your normal activities. See if you can keep some of this mindful awareness going as you move on with your day.

How the Body Scan Fosters Mindful Acceptance

The body scan provides intensive practice of mindful acceptance of the present moment as it is. Consider the many things that can be accepted while doing the body scan:

1 – Aches, pains, itches, feeling too warm or too cold

Physical discomfort provides an excellent opportunity to practise friendly interest and acceptance of bodily sensations, breathing with them, and allowing them to be as they are. This does NOT mean that you have to resign yourself helplessly and passively to feeling uncomfortable. Instead, you're practising willingness to open up to whatever comes along. If you feel an urge to do something about discomfort (change your position, put on a sweater), observe the urge and accept its presence, as if it were a passenger who has boarded your bus. If you decide to act on the urge, do so with non-judgemental awareness.

2 – Sleepiness

Falling asleep during the body scan is common. If you went to sleep, it wasn't a failed practice – you probably *noticed* that you spent some of the time sleeping. On the other hand, you'll get more benefit if you stay awake. When sleepiness arises, see if you can observe the sensations of sleepiness with acceptance and interest. If you consistently fall asleep while practising, try doing the body scan sitting up or with your eyes open. Experiment with different times of day. Perhaps the body scan is telling you that you're sleep-deprived.

3 – Distracting noises

Many people mistakenly believe that meditative exercises require peace and quiet. In fact, noise can be part of the practice. If unpleasant sounds are present, practise accepting them as they are – not in a white-knuckled, clenched-teeth way, but with friendly interest, as best you can. If a dog is barking, observe the sounds. You don't have to be passive or helpless. If it's your dog, and the neighbours will be annoyed, it might be wise to bring the dog in. See if you can do the whole thing mindfully: getting up, walking to the door, opening the door, calling the dog, closing the door, returning to your spot, sitting or lying down, resuming the body scan.

If you're frustrated or angry about sounds you can't control, observe your thoughts and feelings. Remember, you're practising non-judgemental acceptance of *everything* that comes up, including noise, distraction and negative thoughts and emotions. Note their presence and gently return your attention to the body scan, as best you can. The goal is not to make yourself like the sounds or to banish them from your mind; it's OK to hear them, not like them, and not like your reactions to them. Practise acceptance of the entire experience.

4 – Thoughts and feelings about the body scan

Feeling bored and restless and thinking, 'This is silly, I don't see the point,' are common and normal reactions. Your goal is to recognize these experiences for what they are: emotions (boredom, impatience); thoughts (*I don't like this exercise, this won't help me*); and urges (desires to quit and do something else). Observe and accept them, without letting them control your behaviour. Labelling will help: Say to yourself, 'Ah, those are thoughts' (or emotions or urges). You're cultivating one of the most important skills to be learned from practising mindfulness: willingness to do something important, even when it feels unpleasant. Don't give yourself a hard time about not liking it. It's OK to dislike it. Disliking is a normal feeling that comes and goes.

5 – Thoughts and feelings about other things

Everyone's mind wanders. The goal is not to stop your mind from wandering. Instead, observe when it wanders and gently bring it back. If your mind wanders to painful problems or memories and negative emotions arise, notice what's happening. If you're getting swept up in thoughts (*She had no right to treat me that way*, or *The meeting is going to be terrible*), label the experience by saying to yourself, 'Angry thoughts are in my mind,' or 'A feeling of anxiety is here.' Then return your attention to the body scan. Listen closely to what the voice on the recording is saying. Follow its instructions as best you can.

Susan's Experiences with the Body Scan

Susan practised the body scan nearly every day after the first session of her mindfulness class. She didn't like it at first. Rumination and self-criticism flooded her mind. She kept thinking about all the things she hadn't been doing lately, especially household tasks like cooking and participating in her sons' activities. She had strong urges to stop the body scan and do chores instead.

'It's strange,' she said during the second meeting of the class. 'When I'm watching TV in the evenings, I know I should work on the laundry or empty the dishwasher, but I can't make myself do it. But during the body scan I have urges to jump up to do these things. I feel guilty just lying there.'

Susan's teacher assured her that these feelings are normal and common, and encouraged her to persist with the body scan, noticing urges, thoughts and feelings, without being carried away or controlled by them, and gently returning her attention to the sensations in her body.

During the second week of daily body scans, Susan began to notice that she occasionally enjoyed them. At the third session, she told her teacher, 'I'm starting to see that I don't have to do what my thoughts and feelings tell me to do. If I suddenly have an urge to empty the dryer, I notice that it's an urge. I focus on how it feels in my body and I make a mental note to empty the dryer later.' Susan described one especially notable practice:

> 'My younger son, Tim, who's thirteen, was practising the clarinet in his room while I was doing the body scan downstairs. He was working on a difficult piece. I heard squawks and wrong notes. I realized I haven't talked with Tim for ages about how it's going in his band, what music they're working on, whether he's enjoying it. I started thinking about what a bad mother I've been. But I didn't go down that road in my mind. I firmly told myself to come back to my body. I observed the sinking feeling in my stomach and breathed with it.

'Then I started listening to the clarinet again and I realized Tim was making progress with the difficult passage. I felt happy and proud of him. I wanted to jump up and tell him how good he sounded. Of course that was also a distraction, so I focused on my body and noticed sensations that were part of the happy feeling. I felt lighter. There was an uplifting feeling in my chest.

'For the last few minutes my mind was alternating between the body scan and the clarinet, but I kept coming back to the body scan until I finished it. I learned that I can keep going with things that are important, even if distracting thoughts and feelings come to my mind. And if I don't get caught up in obsessing and ruminating, I'm more aware of things around me, like what's going on with my kids.'

Why It Makes Sense to Focus on the Body

Let's look closely at what happens to Susan when she wakes up on a typical morning. First, she notices a feeling of fatigue. Immediately, she has thoughts about it: *I didn't sleep well, today will be terrible. I'll be so exhausted. Why does this keep happening? I hate feeling this way. What's the matter with me? Why can't I be normal?*

This is rumination and makes her feel worse. Then she tells herself not to think about it. 'Come on, get going, you're wasting time,' she tells herself harshly, and forces herself out of bed. The self-critical tone adds to her feelings of unworthiness. She showers and dresses in a bad mood, then goes into the kitchen for coffee and a quick breakfast. Her sons appear at about this time, with their minds on the school day ahead. She'd like to have a cheerful word with them before they leave for the bus stop, but she's preoccupied and misses the moment. She drives to work lost in thoughts about how badly things are going.

Now let's consider how mindful attention to the body would help. Susan wakes up and notices a feeling of fatigue. She quickly scans her body, noting sensations of heaviness in her arms, legs and chest. She takes a few mindful breaths, imagining her breath travelling through her arms and legs. A thought appears: *Why am I always so tired?*

'I don't need to get sucked into rumination,' she says to herself. 'I've been a bit depressed lately. Tiredness is part of it.' Gently she stretches her arms and legs, observing the sensations and noticing that she feels slightly more wakeful though still rather blue. 'What do I need?' she asks herself. 'A quick shower and a healthy breakfast, and maybe a walk after dinner tonight for some exercise.'

Feeling more willing to engage with the day, she gets out of bed, feeling the cool floor under her feet. As she follows her morning routine, she's aware of feelings of fatigue and sadness, but doesn't ruminate or criticize. She also notices many other things: the soap and water on her body in the shower; the warm air of her hair dryer; hot coffee moving down her throat. She chats briefly with her sons, says 'Have a good day!' and drives to work, feeling her hands on the steering wheel and observing her surroundings.

Emotions have strong bodily components. Depression, in particular, includes physical sensations of fatigue and heaviness. Sensations can trigger unhealthy behaviour and thinking patterns, especially when we're not paying attention. Observing what's happening in her body helps Susan recognize her emotions as they come and go without falling into the traps of rumination and self-criticism. She hasn't rid herself of all the unpleasant feelings; rather, she's expanded her awareness to make room for them while treating herself with kindness and doing things she values.

What If the Body Scan is Intensely Difficult and Unpleasant?

If you experience very strong negative emotions or traumatic memories during the body scan, you may feel that this practice is too difficult. Before giving up on it, consider the following options:

1. Gentle, compassionate persistence can overcome many difficulties. Experiment with practising for shorter periods, sitting up rather than lying down, or with your eyes open. You might scan only your legs and feet one day, your torso another. See if you can find a way to be kind to yourself without abandoning this exercise.

2. If the body scan is a serious obstacle, postpone working with it for now and try again later. Meanwhile, practise awareness of the body with mindful walking (described in the previous chapter) or mindfulness of other routine activities, such as showering or bathing, brushing your teeth, combing your hair, standing in line, cooking, shopping, or emptying the trash. In addition to the obvious parts of the body, see if you can observe other parts: the sensations in your feet while combing your hair; the opposite hand as you brush your teeth; your abdomen while standing in line.

3. If you've suffered traumatic experiences or are susceptible to intense, negative emotions, consider working with a mental health professional with knowledge of mindfulness-based treatments. An experienced teacher can help you overcome difficulties with the body scan and find ways to benefit from it.

Acceptance and Willingness in Daily Life: Mindful Pausing

Mindful pausing is a way to apply the skills learned from the body scan to ordinary life. The goal of mindful pausing is to step out of automatic pilot, bring mindful awareness into the present moment, and see what the situation requires. Mindful pausing has several steps. Use the word 'SOBER' to remember them. Instructions are in the next box.

MINDFUL PAUSING

S – Stop or slow down. Say to yourself, 'OK, let's pause for a moment', or something similar. Adjust your posture:

- Straighten your spine a bit, with your head directly over your neck.

- Lower your shoulders, unclench your teeth.

- Let your posture reflect your intention to be open to the present moment.

O – Observe. What's happening right now in your body and mind? Notice sensations, thoughts, emotions and urges. It may be helpful to label them:

- Tension in my shoulders.

- Heaviness in my chest.

- A feeling of anger is here.

- Self-critical thoughts are racing around.

- Feeling sad and stressed.

- Wishing I could leave work early.

B – Breathe. Observe the sensations as your breath goes in and out. Focus your attention just on breathing, as best you can. When your mind is pulled away, gently bring it back to breathing. Experiment with silent labelling or counting:

- Breathing in 1, breathing out 1.

- Breathing in 2, breathing out 2.

- Take at least 2 or 3 mindful breaths, 5 or 10 if there's time.

E – Expand your awareness. Observe your body as a whole, including sensations, posture, facial expression. Focus gently and kindly on uncomfortable sensations. Breathe with them. Allow them to be as they are. Say to yourself:

- Let me just notice this.

- It's OK for me to feel this.

- It's already here. Let me go ahead and feel it.

R – Respond mindfully. As best you can, choose wisely what to do.

- In some situations, the wisest option is to allow a situation or feeling to run its natural course.

- In other situations, you may need to take more definite action.

- Mindful pausing helps you remember what you care about and discern what the situation requires.

Mindful pausing allowed Susan to realize what she was feeling and thinking, and how her thoughts and feelings were controlling her behaviour. One day, just as she came into the house after work, her son Tim reminded her that he had a band concert that evening. Her immediate feeling was dread; her first impulse was to say she was too tired to go. But she held back. 'Oh,' she said, standing by the door, looking at Tim.

Silently, she reminded herself to pause. She noticed feelings of fatigue and irritation – with herself for forgetting the concert and with Tim for not reminding her. She noticed a desire to collapse into the recliner and watch TV. 'But I do that every night, and I don't feel any better,' she thought. She stood up a little straighter, took a breath, and observed her body standing in the hall, still wearing her coat, holding her purse and keys, her feet aching in her work shoes.

'Mom,' said Tim. 'Are you OK?' She looked into his concerned face, realizing she'd been staring at him for several seconds.

'Yes,' she said, with a bit more energy. 'Let's have an early supper so we can all get to the concert.' Mindfully, she set down her purse, hung up her coat and changed her shoes. She and her husband organized a quick meal. Susan noticed that everyone seemed cheerful, and she felt a little happier herself.

In the car on the way to the concert, a feeling of exhaustion came over her. She observed a few breaths and allowed her body to sink into the car seat, while her husband drove and the kids chattered in the back. 'The concert is important to Tim,' she told herself. 'He wants me to be there. I might even enjoy it.' And to her surprise, she did. The band played well, several of the parents chatted with her afterwards, and her family seemed very pleased that she was there.

Mindful pausing helped Susan behave consistently with something she cares about: participating in her kids' activities. She accepted the presence of unpleasant emotions and sensations and willingly went to the concert. The following worksheet summarizes some of Susan's experiences practising acceptance and willingness. As with the previous worksheets in this book, make copies of the blank one for your own use.

Worksheet: Acceptance and willingness

****Remember to maintain an attitude of friendly curiosity***

Day & time	In the service of these values and goals . . .	. . . I practised mindful acceptance of these thoughts and feelings . . .	. . . and willingness to do these behaviours or activities:
When did this example occur?	What were the important values and goals you were pursuing? General categories: • Work • Family • Other relationships • Self-care, health • Contributing to others or the community NOTE: For a review of values and goals, revisit chapter 7.	What did you observe in your body and mind? General categories • Body sensations (aching, fatigue) • Thoughts (*I don't feel like doing this, this is going to be terrible*) • Urges (desires or impulses to do something else) • Emotions (sadness, anger, fear) • Other (images, memories) IMPORTANT: Acceptance does NOT mean that you liked, wanted or approved of your thoughts and feelings, only that you acknowledged them and allowed them to come and go on their own, without letting them control your behaviour.	What did you do that was consistent with your values and goals? IMPORTANT: Willingness means that you went ahead with behaviour consistent with your values and goals. It does NOT mean that it necessarily felt good. You may have felt anxious, sad, fatigued, discouraged, frustrated, angry or anything else. However you felt is OK.

Worksheet: Acceptance and willingness

Your name: <u>Susan</u>

Remember to maintain an attitude of friendly curiosity

Day & time	In the service of these values and goals:	I practised mindful acceptance of these thoughts and feelings:	Willingness to do these behaviours or activities:
Saturday 9.00 a.m.	Taking better care of myself, getting exercise.	I thought, I'm too fat and out of shape, there's no point, it'll be embarrassing. I felt heavy, tired, wanted to stay inside, felt dread, gloomy, discouraged.	Went for a walk around the neighbourhood. Observed sensations of walking and my surroundings. Spoke to a couple of neighbours who were out walking.
Thursday 5.30 p.m.	Being a good mother, being involved in my kids' activities.	I thought, I'm too tired to go to Tim's concert tonight. He should have reminded me so I'd be prepared. I felt fatigued and irritated. I wanted to stay home.	Got a quick dinner ready. Went to Tim's band concert. Enjoyed it more than I thought I would.
Monday 2.00 p.m.	Being a good employee, being helpful to others at work.	Felt nervous, anxious, heart going fast, trembly feeling, thought people will get bored or confused.	Gave a training session for my co-workers on how to use a new software programme.

Worksheet: Acceptance and willingness

Your name: _____

Remember to maintain an attitude of friendly curiosity

Day & time	In the service of these values and goals:	I practised mindful acceptance of these thoughts and feelings:	Willingness to do these behaviours or activities:

By practising the body scan and mindful pausing, Susan learned important lessons. Behaving consistently with her values and goals is satisfying, and she doesn't have to feel any particular way to get started. When she feels blue, discouraged, tired and unmotivated, she can turn her attention to the sensations in her body, observe her breath, accept her thoughts and emotions as they ebb and flow, and choose wisely what to do. Although it's difficult to do things when she feels discouraged, fatigued or nervous, it's also empowering. It gives her a feeling of inner strength to realize that her thoughts and feelings don't have to control her behaviour.

As Susan works toward greater willingness to behave consistently with her values and goals, she must be careful to avoid an important pitfall: taking a harsh, self-critical attitude. Forcing herself to do things, telling herself she's an idiot or a failure if she doesn't, and mentally beating herself up is inconsistent with a mindful, accepting attitude and will lead to rumination, avoidance and a worsening mood. Most of us find it difficult to treat ourselves compassionately, and it's even harder if we've struggled with anxiety, depression and other problems.

In the next chapter, we'll consider how self-compassion and mindfulness work together to help us accept ourselves as human beings while building the life we want.

Chapter Summary

- Acceptance of thoughts and feelings is an important mindfulness skill. It means observing them and allowing them to run their natural course, without trying to suppress or get rid of them in unhealthy ways.

- Willingness means going ahead with behaviours and activities that are important to pursuing our values and goals, even when it's difficult and uncomfortable.

- Practising the body scan cultivates acceptance and willingness. When difficult thoughts and feelings arise, mindful observation and acceptance of sensations in the body helps keep us out of the psychological traps discussed earlier: rumination, suppression and avoidance, emotion-driven behaviour and self-criticism.

- Mindful pausing gives us time to see clearly what is happening in the mind and body and choose wisely what to do. Sometimes, the wise choice is to allow difficult feelings and situations to run their natural course. At other times, we need to take more definite action. Keeping our important values and goals in mind helps us choose meaningful and satisfying behaviour.

12 Self–compassion

'True mindfulness is imbued with warmth, compassion and interest.'

Christina Feldman

The importance of compassion has been recognized since ancient times. Most of the world's religions teach that compassion, kindness and caring for others are essential virtues. Modern scientists believe that compassion is a part of human nature that evolved because it helps us survive. Communities in which people care for each other are the most likely to provide a healthy environment for future generations.

What does it mean to be compassionate? Most definitions include both feelings and actions; empathy and concern for people who are suffering, and working to alleviate suffering. Acting with compassion can be difficult. It requires awareness of others' pain and willingness to stay present and try to help, even when turning away would be easier and more comfortable. Despite the difficulties, most people agree that we should aspire to treat others with compassion whenever possible.

We're less convinced that we should be compassionate towards ourselves. We fear that self-compassion will make us lazy and undisciplined, that it's selfish, that we don't deserve it. As a result, we're often harsh and unkind to ourselves during difficult times, blaming and criticizing ourselves in ways that would seem cruel if directed towards others. But research shows that self-compassion is much healthier than self-criticism and that practising mindfulness makes us more self-compassionate. In this chapter, we'll explore the nature of self-compassion and the benefits of treating ourselves kindly.

Dana's Story

Dana is worried about her weight. She's usually on a diet and has many personal rules about foods to eat and to avoid. Like most dieters, she often has a paradoxical reaction when she eats a food she's forbidden herself; rather than returning immediately to her diet plan, she eats *more* of the forbidden food.

This happens because eating food that's usually off limits triggers self-critical thoughts and feelings of regret, shame and inadequacy. Dana tells herself she's hopeless, has no self-control, and might as well eat more. The forbidden food is comforting and temporarily distracts her from her difficulties in living up to her goals. This may sound irrational, but it's a surprisingly common pattern. The same thing happens with people trying to cut back on drinking or smoking. If you've ever behaved in this way, you're not alone.

Dana volunteered for a study at the university. She was told it was about eating while watching TV; in reality, it was about the effects of compassion on eating sweets. When Dana arrived, the researcher asked her to sit alone in a room and eat a doughnut while watching a video. Dana's heart sank; she tries to avoid doughnuts because of the fat and sugar. But she complied. When she'd finished, the researcher entered the room and said, 'You might wonder why we picked doughnuts to use in the study. It's because people sometimes eat unhealthy, sweet foods while they watch TV. But several people have told me they feel bad about eating doughnuts in this study, so I hope you won't be hard on yourself. Everyone eats unhealthily sometimes, so I don't think there's any reason to feel bad about it. This small amount of food doesn't really matter anyway.'

This message was designed to help the participants adopt a self-compassionate attitude – recognizing that eating unhealthy food is common, refraining from excessive self-criticism, and taking a balanced perspective on the situation. After hearing this statement, Dana felt a bit better. 'She's right,' she thought. 'It was just one doughnut, and not a very large one. That's not so bad. I can eat healthy the rest of the day.'

Then the researcher brought three bowls of candy into the room along with a form for rating their taste, texture, appearance and aroma. She asked Dana to taste the candies, complete the rating form, and then fill out some questionnaires. 'You can eat as much of the candy as you like while you're working,' she said. 'I'll be in the next room. Come and tell me when you've finished all the forms.'

All of the participants in this study were concerned about their weight. Half of them, including Dana, heard the compassionate message after eating the doughnut. The others were not given this reassurance. The real purpose of the study was to find out which group would eat more candy during the taste test. Previous studies show that a diet violation, such as eating a doughnut, tends to weaken self-control, causing people to eat more candy than they would otherwise. Would encouragement to adopt a self-compassionate attitude make a difference?

The results were clear. Those who had NOT heard the compassionate message showed the typical pattern; they were more distressed about eating the doughnut, reported more self-criticism about it, and ate *more* candy during the rest of the experiment. Those who had been encouraged to be self-compassionate were less upset, less self-judgemental, and ate less candy. Dana's experience was consistent with this pattern; she was tempted by the candy, but ate only slightly more than necessary to complete the taste test.

After Dana had finished the taste test and questionnaires, the researcher explained the real purpose of the study. Dana was intrigued. 'After you told me not to be hard on myself about the doughnut, it felt easier to resist the candy,' she told the researcher. Dana is realizing what the study confirmed: a self-compassionate attitude helped people with weight concerns eat less of a tempting but unhealthy food.

George's Story

George has been a regular smoker for ten years. He's extremely self-critical about his failure to quit, often berating himself for his lack of self-discipline. He volunteered for a study about ways to reduce smoking and was assigned to a group that learned self-compassion skills. During a forty-five-minute session, the researcher guided him through several activities:

1. First, they discussed the self-compassionate approach to smoking reduction, which has the following elements:

    •   Understanding of how difficult it is to quit.

    •   Wisdom about what's best for one's long-term wellbeing.

    •   Strength to cope with setbacks.

    •   Non-judgement when failures occur.

    •   Warmth in relating to oneself.

2. Next, George visualized adopting these qualities and wrote himself a letter from the perspective of a compassionate person:

    'I'm really glad you're taking steps to help yourself feel better in the long run. Making this decision is difficult and brave and I know it's hard for you. I'd like to help you get through the difficult moments. It will be stressful but let's try to tolerate the short-term pain to feel healthier in the long run. This is hard. Giving up cigarettes is a huge loss. Let's focus on smoking reduction as one of the kindest things you can do for yourself.'

3. Then he practised what to say to himself, from the self-compassionate perspective, when faced with urges to smoke:

    'I know you REALLY want this cigarette. I feel how hard this is for you. Let's focus on your long-term wellbeing. To feel better and be healthier, let's try to resist this cigarette in spite of how hard it is. I know you can do it and in time you'll be grateful that you did.'

George felt sceptical but agreed that for the next three weeks he would give these skills his best effort. He re-read the self-compassionate letter every day and talked to himself in a self-compassionate way whenever he felt an urge to smoke. He kept detailed records of the cigarettes he smoked. The control group kept the same records but didn't learn about self-compassion.

Over the three-week period, the self-compassion group smoked substantially fewer cigarettes. The difference was greatest for people like George who are extremely self-critical. Once again, self-compassion was more effective than self-criticism in helping people change an unhealthy habit.

At the end of the three weeks, George met with the researcher to turn in his forms and discuss the study. 'I have to admit, I'm surprised,' he said. 'I really thought this was silly. I thought I had to beat myself up to make any progress at all. But I've been doing that for years and I'm still a smoker. During these last three weeks I've cut way back. If I keep this up, I might be able to quit completely.'

The Many Benefits of Self-compassion

Most research studies are short-term; George practised self-compassion for three weeks, while Dana was encouraged to be self-compassionate on a single occasion. Studies of people who are naturally self-compassionate, or who've practised it for months or years, show that a general attitude of self-compassion has many benefits. For example, self-compassionate people are less likely to become depressed. They feel the normal ups and downs of daily life and have sad thoughts and feelings when misfortunes occur. But they ruminate less. They don't try to suppress their feelings. They weather emotional storms with acceptance and equanimity, without descending into depression.

Self-compassionate people are also less likely to develop anxiety disorders, especially if something traumatic happens to them. They're less angry and hostile, less perfectionistic. They have less fear of failure and are more open to growth and learning. When they encounter awkward or embarrassing situations, they keep their emotional balance and a healthy perspective. They have lower levels of stress hormones circulating in their bloodstreams.

Concerns about Self–compassion

Is self-compassion selfish? Shouldn't I be more concerned with others' needs?

Studies using brain scans show that the same area of the brain is activated when people are compassionate toward themselves or others. This may explain why self-compassionate people also show more concern for others: they're more compassionate in general. Before criticizing someone, they're more likely to imagine how they'd feel in that person's place. In romantic relationships, they're more supportive of their partner, less aggressive and controlling, and more respectful of their partner's opinions.

People in the helping professions, such as doctors, nurses, therapists and the clergy, are susceptible to compassion fatigue and burn-out – forms of emotional exhaustion brought on by working with suffering people. Research shows that self-compassion *reduces* burn-out, making it easier to continue practising compassion towards others. People who take good care of themselves, accept negative thoughts and emotions as a normal part of their job, and refrain from harsh self-criticism, are less likely to become drained, discouraged and disconnected from the people they work with. They're more likely to find satisfaction in their opportunities to make a difference in the world, despite the inevitable stress.

What if I don't feel kindly or compassionate toward myself?

George didn't always feel self-compassionate when urges to smoke arose. Sometimes he felt self-critical, self-blaming and guilty. We don't have to *feel* kindly toward ourselves in order to *behave* in a self-compassionate way. When we act with self-compassion, we try to find the wisest and most helpful course of action for the circumstances, regardless of how we're feeling at that moment.

You've probably behaved nicely to others when you were annoyed with them and thought they didn't deserve it; perhaps because you value treating people with decency and respect. If you value treating yourself in the same way (and research shows this is beneficial) then the principle discussed in previous chapters applies. Behaving consistently with important values doesn't have to depend on the feelings that are present in any particular moment. If you're feeling undeserving of compassion because you've made mistakes, hurt someone, or caused harm, gently experiment with the following steps:

1.   Remind yourself that everyone makes mistakes, hurts others and causes harm now and then.

2.   Remember that guilt and remorse are built into human nature. Their purpose is to motivate us to apologize, make amends and correct our own mistakes, as best we can. They're useful emotions if we handle them constructively. Mindfulness and self-compassion help us do this.

3.   Observe your thoughts and emotions without judgement, including thoughts such as 'I don't deserve compassion'. Remember that this is a thought.

4.   Observe the sensations in your body. Breathe with them.

5.   Ask yourself: What really matters to me in this situation? What behaviour is consistent with my values and goals?

6.   Remember that *constructive* self-criticism can be helpful, but you're more likely to behave consistently with your values and goals if you're not consumed with *excessive* self-criticism. For a review of constructive criticism, go back to chapter 6.

If you're a highly self-critical person, self-compassion may seem nearly impossible. It's important to understand that self-compassion is a *set of skills* that anyone can practise. In the rest of this chapter, we'll consider how to cultivate these skills. First, here's a summary of what self-compassion is and is not.

Self-compassion includes:	Self-compassion does not include:
Seeing situations clearly, including our own mistakes. This requires mindful observation and keeping a balanced perspective.	Ignoring our mistakes and weaknesses or giving ourselves false praise.
Recognizing that pain, hardships, failures and inadequacies are part of being human – everyone experiences them.	Wallowing in self-pity. While pitying ourselves we tend to forget that many others have similar problems or suffer in their own ways.
Caring for ourselves with kindness and understanding because we're human, not because we're above average or special.	Judging ourselves, either positively or negatively, or evaluating whether we're superior or inferior to others.
Constructive, persistent efforts to change behaviour or correct mistakes that are causing harm.	Being lazy, self-indulgent and undisciplined.

Five Ways to Cultivate Self-compassion

1 – Practise the mindfulness exercises you already know

Research shows that people who consistently practise mindfulness become more self-compassionate. This is not surprising. As we've seen, mindfulness includes a kind, open-hearted and friendly attitude towards ourselves, especially when we're having painful thoughts and feelings. The mindfulness exercises described in the previous chapters will help you develop your self-compassion skills. This will be good for your mental health.

2 – Basic self-care

Eating a nutritious diet, exercising regularly and getting enough sleep are among the kindest things you can do for yourself. You'll still have negative emotions, but there's a good chance they'll be less intense and won't last as long if you're well nourished and rested. You'll cope with them better because you'll have more energy for practising the mindfulness skills you've been learning. You'll think more clearly and make wiser decisions. You may also feel more positive emotions.

Don't try to overhaul your health habits all at once. Behaviour change takes time and patience. Start with small goals, like eating a healthier breakfast, going for a walk after dinner, or going to bed at a reasonable hour. Gradually add more healthy behaviour. Remember to apply the mindfulness skills you've learned to eating and exercising. If you have trouble with sleeping, see the next box for helpful tips.

TIPS FOR HEALTHY SLEEPING

1 – Sleeping environment

- Use a good mattress and pillow.

- Keep the room dark, quiet, and at a comfortable temperature.

2 – Eating, drinking and exercise

- Eat regular, nutritious meals.

- Don't go to bed hungry.

- Avoid heavy or greasy foods before bed; a light snack is preferable.

- Avoid caffeine and alcohol in the evenings; drink other liquids in moderation.

- Exercise regularly, but not within 3 hours of bedtime.

3 – Time spent in bed

- Don't spend extra time in bed. If you need 7 hours of sleep, spend 7 hours in bed.

- Use your bed only for sleeping and sex. Read, eat and watch TV elsewhere.

- Go to bed and get up at roughly the same time every day.

4 – If you can't sleep

- Get up, go to another room, and do something quiet and relaxing, like read a book (not an exciting one). Don't watch TV or use a computer; the bright screen may induce wakefulness. When you feel sleepy, go back to bed.

- Put the clock where you can't see it. Clock-watching during the night can cause frustration and worry, which interfere with sleep.

- Practise mindful acceptance of not sleeping.

3 – Savouring

Imagine going to an excellent restaurant, ordering your favourite dish, eating it mindfully, and relishing the moment, with your attention focused on the delicious tastes, aromas and textures. This is savouring. The alternative is to eat it mindlessly, while checking your messages, reading, talking with someone or thinking of other things.

Now imagine that you've just won an award at work. You've received a glowing letter from your supervisor praising your performance and telling you that your name will be added to the plaque in the main hall. Savour this by allowing yourself to bask in your good feelings.

Some people are wary of savouring. They think that it will bring on bad luck, that they don't deserve their good fortune, that it's unseemly to enjoy things too much, or that they can't live up to the high standard they somehow attained on this unusual occasion. However, research shows that people who consistently enjoy and appreciate their positive experiences are happier, more optimistic, and less likely to be depressed than people who don't. Savouring is an excellent way to be kind to yourself.

Use your mindfulness skills to practise savouring. When you have a pleasant experience, observe it closely and allow the good feelings to flow. If you're having a delightful time at a gathering of family or friends, be present and enjoy it to the fullest. If you've finished a difficult piece of work and you're pleased with how it turned out, relish the feelings of pride and satisfaction. When thoughts arise, such as, 'This won't last,' or 'I can't expect things to keep going this well,' or 'That was just good luck, I don't really deserve this,' label them as thoughts and gently return your attention to enjoying the moment while it lasts.

4 – Self-soothing

Self-soothing is a way of being gentle and kind with yourself when you're under stress and feeling upset. It focuses on the five senses. Instead of waiting for pleasant experiences to come along, intentionally seek out simple comforting things, and attend to them mindfully, to help yourself through difficult moments.

Here's an example: Robin is a fifty-two-year-old woman who found a lump in her breast. She had a biopsy and then had to wait for three days to learn the results. She practised self-soothing during that time.

> 'Waiting for the results of the biopsy was very difficult. I continued to go to work, but in the evenings it was hard to keep myself from obsessing and worrying. I tried to eat healthy, but I was so anxious I didn't have much appetite. I decided that self-soothing might help. I tried all kinds of things. I don't like the winter cold, so I focused on warm things.
>
> 'One evening I took a hot bath with some scented bath oil and listened to my favourite music. I savoured the sensations, sounds and

smells. My mind went back to thinking about cancer at times, but I kept bringing it back. I drank tea and hot chocolate, and I ate soup and toast made from my favourite bread. I tried to eat and drink every-thing mindfully. I watched entertaining movies with my husband Jerry while snuggling in a soft quilt. Jerry had put it in the dryer for a few minutes first so it was nice and warm. We also made fires in the fireplace and I watched the flames, listened to the crackling sounds, and smelled the smoky scent. I mindfully petted our cat a lot. He has a big, soft tummy and a wonderful purr. That was very comforting.

'Self-soothing made those three days a little easier. Staying in the pre-sent was difficult at times but much better than dwelling on the fear and uncertainty for endless hours. On the fourth day, I learned that I have an early-stage cancer that can be treated successfully in most peo-ple. I'll continue being kind to myself while I go through the treatment.'

Self-soothing is not a form of avoidance or suppression; you're not denying that you're in a difficult situation and feeling upset, nor are you avoiding constructive behaviour that might solve the problem. Self-soothing is a way to be self-compassionate when you have a stressful problem that can't be solved right away. It helps you be aware of the present moment without ruminating, obsessing or behaving rashly. It puts you in a better frame of mind for taking wise action when you can.

Suggestions for self-soothing with each of your five senses are in the next box. They're only suggestions; you may have other ideas that would work well for you. The key to self-soothing is to do it mindfully. Closely observe whatever you see, hear, smell, taste or touch. Savour it. When your mind wanders off, gently bring it back, without criticizing yourself.

Self-soothing doesn't have to be time-consuming. If you don't have time for a long bath or sitting in front of a fire, think about ways to make your regular environment more soothing. Photos or pictures, plants or flowers, background music, a more comfortable chair – all can provide brief, soothing moments at home or work. Some people find that self-affectionate behaviour, such as placing your hand over your heart or gently stroking your arm, is soothing.

SUGGESTED ACTIVITIES FOR MINDFUL SELF–SOOTHING WITH THE FIVE SENSES

Choose things you find pleasant and enjoyable

1. Eating, drinking, or cooking:

- See the colours, textures, and shapes of the food; the arrangement on the plate.

- Hear any sounds: chopping, sizzling, fizzing, bubbling.

- Smell the aromas, taste the flavours.

- Notice the temperature, texture, and weight of the food, the feel of utensils, cups, or glasses.

2. Being out in nature or in a park:

- See the trees, flowers, wildlife, or waves if you're near water.

- Hear the breeze, birds, waves, other people, passing cars.

- Smell the air, flowers, water.

- Feel the ground under your feet, the air and sun on your skin, the texture of tree trunks.

3. Being out in your neighborhood, or in a city:

- See houses, trees, gardens, people passing.

- Hear the sounds.

- Smell any scents in the air.

- Feel the ground under your feet.

4. Listening to music you enjoy

- See the musicians playing (if you're at a live performance).

- See images that the music brings to your mind.

- Hear the instruments, melodies, harmonies.

- Feel the rhythm if you like – move to the beat.

5. Being indoors:

- Watch a fire, hear the crackling sounds, smell the smoke.

- Take a bath or shower, feel and hear the water, smell the soap or shampoo.

- Wear your most comfortable clothes, feel the texture on your skin.

- Put flowers around your house, see the colours and shapes, smell the scents.

These are only suggestions. Choose what would be most soothing for you.

5 – Self-validation

Validation is a kind and helpful way of practising mindful acceptance of thoughts and feelings; it means observing them without judgement and recognizing that they're understandable given the circumstances, even if they seem irrational on the surface. We can validate ourselves or other people. In this example, Tony validates his daughter, who's frightened of a bee:

'I was driving with my eight-year-old daughter Lindsey in the back seat and suddenly she started screaming hysterically that there's a bee in the car. I pulled over and waved the bee out the window.

Lindsey was wailing that she didn't want to go to the hospital again. I was confused because she's never been in the hospital. But then I remembered that last year we were on a trip and Lindsey got an insect bite just under her eye. We put ointment on it, but it was uncomfortable and everywhere we went people asked what happened to her eye.

'*So we took her to a clinic. It wasn't a hospital, but maybe Lindsey remembers it that way. She didn't like being there. She was afraid she'd get an injection. The doctor said it was an insect bite, gave us more ointment, and eventually it went away. I'd forgotten all about it but Lindsey remembered.*

'*So I said, "I understand the bee scared you because you ended up at a clinic that time when everyone was looking at the bug bite under your eye. That was no fun." That helped her settle down, so then I said, "Let's figure out what you can do if a bee gets in the car again." Lindsey said she could open the window and she could tell me. She thought she'd be able to stay calmer next time.'*

Tony's behaviour is a good example of validation. He communicated to Lindsey that her emotional reaction was understandable in the circumstances. His behaviour was kind, considerate and constructive: It helped Lindsey feel calmer and make a plan for what to do on future occasions. Tony loves Lindsey deeply, but he didn't *feel* very compassionate during this incident; he was impatient with the delay and irritated with Lindsey for making such a fuss. However, he *behaved* in a kind and compassionate way because he values being a supportive parent. Many psychologists believe that children who grow up with validating adults learn healthy ways for managing upsetting situations and negative emotions.

Lindsey's reaction to the bee seemed irrational and out of proportion at first. Tony had to think for a moment before it made sense to him. As we've seen in previous chapters, emotions may seem illogical on the surface, but they usually make sense for the following reasons:

1. **Emotions are built into human nature; we have them because they serve useful purposes.** Lindsey's emotional reaction was a way of communicating her fear and motivating her father to take action to help her.

2. **Normal learning and conditioning processes have a big impact on our emotional reactions.** Lindsey has learned from experience to associate small flying creatures with uncomfortable bites or stings and scary medical environments.

3. **Brain and body chemistry influence how we feel our emotions.** Some people naturally have intense, easily triggered emotions, whereas others are less sensitive. Lindsey may have an intense, emotional temperament. If so, validation and learning constructive ways to handle upsetting situations will be especially important for her.

4. **Temporary conditions also influence how we think and feel.** If we're tired, hungry, sick or in pain, we're more susceptible to strong negative thoughts and emotions. Perhaps Lindsey was tired or hungry that day.

Validation is not just for children. Research shows that it makes difficult tasks less stressful for adults. In one study, students attempted several sets of challenging mental arithmetic problems. During rest periods, the researcher conversed with them about how it felt to work on the problems. For half the participants, the researcher made validating comments, like, 'It really is hard to do maths problems without pencil and paper,' or 'Most of the other participants have felt the same way you do.'

For the other participants, the researcher was invalidating, saying things like, 'I don't understand why you would feel that way,' or 'They're just maths problems ... there's no point in getting frustrated.' Those who were invalidated got more and more annoyed and stressed as the study went on and their heart rates went up. Those who were validated stayed calm; their heart rates went down.

Validating *ourselves* is just as important as validating other people, though sometimes more difficult. Here's an example of self-validation from Joel, who works in a frozen yogurt shop:

> *'I got to work and found that the guy I was supposed to be working with had called in sick. This meant that I had to do the work of two people all day. I was angry and wanted to take care of only my own responsibilities. Then I felt guilty for thinking that way and told myself I had a bad attitude.*

> *'Then I remembered to validate. My feelings are totally normal and understandable for this situation. Instead of judging myself, I considered the consequences of acting on my wishes. I realized that if I only did my own tasks my boss would be upset with me, for good reason.*

> *'I decided to take care of everything that needed doing, as best I could. I didn't want to jeopardize my job or my reputation as a good worker. It was a hard day but I was able to keep things going pretty well on my own. I stayed focused on what I needed to do and didn't obsess about the situation. I felt proud of myself at the end of the day.'*

Self-validation was kind and constructive – it helped Joel stop criticizing himself for having normal thoughts and feelings. He accepted them as understandable, didn't dwell on them, and willingly took on the tasks consistent with being a responsible employee, one of his important values.

How to Self-validate

Validation includes several steps. It combines self-compassion skills with mindfulness skills you already know: mindful observation and labelling; accepting the reality of a situation; and mindful pausing. Instructions and examples are in the next box. When you talk to yourself in the recommended ways, see if you can use a kind and sympathetic tone.

VALIDATING YOUR THOUGHTS AND FEELINGS IN DIFFICULT SITUATIONS

Step 1 – Mindful observation and labelling

First, you have to recognize when you're having a difficult or stressful experience. It may be helpful to pause and label it, using words that feel natural. Here are some examples:

> *I'm having* (or *this is*) . . .
> > . . . *a difficult* (*painful, upsetting, tough, unpleasant, stressful*) . . .
> > . . . *moment* (or *situation* or *problem*).

Take a few moments to observe your thoughts and feelings, without judging them, or yourself for having them.

Step 2 – Recognizing that this is a common human experience

Remind yourself that everyone goes through difficult and painful situations, has unpleasant thoughts and feelings, and does things they regret – they're part of life.

> *Everyone has difficulties (problems, stressful situations) at some point.*
> *This is a normal part of life.*
> *Everyone makes mistakes.*
> *I'm not the only one . . .*

Step 3 – Expressing kind understanding

Remember that your thoughts and feelings are a result of your brain and body chemistry, your previous learning experiences, and the current situation. They make sense in their own way, even if they seem irrational on the surface. Say something like this:

> *It's understandable (or natural) that I'm feeling this way.*
> *This is normal (to be expected, not surprising) for this situation.*

What If Your Thoughts and Feelings Don't Seem to Make Sense?

- Remember that thoughts and feelings are visitors; we don't always understand how our visitors come to us.

- Don't ruminate or obsess about where your thoughts and feelings came from or criticize yourself for not knowing. Observe them with interest and openness. Practise mindful acceptance of them, and of yourself for having them.

- Think about how you would behave toward a friend whose B&B was suddenly overrun with strange and unexpected guests, some of whom were rude, loud and unpleasant. Practise treating yourself with the same consideration: *My goodness, what a lot of strange, unpleasant visitors. How can I be helpful in this situation?*

Self-validation is useful in several ways. It helps us feel better and see situations more clearly. It helps us get out of psychological traps, such as rumination, avoidance and emotion-driven behaviour. It puts us in a better position to make wise choices about what to do about difficult situations. If there's nothing we can do, it helps us accept the reality of the situation without doing something that makes matters worse.

Next is a self-validation worksheet completed by Susan, the woman from the previous chapter. She has two teenage sons and is susceptible to self-criticism and depression.

Worksheet: Self-validation

Remember to maintain an attitude of friendly curiosity

Day & time	What was the situation?	What did you say to validate your experience?	Did validation help? If so, how?
When did this example occur?	What was going on? What sensations, thoughts, urges, or emotions did you observe? Did you catch yourself falling into any psychological traps? • ruminating • trying to avoid something • acting on your emotions in a way you might regret later • criticizing yourself harshly	Mindful labelling (choose your own words): *This is...* *... a difficult (painful, upsetting) moment.* *... a stressful (unpleasant, tough) situation.* *... a moment of suffering.* *... really hard.* Recognizing common humanity: • *Pain (difficulty, stress) is part of life.* • *I'm not the only one who feels this way in situations like this.* Expressing kind understanding: • *It's understandable that I feel this way, given the circumstances.* • *My feelings are normal (to be expected, not surprising) for this situation.*	• Did it help you see the situation more clearly? • Did you feel better able to handle the situation wisely? • Did it help you out of a trap? ONLY USE THE SKILLS THAT ARE HELPFUL. • If recognizing common humanity does NOT help in this situation, omit it. Try it again in another situation. • If your thoughts and feelings do NOT seem understandable, and it feels false to say that they are, practise mindful acceptance of having puzzling or confusing thoughts and feelings.

Worksheet: Self-validation

Your name: <u>Susan</u>

Remember to maintain an attitude of friendly curiosity

Day & time	What was the situation?	What did you say to validate your experience?	Did validation help? If so, how?
Monday, 6.00 a.m.	I woke up, felt fatigued, depressed, didn't want to get out of bed, started thinking about what's wrong with me.	This is a difficult moment. No one likes feeling like this. I've been a bit depressed lately. Tiredness is a normal part of depression.	Kept me from ruminating about why I'm so fatigued. Helped me focus on what I need – a hot shower and a good breakfast.
Tuesday, 6.00 p.m.	I was grocery shopping after work and suddenly remembered I was supposed to pick up my son Chris at football practice. I called to tell him I'd be 15 minutes late. I felt guilty and told myself what a bad parent I am.	It's natural to be upset about forgetting, but my husband usually picks up Chris from football. We're very busy and it's understandable to forget something now and then, especially a change in the routine.	Helped me realize that all parents make mistakes. Chris has a phone. If I hadn't remembered, he would have called me. Later, Chris showed me how to programme my phone to send me reminders.
Thursday, 3.00 p.m.	I was using a new software programme at work and realized I'd made a mistake and had to repeat 2 hours of work. I was angry at myself and calling myself an idiot.	This is a frustrating situation. It's unfortunate I have to repeat this work, but I'm only human. Mistakes are to be expected when working with something new.	Made me realize I need to take a few minutes to calm down. I went for a walk up and down the hall and did mindful breathing. Then I was able to think about how to correct the error.

Worksheet: Self-validation

Your name: _____

Remember to maintain an attitude of friendly curiosity

Day & time	What was the situation?	What did you say to validate your experience?	Did validation help? If so, how?

Susan learned that when she practised self-validation she was able to think of wise ways to deal with troubling or unpleasant situations. She didn't have to *feel* self-compassionate before she could validate – validation is a skill that we can use any time, regardless of the feelings that might be present. The key is to remember to use it. This improves with practice. The worksheet opposite will help you practise. Remember to make copies.

Looking Ahead

If you've read this far in the book, you've learned about the following mindfulness skills and how to use them:

- Observing and labelling your present-moment thoughts and feelings, without judging them or yourself for having them.

- Paying attention to what you're doing while you're doing it.

- Accepting your thoughts and feelings while acting in ways that are consistent with your long-term goals and values.

- Treating yourself with compassion.

These skills are an excellent collection of useful tools for managing the moments of your life, whether they're painful or joyful, easy or difficult. We've considered the skills separately, but they all work together. In the next chapter, we'll consider several exercises that will help you bring everything together – one exercise each for sensations, thoughts, emotions and urges. They're a little more advanced than the exercises in the previous chapters, but the skills you've learned will help you work with them.

Chapter Summary

- Self-compassion is an important mindfulness skill. It means treating yourself kindly during times of stress and unhappiness, remembering that pain, failure and struggles are part of the common human experience, and keeping a mindful, balanced perspective on the situation and your feelings.

- Self-compassion is good for our mental health. It reduces the risk of depression and anxiety and helps us see more clearly what to do in difficult situations. We're more likely to behave consistently with our values and goals when we're self-compassionate than when we're harshly self-critical.

- Self-compassion is a set of skills that anyone can practise. Mindfulness skills include a self-compassionate attitude. Basic self-care, including eating, exercising and getting enough sleep, makes it easier.

- Self-compassion can also be practised with savouring, self-soothing and self-validation.

Part 4

Putting It All Together

13 Exercises for Combining the Skills

> 'Let me embrace thee, sour adversity, for wise men say it is the wisest course.'
>
> William Shakespeare

Imagine that you're hiking towards a beautiful mountain. The mountain represents something of great value to you; reaching it is an important and meaningful personal goal. As you get closer, you discover that a stinky, mucky swamp lies between you and the mountain. This is annoying and disappointing. Your map shows no swamp.

To get a better view, you climb a tree. From there, you see that if you want to reach the mountain, there's no way to avoid the swamp. You also notice a supply shop not far away. You proceed to the shop for advice.

The shopkeeper confirms that there's no way around the swamp, but offers rubber boots, insect repellent, bottled water, food and a map drawn by a previous traveller showing the easiest way through. You stock up on these supplies and head into the swamp.

We all encounter swamps as we pursue our goals. Getting through them is easier and far less unpleasant if you use the mindfulness skills you've learned so far.

Acceptance and willingness

Accepting that you have to cross the swamp and that it's likely to be unpleasant, you focus on what you need to do. Acceptance does NOT mean that you have to wallow in the swamp or take the most difficult path. You can use all the help that's available to get through as quickly and comfortably as possible. Once you've prepared as best you can, you willingly walk into the swamp – knowing that you're likely to get wet, dirty, insect-bitten and tired – because reaching the mountain is important to you.

Mindful observation

You pay close attention to your surroundings, observing the terrain and how it corresponds to the hand-drawn map. You observe your physical sensations, noticing when you feel hungry, thirsty or tired and pausing to eat, drink or rest. You find that mindfulness of sounds adds a touch of pleasantness to the journey: birds chirp, frogs croak, the breeze rustles in the swamp grass. When you spot a bird, a frog or a dragonfly, you take a few moments to really see it before walking on. You notice that your footsteps make interesting noises. The swamp smells unpleasant at first, but you observe without judgement and begin to appreciate the variety of scents.

Acting with awareness

You walk with awareness of walking, noticing the sensations as your body moves and sensing the swampy ground under your feet. When you stop for a snack, you eat and drink mindfully, appreciating the tastes and textures of the granola bars, the dried fruit and the water. When your mind gets absorbed in angry thoughts (*Why is this swamp here? Why wasn't it on my map? This isn't fair! I shouldn't have to do this!*), you acknowledge the feelings of frustration, observe the sensations, and shift your attention back to walking mindfully. You pull your camera out of a pocket. Taking photographs helps you be mindful of the colours, shapes, textures and patterns in this unusual environment.

Self-compassion

You recognize that everyone has unexpected setbacks while pursuing meaningful goals, that no one likes crossing stinky swamps. You realize that your annoyance, disappointment and aversion to the swamp are normal and understandable. You refrain from self-criticism about feeling this way. You help yourself constructively, as best you can, pacing yourself and using your supplies.

The preceding chapters discussed mindfulness skills separately, but in many situations it's helpful to use all of them simultaneously: observing present-moment experiences with a non-judgemental and self-compassionate attitude; accepting them as they are; willingly taking wise actions even when it's difficult; and acting with awareness of what we're doing. The rest of this chapter describes four exercises that combine these skills: one each for sensations, thoughts, emotions and urges. These exercises can help you with the most difficult situations you face. You may find them more challenging than earlier ones, but the skills you've already learned will help you use them effectively.

Working with Sensations through Mindful Movement

Many mindfulness exercises, like the breathing meditation and the body scan, invite us to sit still. Stillness helps us observe our sensations, thoughts, emotions and urges – coming and going, rising and falling – without reacting to them in impulsive ways. Stillness cultivates strength, equanimity and mindful presence.

On the other hand, we also need ways to practise mindfulness while our bodies are moving. Much of life is not conducted while sitting still, and our bodies are healthier if they move around regularly. In Chapter 10, we explored mindful walking, which cultivates mindful awareness during an ordinary daily activity that we often do mechanically. To sharpen awareness of body sensations, many mindfulness programmes also include gentle movements and stretches.

A series of movements and stretches is presented in the box on page 251. The specific movements are less important than the attitude you bring to the exercise. Mindful movement is a way to combine the skills we've already explored – observing without judgement, acting with awareness, acceptance, willingness and self-compassion. It's an opportunity to let go of goal-setting and problem-solving. There are no standards for how far you should stretch or how long you should balance. As best you can, adopt an attitude of friendly curiosity and acceptance of your body and its sensations while doing these movements.

Before beginning the exercise, consider the following points:

1. This exercise is done in a standing position. Choose a place where you can stand comfortably and gaze straight ahead without getting too distracted. You need room to raise your arms straight out to your sides.

2. It's important to take care of yourself. Recognize your limits and don't push yourself beyond them. Refrain from anything that doesn't feel appropriate for you to do. If you have physical limitations that might make it unwise for you to do these movements, consult with your doctor before trying them.

3. The purpose of this exercise is not to achieve any particular goals, other than awareness and acceptance of the body in each moment. We're not trying to strengthen the muscles, give them a workout, or get the body into shape. We're just noticing sensations and allowing them to be as they are, without judging them or ourselves as good or bad.

4. Don't do anything that causes pain. Other sensations, such as trembling, tingling, pulling, or stretching (within reasonable limits) are normal. Practise observing them mindfully. What do the sensations feel like? Where you feel them? Are they changing or shifting? Are they pleasant, unpleasant or neutral? See if you can adopt an attitude of friendly curiosity.

5. Notice your reactions to the sensations. Judgemental thoughts about your body may arise, such as how it looks; how strong, fit, or flexible it is; or how well it's doing these movements. Remember that this is a mindfulness exercise, not a competition or a performance. Don't stand in front of a mirror. As best you can, let judgemental thoughts pass by like clouds in the sky, and return your attention to observing the sensations. If you have emotions or urges, observe them mindfully, as best you can, focusing on how they feel in your body.

6.   The movements are designed to be practised slowly, with full aware-
     ness of all the sensations that arise. Spend as much time as you like
     with each movement. There are no time limits.

7.   Remember that mind wandering is normal. When your attention
     drifts away, gently bring it back, as best you can, to observing the
     sensations. Let go of judgemental thoughts about the wandering
     mind.

8.   Read through the instructions in the next box a couple of times to
     understand what you're being invited to do, and look at the illustra-
     tions. Then you can refer to the text or the pictures as you go along.
     If you prefer, the website for this book has a recording of the exercise.

MINDFUL MOVEMENT

1 – Standing

Stand with your feet about hip-width apart, your back reasonably
straight but not stiff, shoulders relaxed, arms hanging loosely at your
sides, gazing straight ahead. Feel the sensations in your body as it
stands here. Notice your feet on the floor and the movement of your
breath. Notice any subtle movements as you keep your balance.

2 – Head tilts

Slowly tilt your head to the right. Your eyes and nose continue to face forward; your right ear comes closer to your right shoulder. Feel the sensations that this produces. Tilt only as far as your head wants to go. Gently explore your limit. Breathe in and out. When you're ready, slowly bring your head back to vertical. Breathe. Now tilt your head to the left, in the same way. Breathe in and out. Feel the sensations. Slowly return to vertical. Practise friendly curiosity about whatever you notice.

3 – Head turns

Slowly turn your head to the right, so that your chin comes closer to your right shoulder. Turn only as far as your head wants to go. Carefully explore your limit. Pause here, feel the sensations and breathe in and out. When you're ready, come back to the starting position, facing forward. Now slowly turn your head the other way, so that your chin comes closer to your left shoulder. Feel the sensations. Breathe in and out. Turn back to the starting position, facing forward. Pause and observe the sensations. Allow thoughts to come and go.

4 – Shoulder rolls

Slowly move your shoulders forward and then up toward your ears, giving a gentle squeeze. Move the shoulders softly towards the back, and then down to the starting position. Breathe in and out. Repeat. Move slowly and feel all the sensations as your shoulders go around. Pause at the starting position. Now try coordinating with your breath. Inhale while moving the shoulders forward and up, exhale while moving them back and down. Repeat the cycle at the pace of your breath, as many times as you like.

When you're ready, pause at the starting position and then switch directions. Inhale while your shoulders move back and then up; exhale while they move forward and then down. Repeat as many times as you like, slowly and gently, observing and accepting the sensations as they are. Refrain from anything that feels painful or unsuitable for your body. Pause in the starting position.

5 – Raising arms halfway

As you inhale, slowly raise your arms to the sides until they're parallel with the floor and your fingers are pointing towards the walls. Flex your wrists, so that your fingers point up. Feel the sensations, accepting them as they are and breathing with them. Now bend your wrists the other way, so that your fingers point down. Gently alternate hand positions: fingers pointing up, fingers pointing down, pausing to breathe with the sensations in each position. When you're ready, slowly lower your arms to your sides, feeling every sensation on the way down. Pause with your arms hanging loosely. Breathe. Practise acceptance of whatever you feel now.

6 – Raising arms overhead

As you inhale, slowly raise both arms, keeping your elbows straight, until your hands are over your head and reaching for the ceiling. If you can't reach that high, or prefer not to, practise acceptance of what your arms will do. Pause here, feeling the sensations as you hold your arms overhead. If you're willing, tilt your head up, so that you can see your hands and the ceiling. Feel the sensations. Remember to breathe. When you're ready, return to looking straight ahead and slowly lower your arms all the way down, feeling every sensation along the way.

7 – Balancing on one foot

Imagine that your head is at 12 on a clock; your feet at 6. Raise your arms just enough that your hands are pointing to 4 and 8. Gaze straight ahead, stand tall. Shift your weight to your left foot, making your left leg strong and tight. Bend your right knee and raise your right foot slightly off the ground. Balance here if you can. If you prefer, keep your right toes on the ground. Feel the sensations and breathe with them. Practise non-judgemental acceptance of any wobbling or difficulty keeping your balance.

Now place your right foot back on the floor and shift your weight to the right, making your right leg strong and tight. Gaze straight ahead, stand tall. Bend your left knee and raise your left foot slightly off the floor, or keep your left toes on the floor for balance. Pause here. Breathe with the sensations. Practise willingness to feel whatever is present.

8 – Return to standing

Return your left foot to the floor, hip-width from the right foot. Distribute your weight evenly across both feet. Stand tall but not stiff. Allow the arms and shoulders to relax. Observe how your body feels now that you've done these movements. Practise acceptance of the sensations. Feel your breath moving in and out of your body.

Responses to Mindful Movement

Sometimes mindful movement is pleasant and enjoyable. The movements may be relaxing or soothing, the sensations in the body pleasing or refreshing. Sometimes we feel flexible and stable, mindfully present, awake, calm and alert. If a sense of wellbeing arises, mindful awareness helps us appreciate it.

On the other hand, this exercise can sometimes be uncomfortable. Muscles may ache, pull or tremble in ways we don't like. We may have judgemental thoughts about our bodies; feelings of disappointment, frustration, anger or sadness; urges to quit or to push the body too hard.

Observing these experiences with gentle, friendly awareness cultivates mindful acceptance of the constantly changing nature of thoughts and feelings. It helps us choose wisely how to respond. You might choose gentle perseverance – continuing with the exercise while accepting the body's limits and treating it kindly. Or you might discontinue the exercise for now and come back to it later.

Mindfulness of Thoughts

As we've seen in previous chapters, thoughts can feel compelling. When a thought comes to mind, such as 'I shouldn't have to cross this stinky swamp' or 'I'll never make it' or 'This is going to be horrible', it's easy to forget that these are thoughts. We often assume that they're important and that we should take them seriously.

Of course, it may be true that the swamp is stinky, that the crossing will be difficult and uncomfortable, and that your arrival at the mountain will be delayed. On the other hand, it may not be helpful to dwell on these thoughts. Mindful observation may reveal that the swamp is interesting and the discomfort can be managed. Crossing the swamp may provide great stories to tell when you finally reach the mountain. It may build your strength for the next goal that lies beyond it.

If 'I'll never make it across this swamp' comes to mind, and you believe it without question, you might turn back and never reach your goal. Or you might say, 'Well, I have to make it, so I'll just get it over with,' and rush into the swamp without adequate preparation, fail to cross it, and fear trying again. But if you say, 'Ah, there's a discouraging thought. This swamp looks impossible, but maybe it isn't. Let me consider my options,' you're in a position to gather information that will help you make a wise choice. Maybe it really is too difficult and you need to make a new plan. Or maybe it's worth trying: others have done it, and you can learn from their experiences and prepare.

The Leaves-on-a-Stream exercise cultivates a mindful perspective on thoughts. This exercise works best if you sit with your eyes closed. The

instructions are in the next box. Read them carefully. When you understand them, set a timer for five minutes, close your eyes, and try it. The
timer helps you not worry about when to stop.

LEAVES ON A STREAM

1. Imagine that you're sitting by a beautiful stream passing through
    a valley. In your mind's eye, sit on a blanket, a rock or a chair,
    in sun or shade – wherever you like. Notice that trees overhang
    the stream. Now and then, a leaf falls into the water and is
    carried downstream on the surface. Watch the leaves floating
    by.

2. Now start noticing your thoughts as they arise. As each thought
    comes up, picture it written on a leaf and watch it float by. If your
    thoughts take the form of images, put each image on a leaf. The
    content of the thought doesn't matter. If you think, 'What's for
    lunch?', 'I hope my sister is OK', or 'I'm worthless', put it on a leaf
    and watch it float by. If the same thought keeps popping up, place
    it on a leaf each time, as patiently as you can.

3. If you notice that your mind has wandered off, gently bring it back
    to watching the leaves float by. If you find that you've fallen into
    the stream and have been carried along with your thoughts, gently
    climb out and resume watching.

4. Watch for thoughts like 'I can't do this exercise' or 'This isn't
    working for me'. Treat these thoughts in the same way – write them
    on leaves and watch them float by. If they come back, do this again.

5. Practise acceptance of any thought that comes along. There's no
    such thing as an unacceptable thought.

6. As best you can, practise kindness and patience with yourself as
    you do this exercise.

Variations on This Exercise

If you prefer, use one of these images:

- Visualize a parade in which each person is holding a sign. When a thought or a mental image comes to your mind, picture it on one of the signs and watch it go by.

- Imagine yourself looking up at the sky. Clouds are slowly passing by. When you have a thought or mental image, picture it sitting on a cloud and watch it pass by.

The purpose of practising mindfulness of thoughts is not to get rid of the thoughts or to dismiss all thoughts as unimportant. Leaves, clouds and marchers in the parade pass by, but a particular thought may reappear, perhaps repeatedly. These exercises teach us to recognize thoughts, particularly repetitive ones, so that we can decide how to respond. If the thought is saying something important – 'Don't forget the plumber is coming at 3.00p.m.' – you can make a reasonable plan to meet the plumber. If the thought is not helpful – 'This is going to ruin my whole day' – you can acknowledge the frustration, let the thought pass by, and still make a reasonable plan to meet the plumber.

Mindfulness of Difficult Emotions

This is a meditative exercise for practising mindful observation, acceptance and self-compassion while a troubling situation or problem is in your mind. It incorporates mindful breathing and awareness of the body while sitting in a quiet, dignified posture. The steps are:

- Observing your breath for a few moments.

- Deliberately bringing to mind something that's been distressing you.

- Mindfully observing what happens in your body.

- Breathing with the sensations while allowing them to come and go in their own way and time.

Before beginning, consider the following points:

1. You don't have to bring to mind your most serious or overwhelming problem. You might think about a minor disagreement you had with someone, a small disappointment, or something that annoyed you.

2. This exercise can be uncomfortable. It may be helpful to remember the guest house metaphor. Think of the troubling problem as an invited guest and make room for it. If you prefer, use the passengers-on-the-bus metaphor – you've invited one of the difficult passengers to sit at the front. The goal is not to change your guests or passengers, but to practise relating to them mindfully, even when they're unpleasant.

3. Remember that everyone has difficult thoughts, feelings and situations. You're not alone in this. See if you can adopt an attitude of warmth and kindness about it, as you would for a loved one with the same problem.

4. Watch for the tendency to get caught up in thinking about the troubling situation. Your mind is probably eager to jump into problem-solving mode. This can easily lead to rumination and self-criticism. Instead, gently bring yourself back to mindful acceptance, focusing on sensations in your body and simply observing them, without trying to change or fix them.

The rest of the instructions are in the next box.

MINDFULNESS OF DIFFICULT EMOTIONS

1. Settle into your sitting posture. Gently close your eyes or gaze downward at the floor in front of you.

2. Focus your attention on your breath. Observe the sensations and movements as the breath goes in and out of your body. As best you can, follow the breath all the way in and all the way out.

3. Allow the breath to go at its own pace and rhythm without trying to change it.

4. Expand your awareness to include your body as a whole. Observe the sensations of sitting in the chair and the contact between your feet and the floor. Notice the sensations in your hands.

5. When you're ready, intentionally bring to mind something that's been troubling you; something difficult that's been going on in your life. For example:

    *   My son is having trouble making friends at school.

    *   My boss made unreasonable demands today.

    *   I'm worried about my mother's health.

    *   I'm having trouble deciding what to do about . . .

    *   I regret how I handled . . .

If you can't think of anything current, choose something from the past that was stressful or unpleasant.

6. Scan your body and notice what happens when this difficulty is in your mind. Does your heart rate change? Do you feel tension or tightness anywhere? Does anything feel warm or cold, heavy or light, tingly or numb? Observe closely, with friendly curiosity. Notice where in the body you feel the sensations and whether they're changing from one moment to the next.

7. It may be helpful to apply short verbal labels, such as 'tension' or 'tightness' to the sensations you observe. As best you can, use a gentle, accepting tone as you label.

8. Expand your awareness to include both the sensations and your breath. If you like, imagine your breath going into the part of the body where you feel the sensations, and coming back out from that part of the body.

9. If judgemental thoughts come up, such as 'It's bad (wrong, stupid, etc.) to feel this way' or 'I'm such an idiot' or 'I'm not doing this right', observe and label them ('Ah, judgements') and return your attention to the sensations in your body.

10. The body may try to resist or get rid of the unpleasant sensations. Signs of resistance include clenching your fists or teeth, scowling, tensing the abdomen, or bracing your arms or legs against the floor or chair. If you observe these signs, see if you can gently let go of the tension and open up to the sensations, accepting them as they are.

11. Practise willingness to feel the sensations, allowing them to be just as they are. It may be helpful to remind yourself: *Whatever it is, it's already here. Let me go ahead and feel it.* This doesn't mean you have to like the sensations. It's OK not to like them.

12. Remember the guest house metaphor. Think of the sensations as difficult guests who have come to visit. Be polite to them, as best you can. Make room for them.

13. Observe your thoughts. Are they racing around looking for solutions? If so, gently thank them for their efforts and return your attention to observing the sensations in your body.

14. Remember the attitude of friendly curiosity. Without trying to force yourself to feel a particular way, consider being kind. Statements like these may be helpful:

> *Painful feelings are here.*
> *Problems and difficulties are part of life.*
> *May I be kind to myself, as best I can.*

This exercise can be challenging. Remember that practising mindfulness is a way of taking care of yourself; it's not about tormenting yourself or forcing yourself to do things. Caring for yourself sometimes requires a warm and compassionate persistence with things that are difficult. See if you can find a way to work gently with this exercise, perhaps doing only a few minutes at a time. If it feels too intense, shift your awareness to your breath, or to sounds in the environment. When you feel ready, shift your attention back to the problem. If it's still too difficult, try again another day.

Lydia learned this exercise in a mindfulness class and practised it after a difficult conversation with her boyfriend. Here is her description:

'Eli and I have been dating for almost a year and I thought things were going really well. The idea of moving in together has come up a few times but we hadn't made a decision about it. My lease is about to expire so I brought it up again. Eli seemed unexcited about it. I was surprised and disappointed, and I let the topic drop. We haven't discussed it since then.

'This has been bothering me for a week so I decided to practise bringing it to mind for the exercise. At first it was really difficult. I had a strong, sinking feeling in my stomach and my face felt flushed. I felt shaky. A lot of thoughts went through my mind, like, "Is he about to leave me? Maybe our relationship isn't what I thought it was. I should have seen this coming. I'm not good enough." I felt angry and also afraid.

'My mind wanted to obsess over these thoughts and replay the conversation with Eli. But I kept coming back to the sensations in my body. Breathing with them really helped. I could let them come and go. It's not a catastrophe to feel these things. After a few minutes, I realized it isn't the end of the world if we don't move in together now. I also realized I don't really know what Eli is thinking. I decided to discuss it with him this weekend.'

Lydia found this exercise difficult but useful. She realized that she can observe her feelings of distress without getting caught in rumination and avoidance. It didn't resolve the situation immediately, but helped her see it clearly and make a plan.

Urge Surfing

Mindfulness teachers like to compare thoughts and feelings to waves in the ocean. Depending on weather conditions, the waves vary in size and strength, but they're always present. Nothing can make the ocean completely smooth. Surfing is a skilful way to handle waves. Rather than trying to stop them or getting overwhelmed, we allow them to be as they are and ride them as they rise and fall.

The wave metaphor is especially useful when we have to manage urges and cravings to do things that we know we'll regret later. Like waves, urges start small, get stronger and more intense, and then decline. Then another one comes along. Urge surfing is a mindfulness exercise designed to help people with addictions, but you don't have to be addicted to anything to benefit from urge surfing. If you have temptations or cravings that you give in to more than you'd like, this is a helpful exercise.

To prepare, think of a situation in which you feel urges or temptations to do something you'll regret later – something that's inconsistent with your values or goals. For your first experience with this exercise, choose an urge that's not too difficult, yet not too easy. For example:

- Losing your temper or getting into an argument with someone.

- Playing computer games instead of working.

- Watching another TV show instead of going to bed.

- Drinking or eating more than you think you should.

- Buying something you can't afford.

Before you begin the exercise, remember the following points:

1. Practise while sitting quietly. It's helpful to close your eyes, so that you can imagine your scenario as clearly as possible. If you'd rather not close your eyes, gaze downward at a neutral point, such as the floor a few feet in front of you.

2. If the exercise begins to feel too intense, open your eyes, look around, and move your body a bit. Shift your attention to your surroundings or to your breath. When you're ready, resume the exercise.

3. Remember the image of the wave. Your goal is to ride the wave as it grows and then subsides, observing it mindfully and accepting it as it is.

The rest of the instructions are in the next box. The website for this book includes a recording of this exercise.

URGE SURFING

1. Sit comfortably in a position that feels relaxed and dignified. For a few moments, observe the sensations of your body in the chair.

2. Observe your breath and allow it to flow in and out.

3. Bring to mind the scenario you decided on – a situation that creates urges to do something you'll regret later. Picture the situation in your mind as clearly as you can. Where are you? Is anyone else present?

4. Imagine the events that lead up to this urge. Picture yourself right at the point where the urge is the strongest, but you haven't yet acted on it. Pause here, without giving in to the urge.

5. Notice how your body feels at this point. What sensations are you feeling? Where do you feel them? Are they shifting or fluctuating?

6. Notice what thoughts are going through your mind. Recognize that they're thoughts and observe them.

7. Notice what emotions are present. Are you sad, angry, afraid, hurt, embarrassed or disappointed? Are you happy or excited?

8. As best you can, be gentle with yourself. Let go of judgements. Remember that urges and cravings are normal human experiences – we all feel them.

9. Allow the urge to be there, without trying to change or control it. Observe what it's like to feel the urge but not give in to it. Take your time.

10. Remember to breathe. The breath is your surfboard. Breathe with the urge, the sensations, thoughts and emotions.

11. Linger in this moment in a friendly, interested way. Practise willingness to feel the urge and refrain from the tempting behaviour.

12. Observe: Is there something behind this urge? Something you need or long for? A problem that needs attention?

13. When you're ready, let go of the scenario you were imagining. Shift your attention back to your breathing. Open your eyes and look around.

Nick's Story

Nick has a full-time job and brings work home nearly every day. In forty-five minutes in his home office, he can make more progress than at work, where he is constantly interrupted by employees with questions and concerns. His family wishes he were more involved with them in the evenings, but they've agreed not to disturb him for forty-five minutes after dinner.

Lately, Nick has been playing an online computer game during his evening work time. At first, he limited his game playing to ten minutes and was able to finish most of his other work in the remaining time. But the game has become more engrossing, and his playing time has crept up. Now he often plays for thirty minutes, sometimes more. He's not getting his work done and feels significantly more stressed during the day. Sometimes he extends his work time at home, but his family complains. He hasn't told them about the computer game.

Nick is working with the urge surfing exercise. Here are his observations after trying it several times:

> 'As I'm about to call up the game on my computer, I'm feeling several things. There's a sense of excitement about starting the game. I feel sort of energized by it. I also feel resentful that I have to work at home. I think I deserve some free time to do something fun, that it's not fair that I have this extra work to do. I've noticed some angry thoughts about various employees who stop by my office so often that I can't get much done there.

> 'During the last week I've been able to stick to a rule: I have to finish the work I brought home, and then I can play the game if there's any time left. Urges to play the game come up while I'm working. I try to be mindful of them. At first I didn't believe the urges would get weaker if I just watched them, but it's really true. They're like waves. They go away and then another one comes along. Observing them helps me see that I don't have to act on them.

> 'I'm not sure I can keep to my rule consistently. I think I could solve

this problem better if I changed some things at work. I decided to tell my employees that the last hour of the day is off-limits for questions. I'll close my door and use a do-not-disturb sign. Then I won't have to bring as much work home, and I can be with my family after dinner.'

Nick's experience illustrates important points about urge surfing:

- Urge surfing doesn't get rid of urges. Nick continued to feel urges to play the game. Yet over time, as Nick observes the urges without acting on them, there's an excellent chance they'll become less frequent and intense. Giving in to urges makes them stronger. Trying to suppress or deny them also makes them stronger. Mindful acceptance of urges is the healthy alternative.

- Urge surfing makes urges feel less overwhelming. Once he observed the thoughts, emotions and sensations, Nick found them less intimidating and felt more confident that he could handle them.

- Sometimes, urges are covering up another problem. Nick realized that beneath his urge to play the computer game was resentment about his employees constantly interrupting him at work. He needed to take steps to change this situation. Mindful observation of urges to play the computer game helped him devise a promising plan.

How These Exercises Help with Daily Life

The exercises in this chapter invite you to take a few minutes out of your normal routine. You may be wondering how they will help with daily life, when you may not have time to sit quietly or practise mindful movement before taking action in a troubling situation. These exercises cultivate mindful awareness that can be applied in countless situations:

- They refine our awareness of whatever is happening in the mind and body.

- They help us learn to stop fighting against or struggling with normal emotions and sensations, even when we don't like them.

- They help us remember that problems and difficulties are part of being human and living a full life, that we don't have to respond with harsh judgement toward ourselves, that kindness and compassion are often more helpful.

- They provide a way to stay out of psychological traps when we're upset. Instead of ruminating about the problem, trying not to think about it, criticizing ourselves for having it, or behaving rashly, we learn that we can face difficulties and respond constructively.

If we practise consistently, we're better prepared for any problematic situation. We're more likely to pause, see the situation clearly, and make a wise choice about what to do. Practising mindfulness is like strengthening muscles. As the muscles of mindfulness get stronger, our lives become happier and more satisfying.

Most people long for happy, meaningful and satisfying lives. In the final chapter, we return to the topic of happiness and how mindfulness helps us cultivate it.

Chapter Summary

- Although it's helpful to study mindfulness skills separately, as we did in the previous chapters, in reality, the skills work together.

- The exercises in this chapter cultivate the ability to adopt a mindful perspective when something unpleasant is happening – troubling emotions or thoughts, unwanted urges or discomfort in the body.

- Each exercise provides the opportunity to combine the skills previously described: observing without judgement; using mindful labels when helpful; and acting with awareness, acceptance, willingness and self-compassion.

- The exercises in this chapter require taking a few minutes out of your daily routine to practise, but the lessons learned can readily be applied to everyday situations and build strength and skills for handling life in the long term.

14 Mindfulness and Happiness

'Happiness is not a goal, it's a by-product.'

Eleanor Roosevelt

Throughout history, deep thinkers have debated what it means to live a happy, satisfying life. Ancient Greek philosophers wrote about two perspectives on happiness that psychologists still study today: one based on pleasure and enjoyment, the other on meaning and purpose. According to the first perspective, a happy life includes mostly positive emotions and more pleasure than pain. The second perspective says that true happiness comes from living in accordance with deeply held values and fulfilling one's inner potential, even when doing so is stressful and uncomfortable.

Mindfulness experts remind us that life is a constantly changing stream of pleasant, unpleasant and neutral experiences. We all have joys and sorrows, successes and failures, gains and losses. Positive emotions come and go; sometimes we don't achieve our goals. Real happiness, from this perspective, comes from knowing that we can keep our balance and find peace of mind despite changing conditions, just as a mountain remains strong and stable during sunshine and storms.

Fortunately, we don't have to choose a single definition of happiness. We all want joy and contentment, meaning and purpose, and the inner strength to respond wisely to pain and misfortune. Practising mindfulness cultivates happiness in all of these forms. In this chapter, we'll see how the mindfulness skills you've learned so far will help you find the happiness you seek.

Mindfulness and Positive Emotions

In the late 1990s, I realized that if I wanted to understand mindfulness, I should practise consistently. I started meditating for 10–15 minutes each morning, observing my breath and watching my sensations, thoughts and emotions come and go. I found it relaxing, but at first I didn't notice any other effects.

After a few weeks, I realized that I was noticing more pleasant moments during the day. I enjoyed the feel of the air when I stepped outdoors, the colours and shapes of the clouds, the patterns of tree branches against the sky, the sounds of birds or people passing by. The indoor world also seemed richer. Ordinary experiences, like listening to cats purr, chopping garlic and sautéing it in olive oil, and rinsing fruit at the kitchen sink with the sun shining through the window, were more vivid.

My life was already satisfying in many ways, but mindfulness of daily experiences made me feel happier. Research shows that I'm not alone.

A Study of Mindfulness and Enjoying Daily Life

For most people, unpleasant events, emotions and circumstances are more attention-grabbing than pleasant ones. We tend to focus on the negative while ignoring the positive. This is especially true for people susceptible to depression. A recent study showed that practising mindfulness helps us appreciate moments of pleasure and enjoyment in daily life, even if they're fleeting.

For six days, 130 adults with a history of depression wore digital wristwatches programmed to beep 10 times a day during waking hours. At each beep, participants completed a short questionnaire about their mood at that moment and the pleasantness of their current activity.

After this six-day period, half the participants completed an eight-week mindfulness programme that teaches many of the skills and exercises described in this book. They attended weekly two-hour sessions and were encouraged to practise daily. The other participants, who served as the control group, continued with their normal routines and did not attend the mindfulness course.

After eight weeks, all participants repeated the six-day procedure with the digital watches, reporting on their feelings and activities throughout each day. Results confirmed the hypothesis: participants in the mindfulness course showed significant increases in their positive emotions, moments of pleasantness and enjoyment of ordinary activities in their daily lives, while those in the control group showed no change over the eight-week period.

Enjoyment of ordinary activities increases resilience to life's normal ups and downs and helps prevent depression. The participants in this study had experienced severe depression in the past and were at high risk of future episodes. Practising mindfulness for eight weeks substantially lowered their risk.

The Benefits of Positive Emotions

We think of positive and negative emotions as opposites, but they're alike in a very important way: they're built into human nature because they can be useful if we handle them constructively. Pleasant feelings like happiness, contentment and interest motivate us to explore the environment, participate in valued activities and bond with others. They increase creativity, openness to new experiences and receptiveness to feedback. As a result, we gain knowledge, skills and social support that enrich our lives and help us recover more quickly from stressful events.

Positive emotions don't have to be intense to provide these benefits. We don't have to seek out unusual or thrilling activities. We also don't have to get rid of negative emotions. The positive ones are still beneficial, even as the negative ones continue to come and go. Mindfulness of the simple, momentary pleasures of normal daily life can have a big impact on the overall quality of our lives. This idea is beautifully communicated by the following poem by Linda Pastan:

The Happiest Day

It was early May, I think
a moment of lilac or dogwood
when so many promises are made
it hardly matters if a few are broken.
My mother and father still hovered
in the background, part of the scenery
like the houses I had grown up in,
and if they would be torn down later
that was something I knew
but didn't believe. Our children were asleep
or playing, the youngest as new
as the new smell of the lilacs,
and how could I have guessed
their roots were shallow
and would be easily transplanted.
I didn't even guess that I was happy.
The small irritations that are like salt
on melon were what I dwelt on,
though in truth they simply
made the fruit taste sweeter.
So we sat on the porch
in the cool morning, sipping
hot coffee. Behind the news of the day –
strikes and small wars, a fire somewhere –
I could see the top of your dark head
and thought not of public conflagrations
but of how it would feel on my bare shoulder.
If someone could stop the camera then . . .
If someone could only stop the camera
and ask me: are you happy?

perhaps I would have noticed
how the morning shone in the reflected
colour of lilac. Yes, I might have said
and offered a steaming cup of coffee.

Practising mindfulness teaches us how to stop the camera and notice the simple joys of daily life.

Mindfulness, Meaning and Purpose

Of course, not all moments of daily life are full of simple joys. A sense of meaning and purpose can provide a different form of happiness and satisfaction, even when the present moment is stressful or painful. Many psychologists use the term 'wellbeing' for the type of happiness based on meaning, purpose and fulfilling one's potential. Research on psychological wellbeing has identified six important components:

1. **Autonomy** – acting in accordance with your own inner standards and preferences, pursuing your own goals, resisting social pressures.

2. **Competence** – having knowledge and skills, managing the demands and responsibilities of daily life.

3. **Healthy relationships** – warm, trusting, satisfying relationships; concern, empathy and care for others.

4. **Self-acceptance** – understanding and accepting all aspects of yourself, including your strengths and weaknesses.

5. **Personal growth** – openness to new experiences, learning and self-improvement; seeking challenges, broadening your horizons.

6. **Purpose in life** – having goals, direction and a sense of meaning in your life.

Cultivating these elements of wellbeing is not always pleasant or enjoyable. Standing on one's own principles and managing daily demands can be stressful. Even the healthiest relationships have awkward, uncomfortable moments. It's painful to face up to our failures and shortcomings, to feel clumsy and nervous while learning new skills. Yet research shows that people who act in accordance with these six elements of wellbeing have higher overall life satisfaction, fewer symptoms of depression, and higher self-esteem.

Studies also show that practising mindfulness improves all six elements of psychological wellbeing. The same pattern is seen in people who take eight-week mindfulness courses and in people who've meditated for years. The more they practise, the more their wellbeing improves. Mindfulness makes it easier to act autonomously, with purpose, in ways that lead to personal growth, even though it's sometimes painful to do so. Mindfulness makes us more aware of what's actually happening in the present moment so that we can pursue what really matters and handle difficulties constructively.

I experienced the effects of mindfulness on wellbeing while writing this book. I was passionate about doing it, and yet it wasn't always pleasant. At times, I felt stressed and discouraged. I had doubts about whether it's any good and fears that I would never finish it. Sometimes I ruminated about whether readers would like it, avoided it by doing other things, and criticized myself for writing too slowly or being unclear.

Again and again, mindfulness enabled me observe what was happening, let go of unhelpful patterns, and redirect my attention to the writing process, with acceptance of the difficulties and willingness to keep working at it. This had a big impact on my wellbeing.

For example, when I wasn't caught in psychological traps, I could think more clearly about what I wanted to say (autonomy) and manage the demands of my life to create time to write (competence). Willingness and self-compassion helped me stretch my mind, develop new writing skills (personal growth), and work constructively with my strengths and weaknesses as a writer (self-acceptance). Awareness of the writing experience helped me talk about it with friends and develop connections with other authors (relationships). It also kept me focused on my goal: to share my understanding with readers in ways that I hope will be helpful and interesting (purpose).

In exchange for these benefits to my wellbeing, I was willing to feel tired, stressed, doubtful and nervous at times. At other times, I felt pleased, excited and energized. Sometimes I felt neutral. All of these feelings came and went, repeatedly, like waves whipped up by the wind on the surface of a lake. Below the surface, where the water was clear and calm, I found great satisfaction in writing this book, no matter how it felt at any given moment.

Mindfulness and Wellbeing in Unpleasant Situations

To deepen my practice of mindfulness, over the years I've attended several week-long meditation retreats at the Insight Meditation Society in Massachusetts. Each retreat has 75–100 participants and several teachers, and is conducted mostly in silence. The daily schedule includes periods of sitting and walking meditation, small-group meetings for questions and discussion, interviews with teachers, mindful meals, and a talk each evening. The atmosphere is caring and peaceful. It's an excellent way to practise intensively.

To keep the price affordable, each participant is given a daily housekeeping task. On one of my retreats, I was assigned to vacuum a long corridor lined with dormitory rooms. The vacuum cleaner was heavy and awkward. On my first day, I had trouble steering it and got into a struggle – yanking, shoving and inadvertently banging it on several people's doors. When I finally finished, feeling sweaty and irritated, I wrestled the vacuum cleaner into its closet and forgot about it.

Late that night, I awoke with a sharp pain in my right shoulder. I didn't understand the source of the pain until after breakfast when I started vacuuming again. I found it necessary to vacuum with my left arm, slowly and gently.

I realized I should vacuum mindfully. As best I could, I let go of judgements, observed the sensations, listened to the sounds, and watched the dirt disappear. I practised acceptance of the lumbering vacuum cleaner and stopped trying to force it. By acting with awareness, I found a way to move without struggle that resulted in a clean floor and allowed my sore shoulder to heal. Vacuuming this way was slow, but there was no need to hurry. Mindful vacuuming began to feel graceful – a bit like dancing. By the end of the week, I felt peaceful and content while vacuuming.

We're all happier when engaged in rewarding, satisfying activities but, for most of us, unpleasant or tiresome tasks are not entirely avoidable. The question is how to manage them skilfully. Doing these tasks mindfully is often more effective than trying to force things to be different or ruminating about how unpleasant they are. As an experiment, try doing the unpleasant tasks in your life mindfully and notice what happens. See if you can find ways to make them less irksome.

In addition, notice your facial expressions while doing your unpleasant tasks. Are you scowling, frowning or clenching your teeth? This might be making matters worse. We think of facial expressions as outward signs of our inner states; we scowl because we're frustrated, smile because we're happy. However, research shows that facial expressions also *influence* emotional states by providing information to the brain. According to several studies, if you smile, you'll feel a little happier. If you frown, you'll feel more sad and anxious. If you raise your eyebrows, you'll find new facts more surprising. If you wrinkle your nose, you'll find disgusting odours more unpleasant.

Half-smiling is an exercise that takes advantage of this interesting aspect of human physiology.

Half-smiling

Relax your shoulders, neck and face. Make your facial expression neutral. Now turn the corners of your mouth up gently, just a little, to make a soft, pleasant, relaxed expression that won't tire your facial muscles. Keep your jaw relaxed. Don't freeze your face; allow it to move naturally.

Half-smiling creates a facial expression of calm and serenity. It influences your brain, so that you *feel* a little more calm and serene. Half-smiling won't get rid of your negative emotions, but it will help you accept the present moment with equanimity.

Caroline's experience with half-smiling

'A new manager was hired where I work. It's the same woman who was in charge of firing people, including me, from my previous job when the company downsized. Last week we were all notified of a staff meeting to introduce her. I still have a lot of bad feelings about losing my previous job. I know it wasn't this woman's fault, but I really didn't want to go to the meeting.

'However, it would be unprofessional to skip it, and I can't avoid her for ever, so I decided I was willing to go. I observed my feelings of anger, dread and reluctance. I told myself it's completely understandable that I feel this way. I also decided to half-smile.

'I got to the meeting room a couple of minutes early. I relaxed my face and shoulders, sat in a dignified posture, and smiled just a little. I looked around and said hello to a few of my co-workers. Then my friend Jane came and sat next to me. She knows how I feel about the new manager. She also knows I'm learning about mindfulness. One day I told her about half-smiling and we tried it. It made us giggle.

'"I was expecting you to be stressed, but you look positively serene," she said.

'"I'm half-smiling," I told her.

'She stared at me. "Oh, gosh!" she said. "You are, aren't you? I'm so impressed!" This made me chuckle.

'Then the boss came in with the new manager and introduced her to the staff. The rest of the meeting was routine, except the new manager was there. A few times I reminded myself to keep a pleasant expression, without being stiff and unnatural.

'When I first learned about half-smiling, I thought it was fake and insincere, like papering over my true feelings. But it wasn't like that at all. My negative feelings about the new manager didn't go away, but half-smiling made me feel a little calmer. It helped me realize that I can handle it if she works here. It gave me a feeling of inner strength.'

Caroline is not happy about the new manager, for good reason. But she's pleased with how she's handling the situation. She reminded herself of something she values: behaving professionally at work. This helped her resist the temptation to avoid an unpleasant situation by skipping the meeting. Mindfully half-smiling helped her feel autonomous, competent and self-accepting. It showed her that she can have strong feelings of wellbeing in an unpleasant situation.

Mindfulness and Facing Adversity

No matter how much we practise mindfulness, we can't escape real misfortune and tragedy, such as sickness, loss, rejection and pain. Here we'll consider serious illness – cancer in particular – for several reasons. First, cancer affects many people. In the US, 46 per cent of men and 38 per cent of women will be diagnosed with cancer at some point in their lives. Of those, 64 per cent will survive for five years or more. Second, cancer patients face extremely distressing circumstances: difficult and painful treatments, reduced ability to work, disruptions in their family and social lives, and uncertainties about how long they will survive. Third, researchers have studied the benefits of mindfulness for people with cancer.

Being diagnosed with cancer can feel like the end of happiness and wellbeing. Yet studies show that cancer patients who participate in mindfulness training feel more cheerful, relaxed and vigorous. Their daily lives feel more interesting. They find more satisfaction in the work they're able to do. Their relationships feel closer and more supportive.

Reflections of cancer patients after practising mindfulness

In the next box are reflections of several cancer patients who completed an eight-week course of mindfulness-based stress reduction (MBSR) at a leading cancer centre in Canada and continued to attend weekly sessions afterwards, some for several years. Participants ranged in age from 43–77 and had a variety of cancers, including breast, prostate and ovarian cancer, malignant melanoma, and Hodgkin's disease. They were interviewed for a study of the effects of mindfulness on their mental health.

REFLECTIONS OF CANCER PATIENTS AFTER MINDFULNESS TRAINING

- I don't think the disease has gotten to me as stressfully and horribly as it could have. I am a fairly emotional woman. If I hadn't taken mindfulness I would be a mess.

- What the meditation does is give me time to look within. By looking within, that gives me control.

- Meditation means taking time out of all the chaos. Meditating gave me the chance to give the chaos some kind of meaning.

- It's changed my outlook on life, my relationship to other people and, most importantly, my relationship to myself. That's the one person I have to deal with every day.

- This whole notion of embracing change as the constant, I'd never really thought of it that way before.

- The ideas actually have a physical embodiment. That's what is so powerful about this –you don't just read it. It's about how you take those ideas and actually do what you have to do. It's very simple what you have to do. You have to sit, you have to be quiet and you have to listen to your breathing. That is really beautifully simple.

- The way I look at cancer is that once you get through the awfulness it's a very powerful motivator to live your life. I'm grateful I can come up here (to the mindfulness group at the cancer centre) and be reminded of that.

- I'm a much happier person than I ever thought I could be with the disease . . . the programme has really transformed my life. I've got a much better life for it.

Despite having a serious illness, the people in this study found that mindfulness helped them develop many of the elements of psychological wellbeing: autonomy, personal growth, healthier relationships and purpose in life. They also felt more positive emotions and fewer negative ones.

Summary: How Mindfulness Contributes to Happiness

We've seen that mindfulness contributes to happiness in several ways:

- Mindfulness makes us aware of simple pleasures and momentary joys that are already part of ordinary life, but that we often overlook. Savouring these experiences increases happiness and satisfaction with life.

- Mindfulness cultivates important elements of psychological wellbeing. It helps us identify and pursue our own goals and values, learn and grow, cultivate relationships, accept our strengths and weaknesses, and respond wisely to the inevitable discomforts.

- In some cases, mindful awareness can transform an unpleasant task or situation into a source of contentment.

- Mindfulness can help us find happiness and wellbeing in the midst of serious adversity.

The Mountain Meditation

Before ending this book, I offer one more exercise. The mountain meditation, originally developed by Jon Kabat-Zinn and used in several mindfulness programmes, cultivates the inner strength and stability to find various types of happiness – peace of mind, contentment, wellbeing, even joy – in the constantly changing conditions of life. Read through it carefully before trying it. There's a recording on the website for this book.

MOUNTAIN MEDITATION

Sit in a comfortable position that feels relaxed yet awake, with your back relatively straight, but not stiff or tense, your hands resting comfortably. If you can, allow your spine to be self-supporting, rather than leaning against the back of a chair.

Close your eyes, or gaze softly at a spot on the floor.

For a few moments, observe the sensations and movements as the breath goes in and out of your body, allowing the breath to go at its own pace and rhythm.

Now imagine a large, beautiful mountain. It might be a mountain you've seen before, or it might be an imaginary mountain. Picture it as best you can. Notice the mountain's peak, perhaps with snow on it, or with rocks showing through the snow. Notice the sides of the mountain. There may be trees growing or sheep grazing. Or perhaps the slopes are snow-covered. Notice that the base of the mountain is solidly embedded in the earth. The mountain is stable, unmoving and beautiful.

Imagine that a wizard has granted you a wish, and you wished to become the mountain. Now you are the mountain, and you share its qualities. You are solidly rooted, still, stable, large, dignified and beautiful. Your head is the top of the mountain and has a wide view of the surrounding

---

area. Your shoulders and arms are the sides of the mountain, and your lower body is the base, firmly embedded in your chair or the floor. Your spine is straight, just as the mountain seems to reach for the sky, yet it is not straining. It is simply being itself.

And now as you are sitting here, notice that during each day, the sun and clouds move across the sky, making patterns of light, shadows and colours that are constantly changing. As the sun moves below the horizon, the sky becomes dark and stars emerge. The moon may appear. The stars and the moon also move across the sky. Sometimes the moon is full; sometimes it's a tiny crescent. Sometimes the stars are numerous and bright; at other times, they're hidden by clouds.

In summer, there may be no snow at all on the mountain, or perhaps only at the very top or in deep crevices where the sun can't reach it. In the autumn, the trees on the mountain may change into bright colours, and then gradually lose their leaves, which fall to the ground and turn brown. In winter, the mountain is covered with snow and ice. In spring, the flowers bloom all over the mountainsides, the leaves return to the trees, the birds sing, the snow melts, and the streams are overflowing with melted snow. In any season, the mountain may be covered with clouds, or fog, or rain. In any season, there may be violent storms, with powerful winds, lightning, thunder, rain, snow or sleet.

People may come to look at the mountain. Sometimes they talk about how beautiful it is, or how majestic, or how inspiring. At other times, they complain that there are too many tourists on the mountain, or that the weather is too cold, cloudy, stormy or wet, to enjoy the mountain today.

None of this makes any difference to the mountain, which remains beautiful and majestic and strong regardless of the changing conditions. The mountain continues to sit, simply being itself, whether anyone sees it, or whether they like what they see. No matter the season or the weather, the mountain is itself – stable, unwavering and strong.

Practising mindfulness teaches us to develop the qualities of the mountain – stillness, rootedness, stability, and simply being ourselves, though many things in our lives are constantly changing. We all have times of light and darkness, calm and storms, intensity and dullness. The thoughts and feelings that we experience, the emotional storms and crises, the periods of joy and excitement, are like weather on the mountain.

This does not mean that we ignore the weather, deny it, or pretend it isn't there. We *observe* the weather, in all of its variations. We accept the weather for what it is. We know that the mountain is not the weather. The mountain remains while the weather comes and goes. The mountain continues to be itself.

Continue to sit and breathe for a few more moments, contemplating the lessons that can be learned from the mountain.

The image of the mountain can remind us of important aspects of human nature: stability, dignity, balance, presence, stillness. At the same time, people are more complex than mountains. We move around, breathe, talk, see, hear and feel. Do the mountain meditation in the spirit of exploration and interest and see if it's meaningful to you.

Summing Up and Looking Ahead

Good mental health is not a matter of what comes to our minds. We all want positive emotions, pleasant thoughts and urges to do sensible things, and sometimes we have those. But we also have painful emotions, dark thoughts and destructive urges. What matters is how we respond to them. Do we ruminate, try to suppress or avoid them, give in to destructive urges, and criticize ourselves harshly? We've seen that these are traps that make matters worse. The alternative is to respond with mindful awareness, observing with friendly curiosity to see what's happening, accepting with compassion the reality of the present moment, and choosing with awareness to do something consistent with what we truly value.

In the previous chapters, we've discussed how to use mindfulness skills to respond to stress and difficulties and build a happier, more satisfying life. Now that you've reached the end of the book, you may be wondering how to maintain your new skills. The most important thing is to keep practising. How to practise is up to you. Having worked your way through this book, you have many options. The following suggestions may be helpful.

1 – Formal practice

If you can, it's helpful to do formal practices regularly. Formal practice means taking time to do a mindfulness exercise while not doing anything else; to sit quietly and observe your breath, do a body scan, or practise mindful movement. You can use the recordings on the website for this book, or you may find that you no longer need them.

If it's difficult to find time for formal practice, remember that even a very short practice is better than none at all. If you intended to practise but the day got away from you, try practising for two minutes before getting into bed. Sit quietly and watch your breath or do some mindful neck stretches or shoulder rolls. Just for two minutes – you can set a timer. This won't interfere with your sleep. In fact, you may sleep better.

Another option is to practise for short periods during the day. Before you get out of bed, do a short body scan or take five or ten mindful breaths. Look for pauses during your workday when you can do the same.

You also might consider practising with a group. Look online for mindfulness groups in your area. Or form your own group with friends. Research shows that support and community greatly contribute to maintaining skills over the long term.

2 – Mindfulness of daily activities

As we've seen, any activity can become a mindfulness exercise: walking, eating, brushing your teeth, washing the dishes. When you walk, see if at least the first ten steps can be a mindfulness practice. At meals, try eating the first two bites mindfully. Try driving mindfully, without the radio. Wherever you are, observe your surroundings.

3 – Savouring pleasant experiences

Mindfulness of ordinary moments of everyday life can improve overall happiness. Pay attention to life's small, pleasant experiences: the smell of tea or coffee; a child's smile; the sun streaming through a window. Savour them.

4 – Remembering your breath

Even if you can't stop what you're doing to sit quietly with your eyes closed, you can direct your attention to your breath throughout the day. Try taking a mindful breath or two at every red light, whether you're driving or on foot. Observe your breath while standing in lines, sitting in waiting rooms, while your computer warms up, or during meetings. When pain, stress and discomfort arise, breathe with them.

5 – Befriending your emotions

Remember that emotions are built into human nature because they serve useful purposes if we handle them wisely. Instead of ruminating, trying to get rid of them, or criticizing yourself for having emotions, observe what's happening in your body. Breathe with it. Give yourself a little space to decide what to do, if anything.

6 – Remembering that thoughts are thoughts

We all have a strong tendency to believe our thoughts. When 'This is awful', 'I'm an idiot', or 'The future is hopeless' come to mind, remember that they're only thoughts. Labelling them (*Those are thoughts*) can be very helpful. This doesn't mean you have to ignore them. Sometimes thoughts are useful. If you act on them, do so with awareness.

7 – Mindful pausing

When thoughts and feelings are difficult, slowing down, even for a brief moment, often provides enough time to see what's happening – in the situation, your mind and your body. Taking a mindful breath (or several) gives you a chance to remind yourself of what's truly important and choose what to do. Remember that sometimes the wise choice is to allow a situation to run its natural course without doing anything about it.

8 – Remembering the guest house and the bus

You are the guest house. Your thoughts and feelings are visitors. You can allow them to be themselves, with acceptance and kindness, without being controlled by them. Or, if you prefer, think of your life as the bus, with your thoughts and feelings as the passengers, and you as the driver. You decide where to drive. You don't have to control the passengers, and they don't have to control you.

Remember that guest house proprietors and bus drivers need kindness, just like everyone else.

Finally, and most importantly, remember that you can start now. As many teachers say, mindfulness is only one breath away. Every moment is an opportunity to start transforming your life.

Notes

Chapter 1

Happiness is not a station you arrive at

M. L. Runbeck, *Time For Each Other* (New York: D. Appleton, Century Co., 1944)

Mindfulness helps with all of the problems listed above

K. W. Brown, R. M. Ryan & J. D. Creswell, 'Mindfulness: Theoretical Foundations and Evidence for its Salutary Effects', *Psychological Inquiry*, 18 (2007), 211–37

R. Davidson, J. Kabat-Zinn, J. Schumacher, M. Rosenkranz, D. Muller, S. Santorelli, F. Urbanowski, A. Harrington, K. Bonus & J. Sheridan, 'Alterations in Brain and Immune Function Produced by Mindfulness Meditation', *Psychosomatic Medicine*, 65 (2003), 567–70

J. Eberth & P. Sedlmeier, 'The Effects of Mindfulness Meditation: A Meta-Analysis', *Mindfulness*, 3 (2012), 174–89

P. Grossman, L. Niemann, , S. Schmidt & H. Walach, 'Mindfulness-Based Stress Reduction and Health Benefits: A Meta-Analysis', *Journal of Psychosomatic Research*, 57 (2004), 35–43

S. Keng, M. Smolski & C. Robins, 'Effects of Mindfulness on Psychological Health: A Review of Empirical Studies', *Clinical Psychology Review*, 31 (2011), 1041–56

M. Levin, J. Hildebrandt, J. Lillis & S. C. Hayes, 'The Impact of Treatment Components Suggested by the Psychological Flexibility Model: A Meta-Analysis of Laboratory-Based Component Studies', *Behavior Therapy*, 43 (2012), 741–56

S. Shapiro, G. Schwartz & G. Bonner, 'Effects of Mindfulness-Based Stress Reduction on Medical and Premedical Students', *Journal of Behavioral Medicine,* 21 (1998), 581–99

Mindfulness-based programmes with strong scientific support

S. Bowen, N. Chawla & G. A. Marlatt, *Mindfulness-Based Relapse Prevention for Addictive Behaviors: A Clinician's Guide* (New York: Guilford Press, 2011)

S. C. Hayes, K. D. Strosahl & K. G. Wilson, *Acceptance and Commitment Therapy: The Process and Practice of Mindful Change* (New York: Guilford, 2012)

J. Kabat-Zinn, *Full Catastrophe Living: Using the Wisdom of Your Body and Mind to Face Stress, Pain and Illness* (New York: Delacorte, 1990)

J. Kristeller, R. Wolever & V. Sheets, 'Mindfulness-Based Eating Awareness Training (MB-Eat) for Binge Eating: A Randomized Clinical Trial', *Mindfulness* (2013)

M. M. Linehan, *Cognitive Behavioral Treatment of Borderline Personality Disorder* (New York: Guilford, 1993)

S. M. Orsillo & L. Roemer, *The Mindful Way through Anxiety: Break Free from Chronic Worry and Reclaim Your Life* (New York: Guilford Press 2011)

Z. V. Segal, J. M. G. Williams & J. D. Teasdale, *Mindfulness-Based Cognitive Therapy for Depression* (2nd ed, New York: Guilford Press, 2013)

Chapter 2

The content and quality of our lives . . .

S. Salzberg, Real Happiness: The Power of Meditation (New York: Workman Publishing, 2011)

Problem-solving mode – this discussion of problem-solving mode and mindful acceptance mode is inspired by material in:

Z. V. Segal, J. M. G. Williams & J. D. Teasdale, *Mindfulness-Based Cognitive Therapy for Depression: A New Approach to Preventing Relapse* (New York: Guilford Press, 2002)

M. Williams & D. Penman, *Mindfulness: A Practical Guide to Finding Peace in a Frantic World* (London: Piatkus 2011)

Mindfulness of sounds and sensations – these exercises are inspired by material in:

S. C. Hayes & S. Smith, *Get Out of Your Mind and into Your Life: The New Acceptance and Commitment Therapy* (Oakland California: New Harbinger Publications, 2005)

M. M. Linehan, *Skills Training Manual for Treating Borderline Personality Disorder* (New York: Guilford Press, 1993)

Z. V. Segal, J. M. G. Williams & J. D. Teasdale, *Mindfulness-Based Cognitive Therapy for Depression: A New Approach to Preventing Relapse* (New York: Guilford Press, 2002)

M. Williams, J. Teasdale, Z. Segal & J. Kabat-Zinn, *The Mindful Way through Depression: Freeing Yourself from Chronic Unhappiness* (New York: Guilford Press, 2007)

For most people, a meaningful and satisfying life includes stressful, challenging, even painful experiences

S. C. Hayes, K. D. Strosahl & K. G. Wilson, *Acceptance and Commitment Therapy: The Process and Practice of Mindful Change* (New York: Guilford, 2012)

The Guest House

C. Barks, *The Essential Rumi* (New York: HarperCollins, 2004) Reprinted with permission.

Chapter 3

Helpful and unhelpful ways of thinking about problems

E. R. Watkins, 'Constructive and Unconstructive Repetitive Thought', *Psychological Bulletin*, 134 (2008), 163–206

Constructive problem-solving

A. N. Nezu, C. M. Mezu & M. McMurran, 'Problem-Solving Therapy', in W. T. O'Donohue & J. E. Fisher (Eds.), *Cognitive Behavior Therapy: Applying Empirically Supported Techniques in Your Practice* (2nd edition, Hoboken, New Jersey: John Wiley & Sons, 2008), 402–7

Common types of rumination

T. Borkovec, W. Ray & J. Stober, 'Worry: A Cognitive Phenomenon Intimately Linked to Affective, Physiological and Interpersonal Behavioral Processes', *Cognitive Therapy and Research*, 22 (1998), 561–76

F. Brozovich & R. G. Heimberg, 'An Analysis of Post-Event Processing in Social Anxiety Disorder', *Clinical Psychology Review*, 28 (2008), 891–903

B. J. Bushman, A. M. Bonacci, W. C. Pederson, E. A. Vasquez & N. Miller, 'Chewing On It Can Chew You Up: Effects of Rumination on Triggered Displaced Aggression', *Journal of Personality and Social Psychology*, 88 (2005), 969–83

P. Costas & A. Wells, *Depressive Rumination: Nature, Theory and Treatment* (Chichester, UK: John Wiley & Sons, 2004)

M. S. Robinson & L. B. Alloy, 'Negative Cognitive Styles and Stress-Reactive Rumination Interact to Predict Depression: A Prospective Study', *Cognitive Therapy and Research*, 27 (2003), 275–92

Self-test: Rumination – based loosely on ideas and material in:

M. Conway, P. Csank, S. Holm & C. Blake, 'On Assessing Individual Differences in Rumination on Sadness', *Journal of Personality Assessment*, 75 (2000), 404–25

T. Meyer, M. Miller, R. Metzger & T. Borkovec, 'Development and Validation of the Penn State Worry Questionnaire', *Behaviour Research and Therapy*, 28 (1990), 487–95

S. Nolen-Hoeksema & J. Morrow, 'A Prospective Study of Depression and Post-traumatic Stress Symptoms after a Natural Disaster: The 1989 Loma Prieta Earthquake', *Journal of Personality and Social Psychology*, 61 (1991), 115–21

D. G. Sukhodolsky, A. Golub & E. N. Cromwell, 'Development and Validation of the Anger Rumination Scale', *Personality and Individual Differences*, 31 (2001), 689–700

P. D. Trapnell & J. D. Campbell, 'Private Self-Consciousness and the Five-Factor Model of Personality: Distinguishing Rumination from Reflection', *Journal of Personality and Social Psychology*, 76 (1999), 284–304

Consequences of rumination

B. J. Bushman, A. M. Bonacci, W. C. Pederson, E. A. Vasquez & N. Miller, 'Chewing On It Can Chew You Up: Effects of Rumination on Triggered Displaced Aggression', *Journal of Personality and Social Psychology*, 88 (2005), 969–83

S. Lyubomirsky & C. Tkach, 'The Consequences of Dysphoric Rumination', in C. Papageorgiou & A. Wells (Eds.), *Depressive Rumination: Nature, Theory and Treatment* (Chichester, UK: John Wiley & Sons, 2004)

P. M. McEvoy & P. Kingsup, 'The post-event processing questionnaire in a clinical sample with social phobia', *Behaviour Research and Therapy*, 44 (2006), 1689–97

R. D. Ray, F. H. Wilhelm & J. J. Gross, 'All in the Mind's Eye? Anger Rumination and Reappraisal', *Journal of Personality and Social Psychology*, 94 (2008), 133–45

C. L. Rusting & S. Nolen-Hoeksema, 'Regulating Responses to Anger: Effects of Rumination and Distraction on Angry Mood', *Journal of Personality and Social Psychology*, 74 (1998), 790–803

Rumination is a psychological trap

S. Nolen-Hoeksema, B. E. Wisco & S. Lyubomirsky, 'Rethinking Rumination', *Perspective on Psychological Science,* 3 (2008), 400–24

C. Papageorgiou & A. Wells, 'Positive Beliefs about Depressive Rumination: Development and Preliminary Validation of a Self-Report Scale', *Behavior Therapy,* 32 (2001), 13–26

E. Watkins & S. Baracaia, 'Why Do People Ruminate in Dysphoric Moods?', *Personality and Individual Differences,* 30 (2001), 723–34

Mindfulness – an alternative to rumination

S. Jain, S. Shapiro, S. Swanick, S. Roesch, S. Mills, P. Bell & G. Schwartz, 'A Randomized Controlled Trial of Mindfulness Meditation Versus Relaxation Training: Effects on Distress, Positive States of Mind, Rumination and Distraction', *Annals of Behavioral Medicine,* 33 (2007), 11–21

P. Broderick, 'Mindfulness and Coping with Dysphoric Mood: Contrasts with Rumination and Distraction', *Cognitive Therapy and Research,* 29 (2005), 501–10

Choosing a new activity

M. Addis & C. Martell, *Overcoming Depression One Step at a Time: The New Behavioral Activation Approach to Getting Your Life Back* (Oakland, California: New Harbinger, 2004)

Chapter 4

Try to pose for yourself this task

F. Dostoyevsky, *Winter Notes on Summer Impressions* (D. Patterson, Trans.), Evanston, Illinois: Northwestern University Press (1988 – original work published 1863).

In a famous experiment, university students were asked to sit alone in a room for five minutes and try not to think of a white bear

D. M. Wegner, D. J. Schneider, S. Carter & L. White, 'Paradoxical Effects of Thought Suppression', *Journal of Personality and Social Psychology*, 53 (1987), 5–13

Most of us have thoughts we'd like to avoid

S. Najmi & D. M. Wegner, 'Thought Suppression and Psychopathology', in A. J. Elliott (Ed.), *Handbook of Approach and Avoidance Motivation* (New York: Psychology Press, 2008), 447–59

Nearly everyone has the occasional unwanted thought that seems bizarre or even shameful

L. Baer, *The Imp of the Mind: Exploring the Silent Epidemic of Obsessive Bad Thoughts*, New York: Plume (2001)

Those told not to think about smoking reported more smoking-related thoughts

P. Salkovskis & M. Reynolds, 'Thought Suppression and Smoking Cessation', *Behaviour Research and Therapy*, 32 (1994), 193–201

Other studies show similar patterns in heavy drinkers trying not to think about alcohol and in people trying to suppress memories of stressful or traumatic events

T. P. Palfai, P. M. Monti, S. M. Colby & D. J. Rohsenow, 'Effects of Suppressing the Urge to Drink on the Accessibility of Alcohol Outcome Expectancies', *Behaviour Research and Therapy*, 35 (1997), 59–65

J. C. Shipherd & J. G. Beck, 'The Role of Thought Suppression in Post-Traumatic Stress Disorder', *Behavior Therapy*, 36 (2005), 277–87

Self-test: two types of avoidance

W. Gamez, M. Chmielewski, R. Kotov, C. Ruggero & D. Watson, 'Development of a Measure of Experiential Avoidance: The Multi-dimensional Experiential Avoidance Questionnaire', *Journal of Consulting and Clinical Psychology*, 23 (2011), 692–713 Adapted with permission.

Why we fall into the avoidance trap

S. C. Hayes & S. Smith, *Get Out of Your Mind and into Your Life: The New Acceptance and Commitment Therapy* (Oakland, California: New Harbinger Publications, 2005)

The Passengers on the Bus *exercise*

S. C. Hayes, K. D. Strosahl & K. G. Wilson, *Acceptance and Commitment Therapy: An Experiential Approach to Behavior Change* (New York: Guilford, 1999)

S. C. Hayes & S. Smith, *Get Out of Your Mind and into Your Life: The New Acceptance and Commitment Therapy* (Oakland, California: New Harbinger Publications, 2005)

Chapter 5

Cherish your own emotions . . .

R. Henri, *The Art Spirit* (New York: Lippincott, 1923)

Psychologists call this 'emotion-driven behaviour'

L. B. Allen, R. K. McHugh & D. H. Barlow, 'Emotional Disorders: A Unified Protocol', in D. H. Barlow (Ed.), *Clinical Handbook of Psychological Disorders: A Step-by-Step Treatment Manual* (4th edition, New York: Guilford Press, 2008), 216–49

The following self-test will help you determine whether you're susceptible to unconstructive emotion-driven behaviour – based loosely on:

S. P. Whiteside & D. R. Lynam, 'The Five Factor Model and Impulsivity: Using a Structural Model of Personality to Understand Impulsivity', *Personality and Individual Differences*, 30 (2001), 669–89

The English language includes more than 500 emotion words

J. R. Averill, 'A Semantic Atlas of Emotional Concepts', *Catalog of Selected Documents in Psychology*, 5 (2002), 30. Cited in R. J. Larsen & D. M. Buss. *Personality Psychology: Domains of Knowledge about Human Nature* (New York: McGraw-Hill, 1975)

Emotion terms – based on material in:

D. Goleman, *Emotional Intelligence: Why It Can Matter More Than IQ* (New York: Bantam Books, 1995)

M. M. Linehan, *Skills Training Manual for Treating Borderline Personality Disorder* (New York: Guilford Press, 1993)

S. E. Spradlin, *Don't Let Emotions Run Your Life: How Dialectical Behavior Therapy Can Put You in Control* (Oakland, California: New Harbinger Publications, 2003)

Components of emotion

D. Barlow, K. Ellard, C. Fairholme, T. Farchione, C. Boisseau, L. Allen & J. Ehrenreich-May, *Unified Protocol for Transdiagnostic Treatment of Emotional Disorders* (New York: Oxford University Press, 2011)

Why do we have emotions?

M. M. Linehan, *Skills Training Manual for Treating Borderline Personality Disorder* (New York: Guilford Press, 1993)

D. Barlow, K. Ellard, C. Fairholme, T. Farchione, C. Boisseau, L. Allen & J. Ehrenreich-May, *Unified Protocol for Transdiagnostic Treatment of Emotional Disorders* (New York: Oxford University Press, 2011)

Research shows that basic emotions

P. Ekman, 'Cross Cultural Studies of Facial Expression', in P. Ekman (Ed.), *Darwin and Facial Expression: A Century of Research in Review* (New York: Academic Press, 1973), 169–222

Secondary emotions

M. M. Linehan, *Cognitive Behavioral Treatment of Borderline Personality Disorder* (New York: Guilford, 1993)

If you have strong emotions, you may already be very much aware of them

S. M. Orsillo & L. Roemer, *The Mindful Way through Anxiety: Break Free from Chronic Worry and Reclaim Your Life.* (New York: Guilford Press, 2011)

Worksheet: Understanding an emotional experience

This worksheet was adapted with permission from McKay, M., Wood, J. C. and Brantley, J., *The Dialectical Behaviour Therapy Skills Workbook* (Oakland, CA: New Harbinger, 2007) inspired by M. M. Linehan, *Skills Training Manual for Treating Borderline Personality Disorder* (New York: Guilford Press, 1993)

Chapter 6

If we treat ourselves harshly . . .

K. Armstrong, *Twelve Steps to a Compassionate Life* (New York: Anchor Books, 2010)

The inner critic

M. McKay & P. Fanning, *Self-Esteem* (3ʳᵈ edition, Oakland, California: New Harbinger, 1992)

Constructive criticism

R. M. Bergner, *Pathological Self-Criticism* (New York: Plenum, 1995)

P. G. Ossario, 'Appraisals', in A. Putman & K. Davis (Eds.), *Advances in Descriptive Psychology* (Ann Arbor, Michigan: Descriptive Psychology Press, 1990)

Research confirms the benefits of constructive criticism

R. A. Baron, 'Negative Effects of Destructive Criticism: Impact on Conflict, Self-Efficacy, and Task Performance', *Journal of Applied Psychology*, 73 (1988), 199–207

Self-test: Self-criticism – based loosely on ideas suggested by:

S. J. Blatt, J. P. D'Afflitti & D. M. Quinlan, 'Experiences of Depression in Normal Young Adults', *Journal of Abnormal Psychology*, 85 (1976), 383–89

P. Gilbert, M. Clarke, S. Hempel, J. Miles & C. Irons, 'Criticizing and Reassuring Oneself: An Exploration of Forms, Styles, and Reasons in Female Students', *British Journal of Clinical Psychology*, 43 (2004), 31–50

K. D. Neff, 'The Development and Validation of a Scale to Measure Self-Compassion', *Self and Identity*, 2 (2003), 223–50

180 overweight adults signed up for a weight-loss programme

T. Powers, R. Koestner, D. Zuroff, M. Milyavskaya & A. Gorin, 'The Effects of Self-Criticism and Self-Oriented Perfectionism on Goal Pursuit', *Personality and Social Psychology Bulletin*, 37 (2011), 964–75

University athletes in swimming or track and field showed a similar pattern

T. Powers, R. Koestner, N. Lacaille, L. Kwan & D. Zuroff, 'Self-criticism, Motivation, and Goal Progress of Athletes and Musicians: A Prospective Study', *Personality and Individual Differences*, 47 (2009), 279–83

Why do highly self-critical people make less progress?

T. Powers, R. Koestner & D. Zuroff, 'Self-criticism, Goal Motivation, and Goal Progress', *Journal of Social and Clinical Psychology*, 26 (2007), 826–40

Unconstructive self-criticism has many other negative effects

A. Besser, G. Flett & R. Davis, 'Self-criticism, Dependency, Silencing the Self, and Loneliness: A Test of a Mediational Model', *Personality and Individual Differences*, 35 (2003), 1735–52

B. Cox, C. Fleet & M. Stein, 'Self-Criticism and Social Phobia in the US National Comorbidity Survey', *Journal of Affective Disorders*, 82 (2004), 227–34

B. Cox, P. MacPherson, M. Enns & L. McWilliams, 'Neuroticism and Self-Criticism Associated with Post-traumatic Stress Disorder in a Nationally Representative Sample', *Behaviour Research and Therapy*, 42 (2004), 105–114

D. Dunkley, R. Masheb & C. Grilo, 'Childhood Maltreatment, Depressive Symptoms, and Body Dissatisfaction in Patients with Binge Eating Disorder: The Mediating Role of Self-Criticism', *International Journal of Eating Disorders*, 43 (2010), 274–81

R. Harman & D. Lee, 'The Role of Shame and Self-Critical Thinking in the Development and Maintenance of Current Threat in Post-Traumatic Stress Disorder', *Clinical Psychology and Psychotherapy*, 17 (2010), 13–24

D. Lassri & G. Shahar, 'Self-criticism Mediates the Link between Childhood Emotional Maltreatment and Young Adults' Romantic Relationships', *Journal of Social and Clinical Psychology*, 31 (2012), 289–311

Why do we criticize ourselves so harshly?

P. Gilbert, 'Compassion and Cruelty: A Biopsychosocial Approach', in P. Gilbert (Ed.), *Compassion: Conceptualizations, Research and Use in Psychotherapy* (London: Routledge, 2005), 9–74

P. Gilbert & C. 'Irons, Focused Therapies and Compassionate Mind Training for Shame and Self-attacking', in P. Gilbert (Ed.), *Compassion: Conceptualizations, Research and Use in Psychotherapy* (London: Routledge, 2005), 263–325

Shame and fear of rejection

P. Gilbert, 'The Evolution of Social Attractiveness and its Role in Shame, Humiliation, Guilt and Therapy', *The British Journal of Medical Psychology*, 70 (1997), 113–47

P. Gilbert, M. Clarke, S. Hempel, J. Miles & C. Irons, 'Criticizing and Reassuring Oneself: An Exploration of Forms, Styles, and Reasons in Female Students', *British Journal of Clinical Psychology*, 43 (2004), 31–50

Is shame the same as guilt?

J. P. Tangney & R. L. Dearing, *Shame and Guilt* (New York: Guilford Press, 2002)

How mindfulness helps with self-criticism

This discussion of fusion and defusion, including the exercises in the box, is based on ideas in:

S. C. Hayes & S. Smith, *Get Out of Your Mind and into Your Life: The New Acceptance and Commitment Therapy* (Oakland California: New Harbinger Publications, 2005)

S. C. Hayes, K. D. Strosahl & K. G. Wilson, *Acceptance and Commitment Therapy: An Experiential Approach to Behavior Change* (New York: Guilford Press, 1999)

Z. V. Segal, J. M. G. Williams & J. D. Teasdale, *Mindfulness-Based Cognitive Therapy for Depression: A New Approach to Preventing Relapse* (New York: Guilford Press, 2002)

A two-day experiment

S. M. Orsillo & L. Roemer, *The Mindful Way through Anxiety: Break Free from Chronic Worry and Reclaim Your Life* (New York: Guilford Press, 2011)

Chapter 7
Our souls are hungry for meaning . . .

H. Kushner, *When All You've Ever Wanted Isn't Enough* (New York: Fireside, 2002)

Two ways of defining happiness

C. Peterson, N. Park & M. E. P. Seligman, 'Orientations to Happiness and Life Satisfaction: The Full Life Versus the Empty Life', *Journal of Happiness Studies*, 6 (2005), 25–41

A. S. Waterman, 'Two Conceptions of Happiness: Contrasts of Personal Expressiveness (Eudaimonia) and Hedonic Enjoyment', *Journal of Personality and Social Psychology*, 64 (1993), 678–91

Both ways of defining happiness are useful

R. M. Ryan & E. L. Deci, 'On Happiness and Human Potentials: A Review of Research on Hedonic and Eudaimonic Wellbeing', *Annual Review of Psychology*, 52 (2001), 141–66

Positive emotions ... motivate and energize us for healthy behaviour

B. L. Fredrickson, 'The Role of Positive Emotions in Positive Psychology: The Broaden-and-Build Theory of Positive Emotions', *American Psychologist*, 56 (2001), 218–26

These behaviours build social bonds, cultivate new skills

B. L. Fredrickson, M. A. Cohn, K. A. Coffey, J. Pek & S. M. Finkel, 'Open Hearts Build Lives: Positive Emotions, Induced through Loving-Kindness Meditation, Build Consequential Personal Resources', *Journal of Personality and Social Psychology*, 95 (2008), 1045–62

Values and goals

S. C. Hayes & S. Smith, *Get Out of Your Mind and into Your Life: The New Acceptance and Commitment Therapy* (Oakland California: New Harbinger Publications, 2005)

S. C. Hayes, K. D. Strosahl & K. G. Wilson, *Acceptance and Commitment Therapy: The Process and Practice of Mindful Change* (2nd edition, New York: Guilford Press, 2012)

Autonomy is a basic psychological need

R. M. Ryan & E. L. Deci, 'Self-Determination Theory and the Facilitation of Intrinsic Motivation, Social Development, and Well-Being', *American Psychologist*, 55 (2000), 68–78

People who pursue freely chosen goals that they genuinely value

K. M. Sheldon & A. J. Elliott, 'Goal Striving, Need Satisfaction, and Longitudinal Well-Being: The Self-Concordance Model', *Journal of Personality and Social Psychology*, 76 (1999), 483–97

K. M. Sheldon & L. Houser-Marko, 'Self-Concordance, Goal Attainment, and the Pursuit of Happiness: Can There be an Upward Spiral?' *Journal of Personality and Social Psychology*, 80 (2001), 152–65

Focusing on what you'd like to avoid instead of what you want to pursue

R. Harris, *The Happiness Trap: How to Stop Struggling and Start Living* (London: Robinson, 2008)

Expecting the road always to be clear, straight and enjoyable

S. C. Hayes & S. Smith, *Get Out of Your Mind and into Your Life: The New Acceptance and Commitment Therapy* (Oakland, California: New Harbinger Publications, 2005)

Most people feel a strong need for personal connections

R. M. Ryan, V. Huta & E. L. Deci, 'Living Well: A Self-Determination Theory Perspective on Eudaimonia', *Journal of Happiness Studies*, 9 (2008), 139–70

Most people are happier if they have knowledge, skills and competencies

C. D. Ryff & C. L. M. Keyes, *The Structure of Psychological Wellbeing Revisited: Journal of Personality and Social Psychology*, 69 (1995), 719–27

Psychologists call these extrinsic goals

T. Kasser & R. M. Ryan, 'Further Examining the American Dream: Differential Correlates of Intrinsic and Extrinsic Goals', *Personality and Social Psychology Bulletin*, 22 (1996), 280–7

People who emphasize these goals are less happy and satisfied with their lives

T. Kasser & R. M. Ryan, 'Be Careful What You Wish For: Optimal Functioning and the Relative Attainment of Intrinsic and Extrinsic Goals', in P. Schmuck and K. M. Sheldon (Eds.), *Life Goals and Well-Being: Towards a Positive Psychology of Human Striving* (Goettingen: Hogrefe and Huber Publishers, 2001), 115–29

Worksheet: Describing your values – this worksheet is inspired by:

S. C. Hayes & S. Smith, *Get Out of Your Mind and into Your Life: The New Acceptance and Commitment Therapy* (Oakland, California: New Harbinger Publications, 2005)

Worksheet: Rating your values and behaviour – this worksheet is inspired by:

K. G. Wilson, E. K. Sandoz, M. K. Flunn & R. M. 'Slater, Understanding, Assessing and Treating Values Processes in Mindfulness- and Acceptance-Based Therapies', in R. A. Baer (Ed.), *Assessing Mindfulness and Acceptance Processes in Clients: Illuminating the Theory and Practice of Change* (Oakland, California: New Harbinger, 2010), 77–106

Students completed a mindfulness questionnaire and then were asked to solve some difficult scrambled word puzzles

D. R. Evans, R. A. Baer & S. C. Segerstrom, 'The Effects of Mindfulness and Self-Consciousness on Persistence', *Personality and Individual Differences*, 47 (2009), 379–82

People with emotional problems who were in an angry mood

S. E. Sauer & R. A. Baer, 'Ruminative and Mindful Self-Focused Attention in Borderline Personality Disorder', *Personality Disorders: Theory, Research and Treatment*, volume 3 (4), 434–44 (2012)

Chapter 8

Mindfulness means paying attention in a particular way: on purpose, in the present moment, and non-judgementally

J. Kabat-Zinn, *Wherever You Go, There You Are: Mindfulness Meditation in Everyday Life* (New York: Hyperion, 1994), 4

People who are mindful of the present moment

R. A. Baer, G. T. Smith, E. Lykins, D. Button, J. Krietemeyer, S. Sauer, E. Walsh, D. Duggan & J. M. G. Williams, 'Construct Validity of the Five Facet Mindfulness Questionnaire in Meditating and Non-Meditating Samples', *Assessment*, 15 (2008), 329–42

R. A. Baer, G. T. Smith, J. Hopkins, J. Krietemeyer & L. Toney, 'Using Self-Report Assessment Methods to Explore Facets of Mindfulness', *Assessment*, 13 (2006), 27–45

K. W. Brown & R. M. Ryan, 'The Benefits of Being Present: Mindfulness and Its Role in Psychological Well-Being', *Journal of Personality and Social Psychology*, 84 (4) (2003), 822

Mindful observation: Introductory exercises – these exercises are inspired by practices described by:

M. M. Linehan, *Skills Training Manual for Treating Borderline Personality Disorder*, (New York: Guilford Press, 1993)

Z. V. Segal, J. M. G. Williams & J. D. Teasdale, *Mindfulness-Based Cognitive Therapy for Depression: A New Approach to Preventing Relapse* (New York: Guilford Press, 2002)

Mindful breathing meditation – mindful breathing is used in many mindfulness programmes. The version here is inspired by:

Z. V. Segal, J. M. G. Williams & J. D. Teasdale, *Mindfulness-Based Cognitive Therapy for Depression: A New Approach to Preventing Relapse*, (New York: Guilford Press, 2002)

Mindful breathing with other sensations

M. Williams, J. Teasdale, Z. Segal & J. Kabat-Zinn, *The Mindful Way through Depression: Freeing Yourself from Chronic Unhappiness* (New York: Guilford Press, 2007)

Chapter 9

We can become aware of judgement...

J. Goldstein & J. Kornfield, *Seeking the Heart of Wisdom: The Path of Insight Meditation* (Boston: Shambala Publications, 2001)

One-word labelling worksheet – inspired by and based loosely on a similar worksheet in:

D. Greenberger & C. A. Padesky, *Mind over Mood: Change How You Feel by Changing the Way You Think* (New York: Guilford Press, 1995). Adapted with permission

The purpose of mindfully labelling thoughts and feelings is to recognize that they're distinct from the person who's having them

S. C. Hayes & S. Smith, *Get Out of Your Mind and into Your Life: The New Acceptance and Commitment Therapy* (Oakland, California: New Harbinger Publications, 2005)

More about emotion labelling

M. M. Linehan, *Skills Training Manual for Treating Borderline Personality Disorder* (New York: Guilford Press, 1993)

Working with judgements – this section is inspired by and based on ideas discussed by:

S. C. Hayes, K. D. Strosahl & K. G. Wilson, *Acceptance and Commitment Therapy: An Experiential Approach to Behavior Change* (New York: Guilford Press, 1999)

M. M. Linehan, *Skills Training Manual for Treating Borderline Personality Disorder* (New York: Guilford Press, 1993)

Z. V. Segal, J. M. G. Williams & J. D. Teasdale, *Mindfulness-Based Cognitive Therapy for Depression: A New Approach to Preventing Relapse* (New York: Guilford Press, 2002)

Chapter 10

While washing the dishes

T. N. Hanh, *The Miracle of Mindfulness* (Boston, Massachusetts: Beacon Street, 1976)

Research shows that people who spend less time on autopilot are happier and more satisfied with life

M. A. Killingsworth & D. T. Gilbert, 'A Wandering Mind is an Unhappy Mind', *Science,* 330 (2010), 932

Raisin exercise – this exercise was first described by Jon Kabat-Zinn and is used in many mindfulness programmes. The version here is adapted from:

Z. V. Segal, J. M. G. Williams & J. D. Teasdale, *Mindfulness-Based Cognitive Therapy for Depression: A New Approach to Preventing Relapse* (New York: Guilford Press, 2002)

Mindful walking – mindful walking was first described by Jon Kabat-Zinn and is used in many mindfulness programmes. The version here is adapted from:

Z. V. Segal, J. M. G. Williams & J. D. Teasdale, *Mindfulness-Based Cognitive Therapy for Depression: A New Approach to Preventing Relapse* New Yorkl: Guilford Press, 2002)

Some forms of multitasking are enjoyable or useful, others neutral or harmless, and some unpleasant or risky

D. Crenshaw, *The Myth of Multi-Tasking: How 'Doing It All' Gets Nothing Done* (San Francisco, California: Jossey-Bass, 2008)

E. Ophir, C. Nass & A. Wagner, 'Cognitive Control in Media Multi-Taskers', *Proceedings of the National Academy of Sciences,* 106 (2009), 15583–7

A. Spink, C. Cole & M. Waller, 'Multi-Tasking Behavior', *Annual Review of Information Science and Technology*, 42 (2008), 93–118

D. L. Strayer & F. A. Drews, 'Multi-Tasking in the Automobile', in A. F. Kramer, D. A. Wiegmann & A. Kirlik (Eds.), *Attention: From Theory to Practice* (New York: Oxford University Press 2007), 121–33

Many studies show that immersing yourself in whatever you're doing, so that you're totally focused on it, creates a state called 'flow'

M. Czikszentmihalyi, *Flow: The Psychology of Optimal Experience* (New York: Harper & Row, 1990)

Cleaning became dancing

J. Kabat-Zinn, *Wherever You Go, There You Are: Mindfulness Meditation in Everyday Life* (New York: Hyperion, 1994), 205

Chapter 11

It takes a huge amount of fortitude . . .

J. Kabat-Zinn, *Coming to our Senses: Healing Ourselves and the World Through Mindfulness* (New York: Hyperion, 2005)

A large group of smokers

S. Bowen & G. A. Marlatt, 'Surfing the Urge: Brief Mindfulness-Based Intervention for College Student Smokers', *Psychology of Addictive Behaviors*, 23 (4) (2009), 666

Chocolate lovers

E. M. Forman, K. L. Hoffman, K. B. McGrath, J. D. Herbert, L. L. Brandsma & M. R. Lowe, 'A Comparison of Acceptance- and Control-Based Strategies for Coping with Food Cravings: An Analog Study', *Behavior Research and Therapy*, 45 (10) (2007), 2372–86

Patients at a clinic for chronic back pain

K. E. Vowles, D. W. McNeil, R. T. Gross, M. L. McDaniel, A. Mouse, M. Bates & C. McCall, 'Effects of Pain Acceptance and Pain Control Strategies on Physical Impairment in Individuals with Chronic Low Back Pain', *Behavior Therapy*, 38 (4) (2007), 412–25

People with anxiety and depression

L. Campbell-Sills, D. H. Barlow, T. A. Brown & S. G. Hofmann, 'Effects of Suppression and Acceptance on Emotional Responses of Individual with Anxiety and Mood Disorders', *Behavior Research and Therapy*, 44 (9) (2006), 1251–63

Engaging mindfully in goal-consistent behaviour, even when it's stressful and uncomfortable, is called 'willingness'

S. M. Orsillo & L. Roemer, *The Mindful Way through Anxiety: Break Free from Chronic Worry and Reclaim Your Life* (New York: Guilford Press, 2011)

Practising acceptance with the body scan – the body scan is used in MBSR, MBCT, MBRP, and other mindfulness-based treatments. It was originally described in:

J. Kabat-Zinn, *Full Catastrophe Living: Using the Wisdom of Your Body and Mind to Face Stress, Pain and Illness* (New York: Delacorte Press, 1990)

The version of the body scan used here is inspired by those in:

Z. V. Segal, J. M. G. Williams & J. D. Teasdale, *Mindfulness-Based Cognitive Therapy for Depression: A New Approach to Preventing Relapse* (New York: Guilford Press, 2002)

M. Williams & D. Penman, *Mindfulness: A Practical Guide to Finding Peace in a Frantic World* (London: Piatkus, 2011)

M. Williams, J. Teasdale, Z. Segal & J. Kabat-Zinn, *The Mindful Way through Depression: Freeing Yourself from Chronic Unhappiness* (New York: Guilford Press, 2007)

Acceptance and willingness in daily life: mindful pausing – mindful pausing is based on the three-minute breathing space, which was developed for MBCT:

Z. V. Segal, J. M. G. Williams & J. D. Teasdale, *Mindfulness-Based Cognitive Therapy for Depression: A New Approach to Preventing Relapse* (New York: Guilford Press, 2002)

Mindful pausing has several steps; use the word 'SOBER' to remember them – the SOBER acronym was developed for MBRP:

S. Bowen, N. Chawla & G. A. Marlatt, *Mindfulness-Based Relapse Prevention for Addictive Behaviors: A Clinician's Guide* (New York: Guilford Press, 2011)

Chapter 12

True mindfulness is imbued with warmth, compassion and interest

C. Feldman, *The Buddhist Path to Simplicity* (London, UK: Thorsons 2001), 173

The importance of compassion has been recognized since ancient times

C. K. Germer & R. D. Siegel, *Wisdom and Compassion in Psychotherapy: Deepening Mindfulness in Clinical Practice* (New York: Guildord Press, 2012)

What does it mean to be compassionate?

P. Gilbert, *Overcoming Depression* (3rd edition, London: Robinson, 2009)

We're less convinced that we should be compassionate towards ourselves

C. K. Germer, *The Mindful Path to Self-Compassion: Freeing Yourself from Destructive Thoughts and Emotions* (New York: Guilford Press, 2009)

K. D. Neff, *Self-Compassion: Stop Beating Yourself Up and Leave Insecurity Behind* (New York: HarperCollins, 2011)

K. D. Neff, 'The Development and Validation of a Scale to Measure Self-Compassion', *Self and Identity*, 2 (3) (2003), 223–50

Dana's story is based on:

C. E. Adams & M. R. Leary, 'Promoting Self-Compassionate Attitudes toward Eating among Restrictive and Guilty Eaters', *Journal of Social and Clinical Psychology*, 26 (10) (2007), 1120–44. Quotation reprinted with permission of Guilford Publications; permission conveyed through Copyright Clearance Center, Inc.

George's story is based on:

A. C. Kelly, D. Zuroff, C. Foa & P. Gilbert, 'Who Benefits from Training in Self-Compassionate Self-Regulation? A Study of Smoking Reduction', *Journal of Social and Clinical Psychology* 29 (2010), 727–55. Quotations reprinted with permission of Guilford Publications; permission conveyed through Copyright Clearance Center, Inc.

Other benefits of self-compassion

W. Kuyken, E. Watkins, E. Holden, K. White, R. Taylor, S. Byford, A. Evans, S. Radford, J. Teasdale & T. Dalgleish, 'How Does Mindfulness-Based Cognitive Therapy Work?' *Behaviour Research and Therapy*, 48 (2010), 1105–12

M. R. Leary, E. B. Tate, C. E. Adams, A. B. Allen & J. Hancock, 'Self-Compassion and Reactions to Unpleasant Self-Relevant Events: The Implications of Treating Oneself Kindly', *Journal of Personality and Social Psychology*, 92 (5) (2007), 887

K. D. Neff, 'The Science of Self-Compassion', in C. K. Germer & R. D. Siegel (Eds.), *Wisdom and Compassion in Psychotherapy: Deepening Mindfulness in Clinical Practice* (New York: Guilford Press, 2012), 79–92

Is self-compassion selfish?

L. K. Barnard & J. F. Curry, 'The Relationship of Clergy Burnout to Self-Compassion and Other Personality Dimensions', *Pastoral Psychology*, 61 (2) (2012), 149–63

R. J. Davidson, 'Changing the Brain by Transforming the Mind: The Impact of Compassion Training on the Neural Systems of Emotion' (October 2007). Paper presented at the Mind and Life Institute Conference, Emory University, Atlanta, Georgia.

K. D. Neff & S. N. Beretvas, 'The Role of Self-Compassion in Romantic Relationships', *Self and Identity*, 12 (1) (2013), 78–98

K. D. Neff & E. P. Pommier, 'The Relationship between Self-Compassion and Other-Focused Concern among College Undergraduates, Community Adults, and Practicing Meditators', *Self and Identity.* (2013), vol 12 (2), 160–76

R. Ringenbach, 'A Comparison between Counselors Who Practice Meditation and Those Who Do Not on Compassion Fatigue, Compassion Satisfaction, Burnout and Self-Compassion. Dissertations Abstracts International: Section B: The Sciences and Engineering', 70 (6-B), (2009), 3820

L. M. Yarnell & K. D. Neff, 'Self-Compassion, Interpersonal Conflict Resolutions, and Well-Being', *Self and Identity,* (2013) vol 12 (2), 146–59

Research shows that people who consistently practise mindfulness become more self-compassionate

E. L. B. Lykins & R. A. Baer, 'Psychological Functioning in a Sample of Long-Term Practitioners of Mindfulness Meditation', *Journal of Cognitive Psychotherapy*, 23 (2009), 226–41

S. L. Shapiro, J. A. Astin, S. R. Bishop & M. Cordova, 'Mindfulness-Based Stress Reduction for Health Care Professionals: Results from a Randomized Trial', *International Journal of Stress Management*, 12 (2) (2005), 164–76

S. L. Shapiro, K. W. Brown & G. M. Biegel, 'Teaching Self-Care to Caregivers: Effects of Mindfulness-Based Stress Reduction on the Mental Health of Therapists in Training', *Training and Education in Professional Psychology*, 1 (2) (2007), 105–15

Tips for healthy sleeping

W. R. Pigeon & M. L. Perlis, 'Cognitive Behavioral Treatment of Insomnia', in W. T. O'Donohue & J. E. Fisher (Eds.), *Cognitive Behavior Therapy: Applying Empirically Supported Techniques in Your Practice* (2nd edition, Hoboken, New Jersey: John Wiley & Sons, 2008), 283–95

Savouring

F. Bryant, 'Savouring Beliefs Inventory (SBI): A Scale for Measuring Beliefs about Savouring', *Journal of Mental Health*, 12 (2003), 175–96

D. B. Hurley & P. Kwon, 'Results of a Study to Increase Savoring the Moment: Differential Impact on Positive and Negative Outcomes', *Journal of Happiness Studies*, 13 (4) (2012), 579–88

Self-soothing

M. M. Linehan, *Skills Training Manual for Treating Borderline Personality Disorder* (New York: Guilford Press, 1993)

K. D. Neff, *Self-Compassion: Stop Beating Yourself Up and Leave Insecurity Behind* (New York: HarperCollins, 2011)

Self-validation

M. M. Linehan, *Cognitive Behavioral Treatment of Borderline Personality Disorder* (New York: Guilford Press, 1993)

C. E. Shenk & A. E. Fruzzetti, 'The Impact of Validating and Invalidating Responses on Emotional Reactivity', *Journal of Social and Clinical Psychology*, 30 (2) (2011), 163–83

S. J. Linton, K. Boersma, K. Vangronsveld & A. Fruzzetti, 'Painfully Reassuring? The Effects of Validation on Emotions and Adherence in a Pain Test', *European Journal of Pain* (2012), vol 16 (4), 592–9

Chapter 13

Let me embrace thee, sour adversity

W. Shakespeare, Henry VI Part 3, Act 3, Scene 1

Swamp metaphor

S. C. Hayes, K. D. Strosahl & K. G. Wilson, *Acceptance and Commitment Therapy: An Experiential Approach to Behavior Change* (New York: Guilford Press, 1999)

Mindful movement – mindful movement, based on gentle yoga postures and stretches, is used in MBSR, MBCT, MBRP and other mindfulness-based treatments. It was originally described in:

J. Kabat-Zinn, *Full Catastrophe Living: Using the Wisdom of Your Body and Mind to Face Stress, Pain and Illness* (New York: Delacorte Press, 1990)

The version here is based on descriptions in:

S. Bowen, N. Chawla & G. A. Marlatt, *Mindfulness-Based Relapse Prevention for Addictive Behaviors: A Clinician's Guide* (New York: Guilford Press, 2011)

M. Williams & D. Penman, *Mindfulness: A Practical Guide to Finding Peace in a Frantic World* (London: Piatkus, 2011)

M. Williams, J. Teasdale, Z. Segal & J. Kabat-Zinn, *The Mindful Way through Depression: Freeing Yourself from Chronic Unhappiness* (New York: Guilford Press, 2007)

Leaves on a stream exercise

S. C. Hayes & S. Smith, *Get Out of Your Mind and into Your Life: The New Acceptance and Commitment Therapy* (Oakland, California: New Harbinger Publications, 2005)

Visualize a parade in which each person is holding a sign

S. C. Hayes, K. D. Strosahl & K. G. Wilson, *Acceptance and Commitment Therapy: An Experiential Approach to Behavior Change* (New York: Guilford Press, 1999)

Imagine yourself looking up at the sky

S. Orsillo & L. Roemer, *The Mindful Way Through Anxiety* (New York: Guildford Press, 2011)

Mindfulness of difficult emotions – this exercise is used in several mindfulness-based treatments. The version here is based on descriptions in:

Z. V. Segal, J. M. G. Williams & J. D. Teasdale, *Mindfulness-Based Cognitive Therapy for Depression* (2nd edition, New York: Guilford Press, 2013)

M. Williams & D. Penman, *Mindfulness: A Practical Guide to Finding Peace in a Frantic World* (London: Piatkus, 2011)

M. Williams, J. Teasdale, Z. Segal & J. Kabat-Zinn, *The Mindful Way through Depression: Freeing Yourself from Chronic Unhappiness* (New York: Guilford Press, 2007)

Urge surfing

S. Bowen, N. Chawla & G. A. Marlatt, *Mindfulness-Based Relapse Prevention for Addictive Behaviors: A Clinician's Guide* (New York: Guilford Press, 2011)

Chapter 14

Happiness is not a goal, it is a by-product

F. Roosevelt, *You Learn by Living* (New York: Harper and Brothers Publishers, 1960)

Throughout history, deep thinkers have debated what it means to live a happy, satisfying life

C. Peterson, N. Park & M. P. Seligman, 'Orientations to Happiness and Life Satisfaction: The Full Life Versus the Empty Life', *Journal of Happiness Studies*, 6 (1) (2005), 25–41

A. S. Waterman, 'Two Conceptions of Happiness: Contrasts of Personal Expressiveness (Eudaimonia) and Hedonic Enjoyment', *Journal of Personality and Social Psychology*, 64 (4) (1993), 678–91

R. M. Ryan & E. L. Deci, 'On Happiness and Human Potentials: A Review of Research on Hedonic and Eudaimonic Well-Being', *Annual Review of Psychology*, 52 (2001), 141–66

Mindfulness experts remind us that life is a constantly changing stream of pleasant, unpleasant and neutral experiences

K. W. Brown & M. Holt, 'Experiential Processing and the Integration of the Bright and Dark Sides of the Human Psyche', in K. M. Sheldon, T. B. Kashdan & M. F. Steger (Eds.), *Designing Positive Psychology: Taking Stock and Moving Forward* (New York: Oxford University Press, 2011), 147–59

A recent study showed that practising mindfulness helps us appreciate moments of pleasure and enjoyment in daily life

N. Geschwind, F. Peeters, M. Drukker, J. van Os & M. Wichers, 'Mindfulness Training Increases Momentary Positive Emotions and Reward Experience in Adults Vulnerable to Depression: A Randomized Controlled Trial', *Journal of Consulting and Clinical Psychology*, 79 (5) (2011), 618–28

Positive emotions are built into human nature because they can be useful if we handle them constructively

B. L. Fredrickson, 'The Role of Positive Emotions in Positive Psychology: The Broaden-and-Build Theory of Positive Emotions', *American Psychologist*, 56 (3) (2001), 218–26

Positive emotions don't have to be intense to provide these benefits

M. A. Cohn, B. L. Fredrickson, S. L. Brown, J. A. Mikels & A. M. Conway, 'Happiness Unpacked: Positive Emotions Increase Life Satisfaction by Building Resilience', *Emotion*, 9 (3) (2009), 361–8

The Happiest Day

From L. Pastan, *Heroes in Disguise*, W. W. Norton & Co (1991)

Research on psychological well-being has identified six important components:

C. D. Ryff, 'Happiness Is Everything, Or Is It? Explorations on the Meaning of Psychological Well-Being', *Journal of Personality and Social Psychology*, 57 (1989), 1069–81

Practising mindfulness improves all six elements of psychological wellbeing

J. Carmody & R. A. Baer, 'Relationships between Mindfulness Practice and Levels of Mindfulness, Medical and Psychological Symptoms and Well-being in a Mindfulness-Based Stress Reduction Program', *Journal of Behavioral Medicine*, 31 (1) (2008), 23–33

R. A. Baer, G. T. Smith, E. Lykins, D. Button, J. Krietemeyer, S. Sauer, E. Walsh, D. Duggan & J. M. G. Williams, 'Construct Validity of the Five Facet Mindfulness Questionnaire in Meditating and Non-Meditating Samples', *Assessment*, 15 (2008), 329–42

We're all happier when engaged in rewarding, satisfying activities

N. Cantor & C. A. Sanderson, 'Life Task Participation and Well-Being: The Importance of Taking Part in Daily Life', in D. Kahneman, E. Diener & N. Schwarz (Eds.), *Well-Being: The Foundations of Hedonic Psychology*, (1999), 230–43

Facial expressions influence emotional states by providing information to the brain

F. Strack, L. L. Martin & S. Stepper, 'Inhibiting and Facilitating Conditions of the Human Smile: A Non-Obtrusive Test of the Facial Feedback Hypothesis', *Journal of Personality and Social Psychology*, 54 (5) (1988), 768–77

M. B. Lewis, 'Exploring the Positive and Negative Implications of Facial Feedback', *Emotion*, 12 (2012), 852–9

D. N. McIntosh, 'Facial Feedback Hypothesis: Evidence, Implications and Directions', *Motivation and Emotion*, 20 (2) (1996), 121–47

Half-smiling

T. H. Hanh, *The Miracle of Mindfulness* (Boston, Massachusetts: Beacon Street, 1976)

M. M. Linehan, *Skills Training Manual for Treating Borderline Personality Disorder* (New York: Guilford Press, 1993)

Cancer

L. E. Carlson & M. Speca, *Mindfulness-Based Cancer Recovery: A Step-By-Step MBSR Approach to Help You Cope with Treatment and Reclaim Your Life* (Oakland, California: New Harbinger Publications, 2010)

E. Foley, A. Baillie, M. Huxter, M. Price & E. Sinclair, 'Mindfulness-Based Cognitive Therapy for Individuals Whose Lives Have Been Affected by Cancer: A Randomized Controlled Trial', *Journal of Consulting and Clinical Psychology*, 78 (1) (2010), 72–9

V. Henderson, L. Clemow, A. Massion, T. Hurley, S. Druker & J. Hebert, 'The Effects of Mindfulness-Based Stress Reduction on Psychosocial Outcomes and Quality of Life in Early-Stage Breast Cancer Patients: A Randomized Trial', *Breast Cancer Research and Treatment*, 131 (2012), 99–109

C. Hoffman, S. Ersser, J. Hopkinson, P. Nicholls, J. Harrington & P. Thomas, 'Effectiveness of Mindfulness-Based Stress Reduction in Mood, Breast- and Endocrine-Related Quality of Life, and Well-Being in Stage 0 to III Breast Cancer: A Randomized, Controlled Trial', *Journal of Clinical Oncology*, 30 (2012), 1335–42

M. Speca, L. Carlson, M. MacKenzie & M. Angen, 'Mindfulness-Based Stress Reduction (MBSR) as an Intervention for Cancer Patients', in R. A. Baer (Ed.), *Mindfulness-Based Treatment Approaches: Clinician's Guide to Evidence Base and Applications* (San Diego, California: Elsevier, 2006), 239–61

Reflections of cancer patients after practising mindfulness

M. J. Mackenzie, L. E. Carlson, M. Munoz & M. Speca, 'A Qualitative Study of Self-Perceived Effects of Mindfulness-Based Stress Reduction (MBSR) in a Psychosocial Oncology Setting', *Stress and Health: Journal of the International Society for the Investigation of Stress*, 23 (1) (2007), 59–69. Copyright © 2006 John Wiley & Sons Ltd. Quotations reprinted with permission of John Wiley & Sons; permission conveyed through Copyright Clearance Center, Inc.

The mountain meditation

J. Kabat-Zinn, *Wherever You Go, There You Are: Mindfulness Meditation in Everyday Life* (New York: Hyperion, 1994)

Resources

Websites – Information about Mindfulness

www.umassmed.edu/cfm
Center for Mindfulness in Medicine, Health Care and Society
University of Massachusetts Medical School

www.mbct.com
Information about mindfulness-based cognitive therapy (North America)

http://marc.ucla.edu/
University of California Los Angeles, Mindful Awareness Research Center

www.mindful.org
Information about mindfulness from *Mindful* magazine

www.mindfulnet.org
Comprehensive information about mindfulness

www.mbct.co.uk
Information about mindfulness-based cognitive therapy (United Kingdom)

www.bangor.ac.uk/mindfulness/
Centre for Mindfulness Research and Practice, Bangor University, Wales

www.oxfordmindfulness.org
Oxford Mindfulness Centre, University of Oxford, United Kingdom

www.bemindful.co.uk
Mental Health Foundation, United Kingdom

Websites – Insight Meditation Retreat Centres

www.dharma.org
Insight Meditation Society, Barre, Massachusetts

www.spiritrock.org
Spirit Rock Meditation Center

http://gaiahouse.co.uk/
Insight Meditation Retreat Centre

Books

N. Bardacke, *Mindful Birthing: Training the Mind, Body, and Heart for Childbirth and Beyond* (HarperOne, 2012)

C. K. Germer, *The Mindful Path to Self-Compassion: Freeing Yourself from Destructive Thoughts and Emotions* (Guilford, 2009)

R. Harris, *The Happiness Trap* (Trumpeter, 2008)

J. Kabat-Zinn, *Full Catastrophe Living: Using the Wisdom of Your Body and Mind to Face Stress, Pain and Illness* (Delta, 1990)

J. Kabat-Zinn, *Wherever You Go, There You Are: Mindfulness Meditation in Everyday Life* (Hyperion, 1994)

J. Kabat-Zinn, *Coming to Our Senses: Healing Ourselves and the World through Mindfulness* (Hyperion, 2005)

M. Kabat-Zinn & J. Kabat-Zinn, *Everyday Blessings: The Inner Work of Mindful Parenting* (Hyperion, 1997)

K. D. Neff, *Self-Compassion: Stop Beating Yourself Up and Leave Insecurity Behind* (HarperCollins, 2011)

S. M. Orsillo & L. Roemer, *The Mindful Way through Anxiety: Break Free from Chronic Worry and Reclaim Your Life* (Guilford, 2011)

S. Salzburg, *Real Happiness: The Power of Mediation* (Workman, 2011)

C. Vieten, *Mindful Motherhood: Practical Tools for Staying Sane During Pregnancy and Your Child's First Year* (New Harbinger, 2009)

M. Williams & D. Penman, *Mindfulness: An Eight-Week Plan for Finding Peace in a Frantic World* (Rodale, 2011)

M. Williams, J. Teasdale, Z. Segal & J. Kabat-Zinn, *The Mindful Way through Depression: Freeing Yourself from Chronic Unhappiness* (Guilford, 2007)

Books for Professionals:

R. A. Baer, *Mindfulness-Based Treatment Approaches: A Clinician's Guide to Evidence Base and Applications* (Elsevier, 2006)

S. Bowen, N. Chawla & G. A. Marlatt, *Mindfulness-Based Relapse Prevention for Addictive Behaviors: A Clinician's Guide* (Guilford, 2011)

L. Dimeff & K. Koerner, *Dialectical Behavior Therapy in Clinical Practice: Applications Across Disorders and Settings* (Guilford, 2007)

C. K. Germer & R. D. Siegel, *Wisdom and Compassion in Psychotherapy: Deepening Mindfulness in Clinical Practice* (Guilford, 2012)

C. Germer, R. Siegel & P. Fulton, *Mindfulness and Psychotherapy* (Guilford, 2005)

S. Hayes, V. Follette & M. Linehan, *Mindfulness and Acceptance: Expanding the Cognitive Behavioral Tradition* (Guilford, 2004)

S. C. Hayes, K. D. Strosahl & K. G. Wilson, *Acceptance and Commitment Therapy: The Process and Practice of Mindful Change* (2nd edition, Guilford, 2012)

M. M. Linehan, *Cognitive Behavioral Treatment of Borderline Personality Disorder* (Guilford, 1993)

M. M. Linehan, *Skills Training Manual for Treating Borderline Personality Disorder* (Guilford, 1993)

L. Roemer & S. M. Orsillo, *Mindfulness- and Acceptance-Based Behavioral Therapies in Practice* (Guilford, 2009)

Z. V. Segal, J. M. G. Williams & J. D. Teasdale, *Mindfulness-Based Cognitive Therapy for Depression* (2nd edition, Guilford, 2013)

S. L. Shapiro & L. E. Carlson, *The Art and Science of Mindfulness: Integrating Mindfulness into Psychology and the Helping Professions* (American Psychological Association, 2009)

Recordings of Mindfulness Exercises

www.stressreductiontapes.com/
www.mindfulnesstapes.com
Recordings by Jon Kabat-Zinn

www.octc.co.uk
Recordings by Mark Williams

www.soundstrue.com
Guided meditations by many teachers, including Tara Brach, Pema Chodron, Jon Kabat-Zinn, Sharon Salzburg and Joseph Goldstein

Copyright Acknowledgements

Chapter 1

'Worksheet: Rating your values and behaviour' *Mindfulness for Two*. Copyright © 2009 Kelly G. Wilson with Troy DuFrene. New Harbinger Publications, Inc. Reprinted with permission.

Chapter 2

'The Guest House' by Jalaluddin Rumi, *The Essential Rumi: New Expanded Edition*, translated by Coleman Barks (2004). Reprinted with permission.

Chapter 4

Self-test: Two types of avoidance. Adapted with permission from Gámez, W., Chmielewski, M., Kotov, R., Ruggero, C., & Watson, D. 'Development of a measure of experiential avoidance: The Multidimensional Experiential Avoidance Questionnaire', *Journal of Consulting and Clinical Psychology*, 23, (2011) 692–713. Used and adapted with permission of Dr Gámez.

Chapter 5

'Worksheet: Understanding an emotional experience', *The Dialectical Behaviour Therapy Skills Workbook*. Copyright © 2007 Matthew McKay, Jeffrey C. Wood and Jeffrey Brantley. Reprinted with permission: New Harbinger Publications, Inc.

Chapter 7

'Worksheet: Describing your values', *Get Out of Your Mind and Into Your Life*. Copyright © 2005 Steven C. Hayes with Spencer Smith. Reprinted with permission: New Harbinger Publications, Inc.

Chapter 9

'Worksheet: One-word Labelling' (adapted with permission from work-sheet 4.1: Distinguishing Situations, Mood and Thought), *Mind Over Mood: Changing How You Feel by Changing the Way You Think*, Copyright © 1995 Dennis Greenberger and Christine A. Padesky. Adapted with permission of the Guilford Press.

Chapter 11

'Mindful pausing' (adapted with permission from 'The 3-Minute Breathing Space'), *Mindfulness-based Cognitive Therapy for Depression*. Copyright © 2013 Zindel V. Segal, J. Mark, G. Williams and John D. Teasdale, and 'Sober Breathing Space', *Mindfulness-based Relapse Prevention for Addictive Behaviours*. Copyright © 2011 Sarah Bowen, Neha Chawla and G. Alan Marlatt. Adapted with permission of the Guilford Press.

Chapter 12

'Promoting self-compassionate attitudes toward eating among restrictive and guilty eaters' by Adams, C. E., & Leary, M. R., *Journal of Social and Clinical Psychology*, 26 (10), (2007), 1120–44. Quotation reprinted with permission of Guilford Publications; permission conveyed through Copyright Clearance Center, Inc.

'Who benefits from training in self-compassionate self-regulation? A study of smoking reduction' by Kelly, A. C., Zuroff, D., Foa, C. & Gilbert, P., *Journal of Social and Clinical Psychology* 29, (2010), 727–55. Quotations reprinted with permission of Guilford Publications; permission conveyed through Copyright Clearance Center, Inc.

Chapter 13

'The Mountain Meditation', adapted from 'Mountain Meditation', *Wherever You Go, There You Are*. Copyright © 1994 Jon Kabat-Zinn, PhD. Used by permission of Hyperion. All rights reserved.

Chapter 14

Index

Mindful Compassion

by Paul Gilbert and Choden

ISBN 978-1-78033-087-7
Price: £20.00

Using the power of mindfulness and compassion to transform our lives

In this important book, Professor Paul Gilbert OBE and long-time Buddhist meditator and teacher Choden have brought together Eastern wisdom and Western science to explore how our minds can cause so much suffering and what we can do about it.

Building on Professor Gilbert's groundbreaking book *The Compassionate Mind*, this new book offers practical step-by-step advice for using the skills of mindfulness and compassion to build our inner capacity for responding more wisely and kindly to the stresses of our inner emotional lives and the conflicting pressures of our everyday lives. Recent research has shown that the ability to develop compassion towards oneself and others has a profound impact on our minds, health and happiness and those we relate to, while mindfulness enables us to stand back and be more objective.

Praise for *Mindful Compassion*:

'A precious and most welcome contribution to bringing about a more compassionate society.'
Matthieu Ricard, Buddhist monk and author of *Happiness: A Guide to Developing Life's Most Important Skill*

'An inspiring book that will be deeply appreciated by many therapists and teachers and those who come to them for help with their suffering. . . A book full of wisdom that will be a wonderful resource for a whole generation.'
Mark Williams, Professor of Clinical Psychology, University of Oxford and author of *The Mindful Way through Depression* and *Mindfulness: A Practical Guide to Finding Peace in a Frantic World*